CANADIAN ISSUES / THÈMES CANADIENS

VOLUME XII, 1990

Canada: Traditions and Revolutions

Canada: traditions et révolutions

Proceedings of a Conference sponsored by the International Council for Canadian Studies and the Association for Canadian Studies held at Laval University in Québec on June 3-5, 1989.

Communications présentées lors d'un congrès tenu à l'Université Laval de Québec, du 3 au 5 juin 1989, sous les auspices du Conseil international d'études canadiennes et l'Association d'études canadiennes.

Edited by / sous la direction de

Alan F.J. Artibise - Simon Langlois

Montréal
1990

Canadian Cataloguing in Publication Data

Main entry under title:
    Canada: traditions and revolutions = Canada : traditions et révolutions

(Canadian issues = Thèmes canadiens; vol. XII, 1990)
Text in English and French.
ISBN 0-919363-25-3

1. Canada—Congresses. 2. Canada—Social conditions—1971- —Congresses. 3. Canada—Economic conditions—1971- —Congresses. 4. Canada—Politics and government—1984- —Congresses. I. Artibise, Alan F.J., 1946- II. Langlois, Simon III. International Council for Canadian Studies IV. Association for Canadian Studies V. Title: Canada : traditions et révolutions. VI. Series: Canadian issues (Association for Canadian Studies); vol. XII, 1990.

FC10.C28 1990   971.064'7   C90-090301-5E
F1008.C36 1990

Données de catalogage avant publication (Canada)

Vedette principale au titre:
    Canada: traditions and revolutions = Canada : traditions et révolutions

(Canadian issues = Thèmes canadiens ; vol. XII, 1990)
Texte en anglais et en français.
ISBN 0-919363-25-3

1. Canada—Congrès. 2. Canada—Conditions sociales—1971- —Congrès. 3. Canada—Conditions économiques—1971- —Congrès. 4. Canada—Politique et gouvernement—1984- —Congrès. I. Artibise, Alan F.J., 1946- II. Langlois, Simon III. Conseil international d'études canadiennes IV. Association d'études canadiennes V. Titre: Canada : traditions et révolutions. VI. Collection: Canadian issues (Association d'études canadiennes) ; vol. XII, 1990.

FC10.C28 1990   971.064'7   C90-090301-5F
F1008.C36 1990

Typesetting/Photocomposition: Guy Leclair
Printing/Impression: UQAM, Montréal, Canada

Legal Deposit, National Library of Canada, Third Trimester, 1990
Dépôt légal, Bibliothèque nationale du Canada et Bibliothèque nationale du Québec, troisième trimestre 1990

Canadian Issues / Thèmes canadiens (ISSN 0318-8442) is an annual publication of the Association for Canadian Studies. It features papers presented at the national conference of the Association. This year's issue is published jointly by the Association for Canadian Studies and the International Council for Canadian Studies. Copies of this volume may be purchased for $15Cdn from the: **International Council for Canadian Studies, 2 Daly Avenue, Ottawa, Ontario, K1N 6E2. Tel.: (613) 232-0417, fax (613) 232-2495; or Association for Canadian Studies, P.O. Box 8888, Station A, Montréal, Qc, H3C 3P8. Tel.: (514) 987-7784, fax (514) 987-8210.**

Thèmes canadiens / Canadian Issues (ISSN 0318-8442) est publié annuellement par l'Association d'études canadiennes. Y sont rassemblées des communications présentées dans le cadre du congrès annuel de l'association. Le présent volume, toutefois, est une publication conjoint de l'Association d'études canadiennes et du Conseil international d'études canadiennes. On peut se procurer ce volume au coût de 15 $ Can l'unité en s'adressant au : **Conseil international d'études canadiennes, 2, avenue Daly, Ottawa, Ontario, K1N 6E2. Tél.: (613) 232-0417, téléc.: (613) 232-2495; ou Association d'études canadiennes, C.P. 8888, Succursale A, Montréal, Québec, H3C 3P8. Tél.: (514) 987-7784, téléc.: (514) 987-8210.**

Conference organizing committee / Comité d'organisation du congrès:
Jean-Michel Lacroix, Chair of the committee/président du comité,
    Université de Paris III — Sorbonne Nouvelle
Gladys L. Symons, École nationale d'administration publique, Montréal
Alan F.J. Artibise, University of British Columbia, Vancouver
Simon Langlois, Université Laval, Québec
Jorn Carlsen, University of Aarhus, Denmark
Béatrice Kowaliczko, Executive Director/Directrice générale, ACS/AEC
Christian Pouyez, Executive Director/Directeur général, ICCS/CIEC

Coordinators / Coordinatrices:
Carol Bujeau, ICCS/CIEC
Susan Hoeltken, ACS/AEC

The following have collaborated in the preparation of this volume / *Ont collaboré à la préparation de ce volume* :

Ann Braithwaite, Jill Capri, Claire Martin, Vincent Masciotra

Acknowledgements / Remerciements:

The Association for Canadian Studies and the International Council for Canadian Studies are grateful to the Social Sciences and Humanities Research Council of Canada, the Social Science Federation of Canada, the Canadian Federation for the Humanities, the Department of External Affairs-Canada, the Ministère des Affaires internationales-Québec, Northern Telecom Limited, and the City of Québec, who have contributed financially to the organization of the conference and the publication of this volume.

L'Association d'études canadiennes et le Conseil international d'études canadiennes tiennent à exprimer leur gratitude au Conseil de recherches en sciences humaines du Canada, la Fédération canadienne des sciences sociales, la Fédération canadienne des études humaines, le ministère des Affaires extérieures-Canada, le Ministère des affaires internationales-Québec, la compagnie Northern Telecom Limitée, et la Ville de Québec pour leur aide financière pour la tenue du congrès et la publication de ce volume.

Cover Photo / photographie de couverture :

Québec comme il se voit du côté de l'est
Carte de l'Amérique septentrionale, dressée en 1688 par Jean-Baptiste-Louis Franquelin.
Photo : Claude Paulette
Bibliothèque nationale de Paris

The editors have made every reasonable effort to assure that proper identification and acknowledgement of sources have been made by the various authors in this publication

Le comité d'édition a fait tout son possible pour que les sources citées par les divers auteurs soient correctement identifiées.

TABLE OF CONTENTS — TABLE DES MATIÈRES

Simon Langlois — Alan F.J. Artibise

INTRODUCTION

La Conférence annuelle sur les études canadiennes tenue en 1989 était parrainée et organisée conjointement par l'Association d'études canadiennes et le Conseil international d'études canadiennes. Les articles colligés dans le présent volume ont été choisis, parmi plus de quarante communications présentées, compte tenu de leur qualité savante, de leur discipline et de leur représentativité des pays participants. C'est la marque d'une maturité croissante chez les chercheurs en études canadiennes que ce recueil contienne d'excellentes communications provenant de disciplines diverses telles que l'économie, les relations internationales, les communications, la littérature, les études sur les femmes, le droit et la sociologie. La nature internationale de la conférence — et des études canadiennes en général — ressort du fait que les participants proviennent du Canada, des États-Unis, du Danemark, de l'Allemagne et de l'Union soviétique.

Le thème de la conférence, soit «Canada : Traditions et Révolutions», était vaste conformément à notre intention de rassembler des chercheurs de toute une gamme de disciplines en vue de discuter de questions et de sujets portant principalement sur la continuité et le changement. Il n'est pas étonnant que les premières communications du présent recueil portent sur les échanges commerciaux, étant donné que 1989 a été l'année où a été conclu l'Accord de libre-échange entre le Canada et les États-Unis. C'est également au cours de cette année que l'Europe s'orientait nettement vers de nouvelles ententes commerciales qui auront fort probablement des répercussions importantes sur le Canada. L'article de Boris Alekhin sur «L'Accord de libre-échange entre le Canada et les États-Unis» soutient que le pacte était en fait partie intégrante d'un processus plus vaste synonyme de modifications structurelles au sein de l'économie tant canadienne que mondiale. L'économie du Canada a toujours été ouverte et vulnérable, mais les transformations survenues au cours des dernières décennies l'ont forcée, affirme Alekhin, à trouver de nouveaux moyens de se protéger. Lorsqu'on l'examine du point de vue international, on s'aperçoit que l'Accord de libre-échange met le Canada «à l'avant-garde de l'intégration économique mondiale». Peu de Canadiens voient la situation sous cet angle et cette perspective, peu importe l'opinion qu'on a face à l'Accord, indique qu'il vaut vraiment la peine de repenser les progrès du Canada dans un contexte beaucoup plus large que les préoccupations quotidiennes des milieux politiques canadiens. Une opinion vaste et similaire ressort également de la communication de Diddy Hitchins et de Bertil Liander intitulée «Post W.W. II Patterns of Trade and Aid». Ces derniers examinent les tendances frappant le Canada, les États-Unis et la Communauté économique européenne afin de déterminer s'il existe réellement un lien entre les courants commerciaux (grandement façonnés par les réalités des marchés mondiaux) et les dynamiques de l'aide au développement (résultant de décisions politiques). Fait intéressant à souligner, le lien le plus faible entre le commerce et l'aide se trouve au Canada, mais les justifications de cette réalité découlent en grande partie de la nature même de l'économie canadienne et de facteurs historiques plutôt que des discours officiels énonçant qu'il n'existe aucun lien entre le commerce et l'aide. En fait, il serait préférable, selon les auteurs de l'article, d'étudier séparément ces deux concepts.

Les thèmes des traditions et des révolutions que l'on a relevés dans l'économie du Canada des années 1980 se trouvent également dans les milieux politiques du pays et particulièrement dans deux documents qui ont défrayé les manchettes tout au long de la décennie : la Charte canadienne des droits et libertés et l'Accord du lac Meech. La communication de Martin Thunert situe la Charte dans le contexte d'une transformation de la relation entre la société et l'État au sein des pays occidentaux depuis 1945, et étudie le phénomène à partir de l'expérience canadienne. M. Thunert examine également la question importante à savoir si la Charte conduira à l'américanisation du pays. Il conclut en affirmant : «the Charter is a steering medium of a political community with a fragile consensus». Le pouvoir de ce «mécanisme» dont il parle est toutefois mis au défi par l'avènement de l'Accord du lac Meech. L'article de José Woehrling soutient que l'Accord constitue une sorte de «contre-révolution» à la Charte en permettant aux provinces d'y déroger dans certaines circonstances. En fait, note-t-il, l'Accord peut conduire à une certaine «régionalisation» quant à la mise en oeuvre de la Charte. L'Accord établit sans contredit «la primauté de la dualité linguistique du Canada et le caractère distinct du Québec». À cet égard au moins, l'Accord fait contrepoids à la Charte, en insistant de nouveau sur le fait que les traditions politiques fragiles du Canada ne peuvent être modifiées facilement ni de façon dramatique.

Peu de canadianistes s'étonneront de ce que le Canada est rarement «révolutionnaire» au plan des politiques, mais dans le domaine des communications on peut s'attendre à ce que les changements révolutionnaires soient davantage monnaie courante. Comme le note Jean McNulty dans son article intitulé «The Internationalization of Broadcasting and Its Implications for Canadian Policy», l'industrie de la radiodiffusion fait continuellement face à une révolution technologique. Pour le Canada, cette réalité a toujours signifié la protection et le développement difficile de la culture canadienne, exigeant du pays l'élaboration d'un cadre politique complexe et raffiné. Il est à noter, affirme McNulty, que ce contexte politique a été peu mis en doute par l'internationalisation des services de télévision. En fait, les nouveaux progrès technologiques n'ont pas transformé de façon dramatique les contraintes exercées sur les décideurs politiques. En pleine révolution technologique, les politiques de radiodiffusion traditionnelles du Canada sont demeurées en place.

Les deux articles suivants se fondent sur les écrits de George Grant, en particulier sur ses vues sur la «modernité». Roy Turner souscrit à l'affirmation de Grant selon laquelle la modernité — que Grant redoutait être la source de l'homogénéisation — met au défi la culture canadienne qui, pour appuyer «une nation forte et unie», exige une imagination collective. En d'autres termes, Turner prétend que le Canada ne peut ignorer la modernité mais qu'il peut — et doit — résister au phénomène s'il veut survivre à titre de «nation unie». Les questions que Turner examine sont loin d'être étrangères à la plupart des canadianistes, quoique ses opinions fournissent de nouvelles perspectives permettant certainement d'attiser le débat de longue date sur l'identité du Canada. L'article de Hans Hauge met en doute, pour sa part, la validité fondamentale de la thèse de la modernité par un examen tant des sources de la perspective de Grant que de récentes critiques européennes. Sous diverses rubriques fascinantes, dont «The Canadian Refraction», «The Magi of the North and the Disappearance of Canada» ainsi que «The Ancients and the Moderns», Hauge étudie la thèse de Grant en vue de voir si le diagnostic de ce dernier sur la modernité était juste ou carrément erroné. Il termine en affirmant que la thèse de la modernité est erronée et cette conclusion, soutient-il, signifie que «la survie n'est pas une situation particulière au Canada mais une réalité moderne». Pour arriver à cet énoncé, Hauge passe toutefois en revue une gamme de questions fascinantes touchant la culture canadienne et la «survie», et il n'est possible de bien saisir ses conclusions qu'en parcourant son article étoffé.

Les changements observables dans la condition féminine constituent certes l'une des dimensions les plus importantes des mutations en cours au

Canada, comme dans les autres sociétés développées. Un ouvrage sur la société canadienne, entre la tradition et la révolution aurait été incomplet sans une étude sur les femmes. La condition féminine est ici analysée sous deux angles : le mouvement social des femmes et les changements observables dans les rôles féminins.

L'article de D. Lamoureux porte plus spécifiquement sur le mouvement des femmes du Québec, mais son analyse pourrait être assez facilement étendue à l'ensemble du Canada. Deux constats lui servent de point de départ. Le mouvement des femmes a été, et est encore, très dynamique et très vivant. Il s'est engagé récemment sur la voie de l'expérimentation sociale et il exprime «une volonté de changer la vie». Le mouvement des femmes est resté un véritable mouvement social. Mais il s'est aussi institutionnalisé. Les structures administratives et politiques font une place aux femmes, les réseaux, les programmes et les mesures législatives se multiplient, afin d'apporter les correctifs et les changements revendiqués par elles. D'où une tension entre deux pôles : l'intégration et l'autonomie, tension qui est l'objet de l'étude de Lamoureux. Ces deux pôles caractérisent maintenant le mouvement des femmes qui oscille entre la lutte pour les droits (Women's rights movement) et la lutte pour la libération (Women's liberation movement). En ce sens, le mouvement des femmes se situe quelque part entre la tradition, marquée par l'institutionnalisation, et la révolution ou la poursuite de la libération, qui est le plus souvent au coeur même de tout mouvement social, faut-il le rappeler.

L'étude de Jones, Marsden et Tepperman analyse l'entrée des femmes dans la sphère publique, en insistant sur la croissance et les changements observables dans les choix qu'elles effectuent maintenant. Le thème général du colloque, traditions et révolutions s'applique encore ici avec une grande pertinence. Les modes de vie des femmes sont plus diversifiés et plus fluides. Ils oscillent encore entre la sphère traditionnelle, centrés sur le foyer et la vie familiale, et la marché du travail, où les femmes se trouvent encore en position inégale et très souvent précaire. «More over, we see no sign of linear trend towards gender equalization in our society». L'une des conséquences majeures des changements observables dans les modes de vie: baisse de la fécondité et de la nuptialité, hausse du divorce, augmentation de la participation au marché du travail, est sans conteste l'individualisation, processus social qui résume plus que tout autre les changements qui sont analysés.

Mais on ne saurait étudier les mutations sociales en se limitant aux aspects structuraux et macrosociologiques, ou encore aux seuls comportements. Il est de tradition, dans le domaine des études canadiennes, d'aborder aussi l'imaginaire social et les représentations collectives. Le présent ouvrage n'échappe pas à cette tradition, et on y trouvera cette fois une préoccupation plus marquée pour un domaine souvent négligé : la poésie. Deux articles y sont consacrés.

Le texte de K. Gould porte sur les courants récents en théorie littéraire au Québec, plus précisément sur la pensée de Nicole Brossard, figure de proue de la poésie québécoise contemporaine, et de France Théoret. L'auteure insiste sur la prise de distance vis-à-vis les courants théoriques américains ou français. Se développent plutôt au Québec des tendances ou des courants en littérature qui puisent davantage dans l'expérience quotidienne. Plus spécifiquement, l'auteure se penche sur l'*écriture au féminin*, «the emergence of various attempts to write in the feminine as a response to the erasure of social, historical, individual, and gender-specific forms of inscription in the experimental writings of *la modernité*».

A. Kizuk propose une analyse critique assez dure de l'avant-garde littéraire canadienne. «At least since the 1890s (...) poetry in Canada has been an expression of competing would-be orthodoxies masquerading as avant-gardes». Il décrit les courants de pensée, les rapports entre les groupes et les auteurs, avant de conclure que l'avant-garde d'hier s'est assagi et rangé, au point même de se transformer en nouvelle orthodoxie. «Canadian avant-gardes tend to transform themselves into orthodoxies as the leaders mature and acquire power in literary and academic circles». La poésie canadienne passerait-elle de la révolution à la tradition? La question mérite d'être posée au terme de la lecture de l'étude de Kizuk.

The 1989 annual Canadian Studies Conference was jointly sponsored and organized by the Association for Canadian Studies and the International Council for Canadian Studies. The articles that appear in this volume were chosen from among the more than forty papers that were presented on the basis of scholarly quality, subject area, and representativeness in terms of country. It is a mark of the increasing maturation of Canadian Studies scholarship that this collection contains excellent papers from such diverse disciplines as economics, international relations, communications, literature, women's studies, law and sociology. The international nature of the conference — and of Canadian Studies generally — is reflected in this volume by the fact that the contributors are from Canada, the United States, Denmark, Germany, and the Soviet Union.

Simon Langlois — Alan F.J. Artibise

The theme of the conference — *Canada: Traditions and Revolutions* — was a broad one as it was our intention to attract scholars from a wide variety of disciplines to address issues and topics that focused on both continuity and change. Not surprisingly, the first papers in this collection focus on trade since 1989 was the year of the Canada-US Free Trade Agreement, as well as a time when Europe was clearly moving to new trading arrangements that were sure to have substantial impacts on Canada. Boris Alekhin's paper on "The Canada-US Free Trade Agreement" asserts that the pact was in fact part of a larger process that involved structural changes both in the Canadian and the world economy. Canada's economy had always been both open and vulnerable, but the changes in recent decades forced it— Alekhin argues—to find new ways to protect itself. The Free Trade Agreement then, when viewed from an international context, places Canada "at the forefront of world economic integration." This perspective is one that few Canadians appreciate and, whatever one's view of the FTA, indicates that there is considerable value in rethinking Canadian developments in a context far removed from the day-to-day concerns of Canadian politics. A similar, broad view is continued in the paper by Diddy Hitchins and Bertil Liander on "Post W.W. II Patterns of Trade and Aid". They examine patterns in Canada, the US, and the European Economic Community with a view to determining whether or not trading patterns (largely determined by global market realities) and development aid patterns (determined by political decisions) are linked. Interestingly, the least linkage between trade and aid is found in Canada but the reasons for this fact are largely to be found in the nature of the Canadian economy and historical factors rather than in Canada's avowed statements that aid and trade are not linked; in fact, trade and aid should, the authors assert, be kept distinct.

The themes of traditions and revolutions found in the Canadian economy in the 1980s can also be found in the country's politics and especially in two documents that dominated the news throughout the decade—the Canadian Charter of Rights and Liberties and the Meech Lake Accord. Martin Thunert's paper places the Charter in the context of changing state-society relations in western societies since 1945, as well as examining it from within the Canadian experience. He also examines the important issue of whether the Charter will lead to an Americanization of the country. He concludes by asserting that "the Charter is a steering medium of a political community with a fragile consensus." The power of this "medium," however, is challenged by the Meech Lake Accord. José Woehrling's article argues that the Accord[1] constitutes a kind of "counter-revolution" to the Charter by

---

1. At the time of writing (May 1990) the Meech Lake Accord had not been approved by all the provinces.

permitting provinces to escape its force in certain instances. In effect, he notes, the Accord may lead to a certain "regionalization" in the application of the Charter. The Accord certainly establishes "the primacy of linguistic duality in Canada and the distinct character of Quebec." In this regard, at least, the Accord is a counter-balance to the Charter, emphasizing again that the fragile political traditions of Canada cannot be changed easily or dramatically.

Few Canadianists will be surprised by the fact that Canada is rarely "revolutionary" when it comes to matters of politics, but in the area of communications it might be expected that revolutionary change is more common. As Jean McNulty notes in her contribution of "The Internationalization of Broadcasting and Its Implications for Canadian Policy," the broadcasting industry is continually in a state of technological revolution. For Canada, this has always meant that protecting and developing Canadian culture is difficult, calling upon the country to develop a sophisticated and complex policy framework. It is notable, McNulty asserts, that this policy framework has not been especially challenged by the internationalization of television broadcasting services. In fact, new technological developments have not dramatically changed the constraints on policy-makers; in the midst of a technological revolution, the traditions of Canadian broadcasting policy have remained in place.

The next two articles take as their starting points the writings of George Grant, particularly his views of "modernity." Roy Turner accepts Grant's assertion that modernity— which Grant feared as a source of homogenization—is a challenge to Canadian culture which, if it is to support "a strong united nation," requires collective imagination. Put another way, Turner argues that Canada cannot ignore modernity but it can—and must—resist the phenomenon if it is to thrive as a "united nation." The issues Turner examines will be familiar to most Canadianists, although his insights certainly provide the long-standing debates about the Canadian identity with new perspectives. Hans Hauge's article, however, challenges the fundamental validity of the modernity thesis through an examination of both the sources of Grant's thesis and recent European critiques. Hauge examines Grant's diagnosis of modernity and under a series of intriguing sub-headings—including "The Canadian Refraction," "The Magi of the North and the Disappearance of Canada," and "The Ancients and the Moderns"—the thesis with a view to answering the question of whether Grant's diagnosis of modernity was adequate of simply wrong. He concludes that it was wrong and this conclusion, he asserts, means that "survival is not a specific Canadian stance but the modern one." In arriving at this point, however, Hauge reviews a variety of intriguing issues relating to

Canadian culture and "survival" and his conclusions can only be fully understood in the context of his rich article.

The discernible changes in women's status are certainly one of the main aspects of transformations presently occurring in Canada as in other industrialized countries. A document on traditions and revolutions in Canadian society would have been incomplete without a study on women. Their status is analyzed herein from two standpoints: the social movement of women and the observable changes in women's roles.

D. Lamoureux's paper focusses more specifically on the Quebec Women's movement, but her analysis could also be extended fairly easily to all of Canada. She bases herself on two observations. First, the Women's movement has been and is still very active and very much alive. It has recently headed towards social experimentation and it expresses «a will to change a way of life». Second, the Women's movement has remained a real social movement, but it has also institutionalized itself. The administrative and political structures now make room for women, and the number of networks, programs and legal measures is increasing to bring about the corrections and changes claimed by these women. This leads to tensions between two opposite views: integration vs. autonomy, a confrontation that is the basis of Lamoureux's thesis. These two focal points now characterize the Women's movement which wavers between the Women's rights movement and the Women's liberation movement. Therefore, the Women's movement stands between traditions, marked by institutionalization, and revolutions or the fight for liberation, which is, more often than not, the core itself of any social movement.

Jones, Marsden and Tepperman's study analyses the entry of women on the public scene, insisting on the growth and on the discernible changes in the choices they now make. The main theme of the conference, "Traditions and Revolutions," again applies and with a high level of relevancy. Women's lifestyles are more diversified and flexible. They still oscillate between the traditional realm, focussed on the home and the family, and the market place, where women are still in a disadvantaged and quite often precarious position. "Moreover, we see no sign of a linear trend towards gender equalization in our society." One of the major consequences of discernible changes in the lifestyles—i.e., falling birth and marriage rates, high divorce rate, increasing representation in the work force—is undeniably individualization, a social process which best summarizes the changes examined here.

It is impossible, however, to study the social transformations by looking solely at structural and macrosociological dimensions or behaviour alone. Canadian Studies have a long tradition of also studying social imagination and collective representations. This document is in keeping with this tradition and focusses this time on a concern for a discipline often left aside: poetry. Two papers deal with this issue.

K. Gould's article pertains to the recent trends on the theory of literature in Quebec, specifically to the works of Nicole Brossard, figurehead of contemporary Quebec poetry, and of France Théoret. The author insists on the need to stand aloof from the American or French theoretical trends in literature which dwell more on day-to-day life. More specifically, the author looks into women's writings, "the emergence of various attempts to write in the feminine as a response to the erasure of social, historical, individual and gender-specific forms of inscription in the experimental writings of *la modernité*."

A. Kizuk proposes a critical analysis which is relatively harsh of Canadian avant-garde literature. "At least since the 1890s [...] poetry in Canada has been an expression of competing would-be orthodoxies masquerading as avant-gardes." He describes the theoretical perspectives, the relationships between groups and authors, before concluding that yesterday's avant-garde has quieted down and is now settled, to the point that it is becoming a new orthodoxy. "Canadian avant-gardes tend to transform themselves into orthodoxies as the leaders mature and acquire power in literary and academic circles." Is Canadian poetry going back from revolution to tradition? This is the question that comes to mind after reading Kizuk's paper.

Boris I. Alekhin

The Canada-US Free Trade Agreement: A Response to the Challenge of Global Economic Interdependence

Abstract

For the past quarter century, important changes have taken place in the structure of the Canadian economy and its interaction with the global economy. The major reason for these changes is the technological revolution, which greatly intensified the whole process of capital accumulation and internationalization. The Canada-US Free Trade Agreement was the most important political outcome of this process. The agreement characterizes Canada as a country at the forefront of world economic integration—a country that came closer than many other industrialized nations to seeing the world as an economically indivisible system.

Résumé

Au cours du dernier quart de siècle, d'importantes transformations ont eu lieu dans la structure économique canadienne et dans la place que le Canada occupe dans l'économie mondiale. La cause principale de ces changements est la révolution technologique qui a grandement intensifié le processus d'accumulation du capital et de son internationalisation. Le Traité de libre échange canado-américain est la plus importante conséquence de ce processus. L'accord montre que le Canada est à l'avant-garde de l'intégration économique mondiale et qu'il est beaucoup plus proche d'une vision du monde comme système économique indivisible que plusieurs autres pays industrialisés.

Introduction

During the past quarter century, profound changes have taken place in the structure of the world economy. All nations, to a varying degree, have been involved in the process of global economic interaction, and it is no longer possible for any country, regardless of its geographical location, economic

1

power or political regime, to achieve its goals without close and systematic interaction with the global economy.

The deepening of the international division of labour tends to make domestic economies both more efficient in terms of per capita income and more vulnerable to adverse developments in the rest of the world. Therefore, the prospect of co-existing as parts of one indivisible economic system poses a serious challenge to the ability of nations to adjust to external shocks, to find by way of competition their niches in the world market, and to manage collectively the internationalization process.

Toward a More Open and Vulnerable Economy

Each country responds to this challenge on the basis of its historical experience, political organization, and economic power. For Canada, with its small population and advanced privately owned industry, open and stable relations with the global economy have always played an important part in the process of capital accumulation. As Table 1 shows, in the postwar period, the proportion of foreign trade (exports plus imports) to Canada's gross domestic product has never been lower than 40%. Since 1960, after three decades of instability, foreign trade has been inclined to grow faster than domestic production.

Turning to the export side of Canada's foreign trade, two interrelated developments should be mentioned. First, the manufactured portion of foreign sales has tended to increase, while the share of resource products has tended to decline.

This tendency has been brought about by the growth of organic composition of capital employed in Western economies (value of fixed assets per worker). The growth of organic composition stimulates international trade in those goods which constitute the fixed portion of capital, i.e., machinery and equipment, while playing down the importance of food, raw materials, and consumer items. Another factor to mention in connection with the changing commodity structure of international trade is a relative decline of world demand for resource products caused by the introduction of resource-saving technology and material substitutes. As a result, manufactured goods are making up a growing proportion of world exports.[1]

2

Table 1 Foreign trade in goods and services as a percentage of gross domestic product

Years	Exports	Imports
1955-59	18.9	27.3
1960-64	19.7	21.3
1965-69	22.8	23.7
1970-74	24.3	25.7
1975-79	27.3	29.0
1980-84	29.1	29.8
1985-87	27.2	25.7

Sources: "Canadian Economic Observer," *Historical Statistical Supplement, 1987* (Ottawa: Minister of Supply and Services of Canada 1988), 5.

For countries richly endowed with natural resources, this tendency creates a problem of structural change. Canada has been relatively successful in adjusting the commodity structure of its exports to the changing pattern of world demand. As Table 2 shows, between the first half of the '60s and the second half of the '80s, the share of finished products in Canadian exports quadrupled. Because exporters of manufactured goods face higher trade barriers, the pressure on the Canadian government to promote freer trade has been growing.

The second development is Canada's growing dependence on trade with the United States. The share of Canadian exports accounted for by the US increased from 56.4% in 1960 to 79.8% in 1987.[2] This development has a lot to do with the changing commodity composition of Canadian foreign sales. It is the United States that serves as a major market base for the technological advance and production rationalization of Canada's manufacturing industries. The US accounts for more than 90% of Canadian manufactured exports.[3] This high proportion can be explained primarily by the rapid growth of sales of motor vehicles and parts to the US made possible by the Auto Pact of 1965.

It is important to note that, since all cars and most components are produced in Canada according to American specifications, using American technology and equipment, the growing share of manufactured goods in Canadian exports should not be interpreted solely as the evidence of Canada's technological and engineering competence. This increase should be seen rather as the result of specific functions assigned to Canadian

3

subsidiaries by their US parent companies, within the context of continental production rationalization.

Table 2 Percent distribution of domestic exports by major commodity groups

Commodities	1960-64	1965-69	1970-74	1975-79	1980-84	1985-87
Food, feed, beverages, tobacco	21.0	15.3	12.1	10.9	11.4	8.4
Raw materials	21.0	18.9	20.1	20.6	17.7	14.9
Manufactured materials	47.3	38.7	33.4	34.3	35.6	32.3
End Products	10.5	26.8	33.7	33.9	34.9	44.2
Special transactions	0.3	0.3	0.2	0.2	0.4	0.2

Sources: Economic Council of Canada, *The Bottom Line*, 92; "Canadian Economic Observer," 52

The tendency toward greater export orientation has not been confined to the automobile industry. In fact, we are witnessing the emergence of a group of larger Canadian companies in the manufacturing sector that turned to aggressive export strategies to deal with the problems of technological change and foreign competition. Increased dependence on foreign markets made these companies and entirely Canadian industries much more vulnerable to foreign protectionist measures, particularly to American ones. This explains, at least in part, why the Canadian Manufacturers Association (CMA) endorsed the idea of a comprehensive free-trade agreement with the United States in 1985. One may recall that the CMA rejected this idea in 1980. Given the fact that business associations in resource industries traditionally support free trade, we may conclude that, for the first time in Canadian history, business communities set up a sort of national front to promote a comprehensive free-trade agreement with the United States. This was something the Canadian government should have taken very seriously, which it did when the Conservatives came to power.

There were other factors at work as well. These were both long and short term, economic and political, as well as domestic and foreign. First, during the last several years, Canadian corporations dramatically increased their foreign direct investment, notably in the United States. In 1975, Canada became a net exporter of capital for direct investment and, as a result, Canadian corporations became interested not only in the freedom of trade but also in the freedom of capital exports. This meant increased opposition to Canadian economic nationalism which encourages other governments to retaliate against Canadian corporations.

Second, as a result of the declining competitiveness of Canadian goods, there was a decline in the Canadian share of world exports. Competitors from Japan, Western Europe and newly industrialized countries successfully competed with Canadian firms on all major markets, including the Canadian market. Between 1970 and 1981, the Canadian share of world exports declined from 5.2% to 3.5%.[4] As a result, Canadian companies intensified their pressure on the government to strengthen and secure access to the market where they are most competitive—the American market.

Third, while the Canadian economy needed new technology and equipment to sustain its competitiveness, the required capital was not available because foreign transnational companies were not sure that their Canadian subsidiaries would have extensive and stable access to the American market. Hence the pressure on Ottawa to liberalize and stabilize a continental regime for trade and investment. Fourth, unwillingness to invest was, to a significant degree, related to the feeling of insecurity which was developing due to growing protectionism in the West, particularly in the United States. According to the World Bank, the proportion of imports subject to non-tariff barriers increased by some 20% during the eighties.

Fifth, the GATT, which has been so important to Canada, discontinued negotiations in 1979 and, despite efforts by the US and Canada, did not resume talks until 1986. In other words, the Canadian situation did not correspond to the process of multilateral trade liberalization—four years at work and four years at recess. The Canadian government and business community felt that reliance on the GATT alone could not solve the problem of market access. Perhaps more importantly, the GATT was not designed to deal with non-tariff barriers that are of prime concern to Canadian corporations.

Sixth, the economic crisis of 1981-82 reinforced the integrationist tendency in Canada's relationship with the United States because it inflicted heavy losses on corporations and workers alike. According to public opinion polls, the majority of Canadians supported integrationism because they saw it as a means of attracting increased investment and creating more jobs.[5]

Seventh, as a result of the growing continentalization of the Canadian economy, foreign trade has become very important in terms of jobs and personal incomes. According to an official estimate, exports provide directly and indirectly some 3 million jobs in Canada.[6] It is not surprising that quite recently, perhaps since the latest economic crisis, many Canadians have accepted the idea of free trade as a positive one, as an idea which coincides with their desire for more economic security. In a broader sense, according to sociological research, Canadians are now more confident about the ability of their economy to withstand "the chill winds of international competition."[7]

Eighth, on the other side of the border, American business (which in many industries is fighting rear-guard action against competitors from Europe and Asia) was also testing the possibility of a "fortress North America" in search of a better defence for its domestic base. The US has little to fear from free trade because it has enormous financial and technological advantages over Canada (i.e. many larger Canadian companies are subsidiaries of American corporations). As one official study has shown, out of 35 commodity groups surveyed by the US International Trade Commission, only one group anticipated that the Free Trade Agreement with Canada would have a significant negative effect.[8] As early as 1980, the Reagan administration hinted to its continental neighbours that it was prepared to move forward on the project of North American accord, which meant economic integration between the United States, Canada and Mexico. The US Trade Law of 1984 specifically mentioned Canada along with Israel and Egypt as a possible partner in a free-trade agreement.

Finally, Canadian business reacted to all the changes in its foreign economic position with a demand to start free trade negotiations as early as possible. This demand was reinforced by numerous business associations, quasi-government commissions and committees, and individual economists and politicians who favoured continental integration. Of particular importance to the Mulroney government was the support to free trade given by the MacDonald Commission. Thus integrationists were taking revenge for their defeat under the Trudeau government.

The Free Trade Agreement (FTA)

Following the recommendations of the MacDonald Commission, Canadian trade negotiator Simon Reisman and his experts prepared a rather ambitious agenda for free-trade negotiations with the Americans. The

Canadian delegation sought to establish a new regime for bilateral trade which would protect Canadian interests and be guaranteed by a supranational dispute settlement mechanism. It even considered the idea of eliminating all non-tariff barriers, (anti-dumping duties, for example). More particularly, the Canadian delegation wanted to: mark out clear rules defining fair and unfair trading practices; establish a bilateral dispute settlement mechanism whose decision on emergency protection would be binding for both sides; improve access to each other's agricultural markets; maintain the Auto Pact as is, unless the proposed changes would stimulate trade in the industry; eliminate all tariff and most non-tariff barriers in bilateral trade; and refrain from introducing new barriers.

Canada also refused to discuss the question of cultural industries and promised that social and industrial programs would not be affected by the FTA. Because neither the White House nor the US International Trade Commission gave instructions to US Chief Trade Negotiator Peter Murphy, he turned to the US Congress for encouragement. Congress viewed the agreement as a means of opening up the Canadian market for American goods and services, cutting social and industrial development programs, eliminating marketing boards in Canada (such as the Canadian Wheat Board), changing—according to the American standards—Canadian legislation on intellectual property, and changing the Auto Pact because during recent years it has been largely beneficial to Canada. It proposed, in exchange, to give Canada as little as possible. In the final analysis, argued the Congressmen, it was Canada—not the United States—that wanted the agreement. It seemed that, while the Canadian delegation envisaged a free-trade zone with open boundaries, clear rules of competition, and a bilateral dispute settlement system, the Americans proposed a few minor changes in the existing regime for continental trade and investment and, at the same time, demanded non-trade concessions from Canada. Careful reading of the legal text of the FTA reveals that neither side achieved all its objectives. While the Auto Pact and its safeguards will be maintained under the Agreement, and the Agreement does nothing to prevent present and future measures to protect and promote Canadian culture and the industries that support it, Canada was unable to persuade the United States to clearly define fair or unfair trading practices. Canada also failed to resolve the issue of emergency protection. However, the two sides did agree to hold another round of negotiations to overcome their differences on this important issue. It is crucially important now for Canada to investigate the extent and nature of the subsidies the American industries enjoy. Evidence of compromise and even failure may be found in other sections of the Agreement.

From the Marxist perspective, the idea of free trade between capitalist countries is quite clear. Marx argued that free trade tends to promote the development of productive forces and social change. While he acknowledged that some countries, Germany and Ireland for example, would benefit from protectionism and that free trade may even aggravate the material position of the working class, in the final analysis, Marx endorsed free trade as "a normal condition of modern capitalist production," "a normal, natural atmosphere for historical evolution." Following Marx, Lenin also argued that the proletariat should support the "complete freedom of capitalist turnover" and welcome any assimilation of nations, except for that imposed by the use of force or based on privileges. In short, Marxists treat protectionism as an instrument to encourage industrialization within the framework of free trade. Industrialization creates dependence on foreign markets, and this dependence creates a need for free trade.

It is sometimes argued that this general principle should not be applied to Canada, because with more than 70% of its exports going to the American market, Canada is a special case. There is little logic in this argument. Canada needs free trade, perhaps more than any other industrialized nation, exactly because it depends so heavily on trade with the United States (see Table 3). Other western countries, having much more diversified foreign trade relations, are not as vulnerable to foreign protectionist measures as is Canada. A search for more stable and open access to the US market is one of the major themes in Canadian economic history. The Canada-US Free Trade Agreement is not a break from past tradition: it is its logical culmination.

Free trade will result in a more efficient Canadian economy and higher per capita incomes because it will allow for more production specialization, optimal plant sizes and higher labour productivity. Free trade will force Canadian companies to concentrate on things they can produce best and phase out production of their least-competitive goods. It will also introduce a greater measure of stability into the investment process.

It goes without saying that free trade encourages international specialization, the growth of labour productivity and increased per capita incomes. But it is also quite clear that Canadian corporations will try to make use of restructuring in order to redistribute the expected addition to the national economic pie. A survey of twenty Canadian companies conducted by Don Daly shows that the tripling of output, as a result of specialization to cater to the entire continental market, may produce a significant decline in the share of wages of gross revenues of the firms surveyed, while the share of profits will rise.[9] Moreover, by increasing the organic composition of capital in the manufacturing sector, free trade may aggravate the problem of jobs available for the fast-growing Canadian population. It is extremely important for Canada to work out an adjustment strategy and set up an adjustment mechanism to help workers and firms to deal with the new situation.

Free trade is often criticized on non-economic grounds. Many Canadians believe that free trade will lead to the erosion of Canadian political sovereignty and national identity. They fear complete Americanization of Canadian culture. Despite the fact that the Canadian government has the right to take any measure to protect and promote the country's cultural industries under the Agreement, these side effects of the FTA may be very real and significant.

Two points should be emphasized here. First, limitations on economic and political autonomy is a logical outcome of the world's growing economic interdependence. Economic indivisibility produces political indivisibility of nations. When a country signs an international agreement, it sacrifices part of its independence and sovereignty for the sake of the benefits it expects from the agreement. Canada sacrificed a great deal of its economic autonomy when it entered the GATT, but so did many other nations that are Canada's partners in the process of multilateral trade liberalization. In the Canada-US Free Trade Agreement, the case is different. Canada is placing part of its autonomy in the hands of the single most powerful nation of the world in the hope of obtaining economic benefits from free trade. This is the outcome which seems least desirable.

Second, history does not support the claim that free trade will eventually wipe out Canadian culture. It is interesting to note that, while the Canadian economy has been drawn into the larger US economy during the post-war period, Canada was able to develop a system of institutions and policies to promote its cultural identity and political culture. This negative correlation between economic integration and the ability of individual nations to preserve and develop their national identities is now recognized by leading Soviet social scientists. Speaking at the first Soviet-Canada conference held in Moscow in February 1988, G. Arbatov said:

> There is no evidence to conclude that world development is deter-
> mined by the tendency towards the gradual erosion of historical
> traditions, national identities, and ideological differences, under
> the impact of the global tendency toward standardization and
> unification. . . . Rather, the great diversity and contradictions of

the modern world go hand in hand with the globalization of the most important social and economic processes.[10]

Table 3 Trade among G-7 Nations, 1986: exports

	Canada	USA	Japan	France	FRG	Italy	UK
Canada	—	20.9	2.6	0.1	1.0	1.2	2.3
USA	77.5	—	38.8	7.4	10.4	10.7	14.3
Japan	4.9	12.4	—	1.3	1.7	1.4	1.6
France	0.8	3.3	1.5	—	11.9	15.6	8.5
FRG	1.1	4.9	5.0	16.1	—	18.1	11.7
Italy	0.6	2.2	0.8	11.8	8.2	—	4.8
UK	2.3	5.2	3.2	8.8	8.5	7.1	—

Sources: *Multinational Business* 2 (1988), 9

Conclusion

For the past quarter century, important changes have taken place in the structure of the Canadian economy and its interaction with the global economy. The most important reason for these structural changes is the scientific and technological revolution that greatly intensified the entire process of capital accumulation and internationalization. As Canadian capital spills over international boundaries in search of new trade and investment opportunities, it comes to depend more and more on the American market. The Canada-US Free Trade Agreement was the most important political outcome of this process. The Agreement characterizes Canada as a country at the forefront of world economic integration—a country that came closer than any other industrialized nation to seeing the world as an economically indivisible system. The FTA is a culmination of the experience of a complex and contradictory interaction with the largest economy which made it possible for the former "white colony," a settler country, to create a dynamic and efficient national economy. Called by Ronald Reagan "the new economic constitution of North America," the Free Trade Agreement, is, in some respects, way ahead of world integrationist experience and opens up a new page in Canadian history.

Notes

1. D.J. Daly, *Managerial Macroeconomics: A Canadian Perspective* (Homewood, Illinois 1988), 251.
2. Economic Council of Canada, *The Bottom Line: Technology, Trade, and Income Growth* (Ottawa: Minister of Supply and Services 1983), 91; *Canadian Economic Observer*, "Historical Statistical Supplement, 1987," 52.
3. *Summary of Canadian International Trade, December 1988* (Ottawa: Minister of Supply and Services of Canada 1989), table X-2.
4. *1982 Year-Book of International Trade Statistics*. Vol. 1 (New York: United Nations 1984).
5. *Globe and Mail*, March 30, 1985.
6. *The World—Our Market* (Ottawa: Department of External Affairs 1987), 7.
7. *Financial Post*, September 28, 1987.
8. *Globe and Mail*, March 23, 1985.
9. *Canadian Industry in Transition* (Toronto: University of Toronto Press 1986), 191.
10 *.SSHA—ekonomika, politika, ideologia*, 7 (1988), 119.

Diddy R.M. Hitchins and Bertil Liander

Post World War II Patterns of Trade and Aid: Canada, USA and EEC

Abstract

This paper presents a detailed description of the pattern of trade engaged in by Canada and its record as a donor of Third World aid, and then briefly reviews US and EEC trade and aid patterns for comparative purposes. By contrast and comparison the paper seeks to explain Canada's patterns of trade and aid, looking for parallels between trade and aid figures. Whilst trading patterns are largely determined by global-market realities, development aid decisions are determined by political decisions within the donor nation-states. Despite this dichotomy, linkages are made between the patterns of trade and aid for Canada, the USA and the EEC.

Résumé

Cet exposé présente une description détaillée du commerce exercé par le Canada et de sa politique en matière d'aide au tiers monde, avec un aperçu, à titre comparatif, des politiques des États-Unis et de la CEE dans ce domaine. Par contraste et comparaison, à l'aide de données statistiques qu'il met en parallèle, l'auteur étudie les pratiques du Canada en matière de commerce et d'aide au développement. Alors que les échanges commerciaux sont dans une large mesure déterminés par les réalités du marché, l'aide au développement dépend quant à elle de choix politiques relevant des États donateurs. Malgré cette dichotomie, des relations peuvent être établies entre commerce et aide, aussi bien pour le Canada, les États-Unis que la CEE.

Introduction

The purpose of this paper is to endeavour to gain a better understanding of Canadian patterns of trade and aid and their interrelationships through a descriptive analysis that provides comparisons with the trade and aid patterns of the USA and EEC. The comparisons are provided to demonstrate contrasting patterns that will further illuminate the Canadian situation. Since aid or, as it is now generally called, development assistance, is a post-World War II phenomenon, the analysis and comparison will cover the period from 1945 to 1988.

I. Canada's Record in Trade and Aid 1945-1988

Since long before its existence as a political entity, Canada has been known as a storehouse of resources for economic development. Europeans, from their earliest known contacts with North America, regarded the area that later became Canada as a source of raw materials and economic opportunity. The Vikings came to Canada in pursuit of land that could support human habitation. Other Europeans followed—the Basques from northeastern Spain in pursuit of the whales and their oil; and the French and the British in pursuit of the codfish that were so plentiful on the Grand Banks off the Atlantic coast of Canada, the fur of the beaver found in the remote northlands, and the timber for their ship building. The earliest European settlements in Canada were resource-based. The conflict between French- and English-speaking settlers was as much over control of economic resources as over political control.

The Canada that was created by the British North America Act of 1867, and which subsequently expanded to straddle the continent "a mari usque ad mare," was preeminently a trading state which, from its vast expanse and resources, partially provided the raw materials for British imperial development. Although nominally self-governing in its early stages, Canada's existence in the international arena was as an adjunct of Britain, a colonial element in the British Empire. Not until 1931, with the Statute of Westminster, did Canada achieve an independent international identity, but, even then, economic independence was not a reality and Canada could have been tied in a neocolonial situation of economic dependence indefinitely had it not been for the cataclysmic effect on global economics of the Second World War.

World War II disrupted economic relations throughout the world. The economies of Western Europe were devastated and the British imperial economic and trade network unravelled. In the aftermath of World War II the allied victors, led by the US, set out to create a new global trading system. The US committed itself to reconstruction of Europe through the Marshall Plan. Canada, as one of the few functioning developed economies in the immediate postwar period, seized the chance to work in consort with the US to restore the British economy and assist in developing and rebuilding Europe as well.

The demand from Europe for raw materials and the financial resources to pay for them, provided largely by the US, offered Canada a significant opportunity for trade that could replace wartime demand and offer real growth potential. Thus Canada entered the postwar period as a modern and developed nation-state, in partnership with the western industrialized countries, but unlike them in having a predominantly resource-based economy rooted in raw materials, more akin to a less developed than to an industrialized economy. The explanation for this anomaly lies in Canada's small population relative to its size and resources. The raw materials are available in far greater quantities than the Canadian population can use or develop and are therefore available to generate export earnings. The smallness of the internal market renders most manufacturing uneconomic: economic production is only possible with access to outside markets. Canada is thus a trading nation by necessity. Foreign trade is essential to maintaining the high standard of living enjoyed by the Canadian people. Currently 31% of Canadian GDP is generated by trade. As Table 1 illustrates, that is a far higher level of reliance on foreign trade than is the norm for other developed countries. Despite this heavy reliance on trade, Canada has, nevertheless, been able to maintain its standards largely because of an overall, ongoing, favorable balance of trade.

Table 1 Export as a percent of G.D.P., 1960-1982

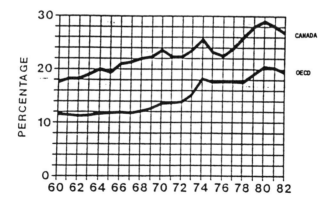

Source: OECD Data Base via I.P. Sharp, 1985

Although, in the past, Canada's exports have been primarily raw materials, since the 1960s the export of manufactured goods has increased so that by 1984 manufactured goods accounted for 42% of Canadian exports (Table 2). The major export products fall into four categories: (i) vehicles, and industrial machinery and equipment, (ii) newsprint, lumber, and wood pulp, (iii) petroleum and minerals, and (iv) wheat. As mentioned previously, the degree of reliance on primary products is rather contradictory to Canada's position as a developed country, making it more difficult for Canada to compete in sales to developing countries: what they need is not more primary products but manufactured goods.

Table 2 Trade by commodity - 1986

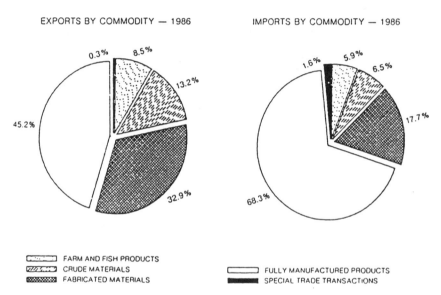

EXPORTS BY COMMODITY — 1986   IMPORTS BY COMMODITY — 1986

FARM AND FISH PRODUCTS
CRUDE MATERIALS
FABRICATED MATERIALS

FULLY MANUFACTURED PRODUCTS
SPECIAL TRADE TRANSACTIONS

Source: Department of External Affairs Annual Report 1986-87

Canadian trade is conducted on a bilateral basis, but in close observance of multilateral trade rules drawn up by such organizations as GATT, OECD and IMF. Canadian trade policy is not of recent origin—its roots go back to the middle of the nineteenth century and it has always embraced a strong element of protectionism. As a British colony, Canada enjoyed protection through the system of imperial preferences. Then, in 1846, the mood in Britain changed towards free trade and Canada became very vulnerable. It concluded a trade agreement with the United States but that did not last more than twelve years, and was cancelled in 1866. This led to the so-called

"National Policy," which was aimed at industrial development in Canada through import substitution and high tariffs to protect the infant industries.

These tariffs are in many cases still in force, albeit reduced in the GATT rounds. Evidence of this is that the majority of Canadian tariffs will take ten years to be dismantled in the context of the US-Canada Free Trade Agreement. The close relationship with the United States, and dependence on them as a trading partner have also affected Canada's trading pattern.

In the 1930s, Canada exported about 40% of its merchandise to the United Kingdom and 25% to the United States. In 1939, it imported about 65% of its needs from the United States and 15% of its imports came from the United Kingdom. Over the years, the relationship with the United Kingdom has changed dramatically, particularly after Britain joined the European Community in 1973 and developed interests and obligations in other markets. The relationship with the United States has, on the other hand, increased significantly (Table 3).

Table 3 Trade by region - 1986

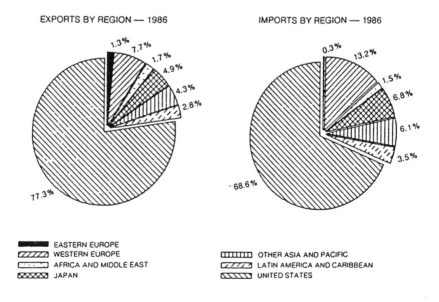

EXPORTS BY REGION — 1986

IMPORTS BY REGION — 1986

EASTERN EUROPE
WESTERN EUROPE
AFRICA AND MIDDLE EAST
JAPAN

OTHER ASIA AND PACIFIC
LATIN AMERICA AND CARIBBEAN
UNITED STATES

Source: Department of External Affairs Annual Report 1986-87

Although dwarfed by the United States, Japan has taken Britain's role as Canada's number two trading partner, and, collectively, the European Community conducts a larger, more balanced trade with Canada, accounting for 12% of exports and 7% of imports in 1986 compared with Japan's 5% of exports and 7% of imports. Trade with the rest of Asia, and particularly the Pacific, has increased, while the relationship with Latin America has diminished. Canada traded more with Asia than with Western Europe for the first time in 1983, and this has continued to be the case in subsequent years. The Middle East, Oceania, Africa and Eastern Europe are still areas of marginal importance for Canadian trade. In the period 1966-70, Canada's exports to developing countries as a share of total exports was 7.52%, and in the period 1971-75, 7.97%.[1] By 1986, this share was virtually unchanged at 8%, distributed as shown in Table 4.

Table 4 Canada's trade % with LDCs

Export	1939		1950	1960	1970	1980	1986
Asia & Oceania	9.8	Asia	2.8	2.2	2.5	4.1	3.6
Africa	2.4	Africa	1.8	1.4	1.0	1.4	0.7
		ME	0.8	0.5	0.8	1.5	0.9
Lat. Am.	1.8	Lat. Am.	6.0	4.8	4.7	5.3	2.8
	14.0		11.4	8.9	9.0	12.3	8.10

Import	1939		1950	1960	1970	1980	1986
Asia & Oceania	7.6	Asia	3.2	1.7	2.2	4.7	5.5
Africa	1.1	Africa	1.1	0.6	0.9	0.8	0.9
		ME	1.0	1.6	0.4	4.3	0.6
Lat. Am.	2.8	Lat. Am.	9.4	7.7	5.1	5.8	3.5
	11.5		14.7	11.6	8.6	15.6	10.5

Source: Calculated from Statistics Canada Yearbook

In 1985, Joe Clark, Canada's Secretary of State for External Affairs, made the following statement:

> It is important to Canada on economic and security as well as humanitarian grounds, that the indebted countries of the Third World grow again economically. Prospects for the growth of Canadian trade and other economic relations with developing

countries will depend in large measure on how the international trade and financial system accommodated those countries' development needs. Their capacity to export to developed countries is an important determinant of their capacity to import our products, to absorb investment productivity and to meet their financial obligations to us. It is also central to their own economic well being.[2]

The philosophy expressed here is quite clear but the question is, has Canada really tried to link aid with trade in a practical and conscientious way? After all, nearly three quarters of the world's population is living in the Third World. That means that regardless of low per capita income, their share of world trade is important, to say the least. Even if oil-exporting countries are not counted, the Third World still offers a larger market for manufactured products than the Japan and the United States markets together.

Since World War II, Canada has not only been remarkable in the world economy in terms of trade, but also for its role in international development assistance, or foreign aid. International Development Assistance, as a Canadian foreign policy objective, only came into being after World War II, with the creation of the United Nations and its agencies devoted to the promotion of economic and social advancement for all peoples. The United Nations Charter assumed development responsibilities and UN agencies were created with development agendas. Canada, as an enthusiastic proponent of the United Nations' initiatives, was among the first UN members to provide technical assistance training and modest financial contributions for the earliest UN initiatives in support of development goals. In creating the Marshall Plan, the United States undertook to play the major role in the reconstruction of Western European economies, while at the same time thwarting any potential spread of Soviet influence as the Cold War started. Canada joined the US in this effort by allocating $2 billion in reconstruction aid for Western Europe.

When, in the aftermath of the war, the British felt constrained to begin to release those of their former colonies demanding independence, they felt some duty, in the light of the prevailing UN development ethic, to provide at least a semblance of both financial support and technical assistance to aid their former colonies in their new-found independence. Discussion of these ideas and needs took place within the framework of the British Commonwealth. Cold War concerns about communist expansionism filling the vacuum created by British withdrawal played a part in the deliberations. Canada, which had been an important, enthusiastic and committed participant in the formation of the UN and its development goals and agencies, also supported the concept of development assistance within the Commonwealth. In 1950, it thus became a founder-partner and contributor to the first formally established development assistance program, the Commonwealth "Colombo Plan," designed to provide assistance to newly independent India, Pakistan and Ceylon (later Sri Lanka), all former British colonies. The Commonwealth donors of the required technical assistance were the UK, Australia, Canada and New Zealand. (The US and Japan became partners in the Colombo Plan in 1951 and 1954 respectively.) Thus began Canadian Development Aid.[3] Since 1950, Canadians have given in excess of $20 billion to fund thousands of projects in more than one hundred countries, and have contributed to sixty or more multilateral development institutions, sending hundreds of tons of food aid and emergency relief. Meanwhile, Canada's aid program has earned a fine reputation abroad: Canada is regarded as a strong supporter of development efforts.

The Colombo Plan became Canada's longest-running and largest aid effort. It was Canada's only bilateral program until 1958, when Canada entered into a Caribbean aid program, closely followed by development assistance to Commonwealth Africa in 1959 and to Francophone Africa in 1961. In the initial stages, Canadian development assistance was mistakenly seen as a one-time effort to get development started through supplying the missing elements of capital and expertise. Development would then, it was felt, become self sustaining and no more aid would be needed. This thinking resulted in a focus in Canadian aid on capital investment in the 1950s, on education in the 1960s, on capital again in the 1970s, and now in the 1980s on human-resource development. Expansion of Canadian development aid beyond South East Asia in the late 1950s followed the earlier practice of supporting British decolonization, but now in the Caribbean and Africa. The basis for Canadian development assistance, provided at Britain's request in the late 1950s and early 1960s, was still to ward off Cold War fears of communist expansion. It was presented to the UN by Canadian Prime Minister Diefenbaker as Canadian "family concern" for the peoples and countries of the Commonwealth. Thus, in 1958, Canada launched its Commonwealth Caribbean Assistance Program. The Caribbean has subsequently been the recipient of the highest per capita allocation of aid from Canada. The Caribbean has also been the Third World region with the highest concentration of Canadian financial and industrial investment.

The inception of Canadian aid to Francophone Africa in 1961 was in response to domestic political concerns related to Quebec (and represented only a token amount prior to 1968). Not until 1964, and then only under considerable pressure from the US, did Canada commit any development assistance to Latin America. Even then, for eight years it took only the form of an annual $10 million contribution to the Inter-American Development Bank of which Canada was, by choice, not a member. Not until 1971 did Canada embark upon bilateral assistance to Latin America, and then in 1972 Canada became a full member of the IADB. These moves were in response to pressure from the Canadian business community, which viewed Latin America as the largest and most promising Third World market for Canadian exports and investment.

From 1950 to 1960 Canada had spent $420 million on aid. Since development assistance had initially been viewed as only a temporary measure, it had been administered under makeshift arrangements. By 1960 the ongoing nature of development assistance had been recognized and more permanent administrative arrangements were made in the formation of the External Aid Office of the Department of External Affairs.

The period 1961 to 1970 saw the expenditure on development assistance of more than three times the amount spent in the previous decade, with annual appropriations rising from $81.9 million in 1961 to $288.6 million in 1969 (Table 5). The Canadian figures reflected a general trend of increased aid giving amongst developed western countries in this period. This increase in development assistance was predicated upon an optimistic view that a sufficient quantity of aid would ensure the necessary "take-off" to development for Third World countries.

Canada's development assistance up until 1968 can be characterized as gradually increasing in quantity, gradually diversifying in its destinations, but fairly stable and fixed in its form. Most development assistance took the form of food aid (wheat and flour), commodity aid (metals, fertilizers, pulp and paper), and economic assistance for infrastructure projects of which the majority were (appropriately, given Canada's expertise and experience) electric-power projects or dams. It was estimated that in 1963 alone, aid projects generated 6000 person-years of work for Canadians.

Canadian Development Assistance came to maturity with the creation of CIDA—the Canadian International Development Agency—in 1968. Creation of CIDA was part of the new thrust in foreign policy introduced by the first Trudeau government. A commitment to increase Canadian development assistance to 1% of GNP, a target identified by the Development Assistance Committee (DAC) of the OECD, of which Canada was a member, was an indication of the Trudeau government's recognition of development assistance as a priority area for Canadian foreign policy. This high profile continued throughout the 1970s, with Canadian contributions to development assistance growing steadily (see Table 5), despite volatility and some declines in US contributions, reflecting some disillusionment with the effectiveness of development assistance in US policy-making circles. Canadian annual contributions to development assistance passed the $1/2 billion mark ($507.3) in 1973 and the $1 billion mark in 1978 ($1050.5 million).

Table 5 Canadian aid 1951-1980

Canadian External Assistance, 1951-1970 Allocation of appropriations by programs ($ millions rounded)											
Fiscal year ending March 31	1951-1960	1961	1962	1963	1964	1965	1966	1967	1968	1969	1970
Bilateral Programs	359.8	61.1	52.9	41.7	45.17	122.1	129.7	199.3	204.7	232.1	269.9
Multilateral Programs	60.8	20.8	16.4	27.8	19.6	26.0	29.8	48.6	48.5	52.2	60.7
Total Allocations	420.6	81.9	69.3	69.5	65.3	148.1	159.5	247.9	253.2	288.6	338.7

Official Development Assistance Disbursements by Program, 1971-1980 ($ millions rounded)										
(Fiscal year ending March 31)	1971	1972	1973	1974	1975	1976	1977	1978	1970	1980
Bilateral Aid (including food aid)	268.8	283.2	329.2	367.7	498.4	525.7	466.5	541.4	559.3	598.8
Multilateral Aid (including food aid)	74.4	97.4	153.8	185.1	200.0	318.5	428.7	425.5	490.4	500.5
Non-Governmental Organizations	8.5	11.9	16.1	20.7	26.0	31.8	41.8	49.1	70.8	78.1
IDRC*	2.5	2.5	8.0	14.0	19.0	27.0	29.5	29.5	35.8	35.6
Other Programs	—	.1	.1	.2	16.5	.4	6.5	4.9	9.6	27.9
Total Disbursements	354.3	395.1	507.3	587.8	760.0	903.5	973.1	1050.5	1165.9	1241.1

* International Development Research Centre

Source: Richard Swift and Robert Clarke, *Ties that Bind.*

Throughout the 1970s development assistance was a key part of Canadian strategy in foreign policy, intended to enhance Canada's independent, middle-power role in international relations. Coupled with the later adoption of Trudeau's "Third Option" strategy to diversify Canadian trade away from dependence on the US market, it made Canadians more receptive to Third World trade possibilities. The 1970s, however, were also marked by the development of major North-South tensions related to the inequities of the global trading system, Third World demands for a New International Economic Order (NIEO), the OPEC oil embargo and oil price shocks, and growing disillusionment with the prospects for development and the effectiveness of aid. Despite Trudeau's efforts and Canada's high profile as an intermediary and conciliator between North and South on these matters, Canada too became more cautious about development assistance potential. Trudeau's early commitment to increase development assistance to 1% of GNP was abandoned in favor of a long-term commitment to the newly adopted, more realistic OECD target of 0.7%. Canadian appropriations peaked in 1975 at 0.54% GNP and had fallen back to 0.42% by 1980.

With the change from Liberal to Conservative governments in Canada in the 1980s, Canadian foreign policy, including development assistance, has come under scrutiny. Government policy statements in 1983 and 1984 first committed Canada to aid targets of 0.5% GNP for 1985-86, rising to the OECD target of 0.7% GNP by 1990. The government then undertook to maintain development assistance at 0.5% through 1990-91, and to raise it to 0.6% by 1995 and to 0.7% by the year 2000. Ultimately, Canada abandoned the 0.7% target altogether while actually achieving 0.46% for 1985-86 and, without a fiscal plan, set a goal of 0.6% to be reached by 1990. Commitment to increasing targets has been abandoned in the 1980s in response to the priority given to reducing the large Canadian federal deficit.

A major trend in Canadian development assistance from its inception to the present has been its diversification in destination. Table 6 identifies major recipients of Canadian development assistance at different stages over the past forty years. From a narrow focus on South Asia, Canadian development assistance has spread to include all of Asia, Africa and the Caribbean. Over the period since 1970, Canadian development assistance has embraced some twenty focus "core" countries each year, in addition to funding a multitude of scattered projects. Many commentators have criticized this dispersion as unlikely to be effective or to have a significant impact.

The global economic malaise of the mid 1980s, highlighted for the Third World in the unresolved debt crisis, has manifested itself in Canada in the form of confusion over the objectives of development assistance. While some have reiterated Canadian idealistic commitment to development, the business community has latched onto development assistance as a lever for Canadian trade promotion and have criticized it for its ineffectiveness in obtaining short-term gains in trade. Several government reviews of foreign policy and aid—the conclusions of which were reflected in the 1987-88 estimates—clarified the situation by setting Canadian development assistance in a clear framework, the primary goal of which is to be human-resource development, while the focus is to be to assist those in absolute poverty, the poorest people in the least-developed countries (LLDCs). In some ways, this suggests that Canadian development assistance has come back to where it started: Canadian commitment, arising from a humanitarian urge, to contribute to development.

Table 6 Major recipients of individual DAC members' aid

Gross disbursements		Canada		*Percentage of total ODA*	
1960-1961		1970-1971		1982-1983	
India	37.4	India	29.0	Bangladesh	6.6
Pakistan	20.4	Pakistan	11.0	Pakistan	4.0
Sri Lanka	3.6	Nigeria	2.7	India	3.3
		Sri Lanka	1.9	Sri Lanka	2.6
		Ghana	1.9	Tanzania	2.6
		Algeria	1.5	Kenya	2.3
		Tunisia	1.5	Egypt	1.5
		Niger	1.3	Indonesia	1.4
		Turkey	1.2	Senegal	1.3
		Morocco	1.1	Zaire	1.4
		Tanzania	1.1	Jamaica	1.1
		Cameroon	1.0	Zambia	1.1
		Senegal	0.9	Ethiopia	0.9
		Colombia	0.9	Sudan	0.9
		Jamaica	0.9	Algeria	0.8
		Guyana	0.9	Haiti	0.8
		Malaysia	0.7	Tunisia	0.8
				Cameroon	0.8
Total above	61.4	Total above	59.6	Total above	34.1
Multilateral ODA	24.9	Multilateral ODA	22.6	Multilateral ODA	35.8
Unallocated	5.9	Unallocated	8.4	Unallocated	15.0
Total ODA $million	65.4	Total ODA $million	363.2	Total ODA $million	1 329.3

Source: OECD, *Twenty-five Years of Development Cooperation.*

II. Trade and Aid: The USA

Throughout the postwar period, the USA has stood like a giant in world trade. Largely responsible for establishing the postwar trading regime by its sponsorship of the Bretton Woods meetings leading to GATT and other significant institutional arrangements in the global economy, the US has dominated global trade since World War II as the single nation-state accounting for the largest volume of world trade. Only since the oil price shocks of the 1970s, the recession of the early 1980s, and the mounting twin deficits of the mid-to-late 1980s has US preeminence begun to diminish. The OPEC oil embargo, followed by the price rises, caused a turn around in the US economic situation, which used to show substantial trade surpluses throughout the 1950s and 1960s. The US has continued to be a major exporter of agricultural products but has become increasingly dependent on imported raw materials and foreign manufactured products, to the detriment of domestic manufacturing industries from automobiles to textiles and footwear.

The US, nevertheless, continues to be *the* nation-state that dominates in world trade. The major trading partners of the US are Canada (accounting for a balanced trade of 20%), the European Community (23%, balanced), South America (15%, balanced), and Japan (12.5% of exports, 22% of imports). Asia (excluding Japan) is becoming an increasingly significant trade partner of the US, accounting in 1986 for 13.5% of US exports and 17% of imports. The Middle East, Africa and Oceania account for only small amounts of US trade. Although the figures indicate that the major focus of US trade is with developed countries, a very significant 35% of US trade is with the LDCs. Whereas US trade with Latin America has, over the period, declined noticeably, the proportion of US exports to developing countries has remained fairly constant, with 35-40% of US exports destined for developing countries. Over the same period, US imports from LDCs have declined fairly steadily (if oil imports in high price years are ignored) from 60% in 1950 to 35% in 1986. US relations with LDCs lie not only within the realm of trade but also in aid. Although virtually the creator of foreign aid via the Marshall Plan, US aid has fluctuated over the years. While still ranking as the single largest contributor, a rank which it is predicted the US will yield to Japan during 1989, the US currently ranks lowest of the OEDC countries in % GNP that is spent on foreign assistance.

It may be said that the forerunners of US foreign-aid programs were the Lend Lease programs of early World War II and the US contributions to UNRRA—the first UN refugee assistance program. UNRAA's goal was to prevent starvation and assist refugees, particularly in Central and Eastern Europe in the closing stages of World War II and during the immediate aftermath. The origins of the bilateral aid programs that came later are to be found in the Marshall Plan, which was aimed at reconstructing the developed but devastated economies of Western Europe. The Marshall Plan's primary motivation was strategic, but it also responded to humanitarian concerns and thereby generated considerable public support. It was a significant weapon in the armory of those Cold War policy-makers who feared that European populations might turn to communism if economic recovery and redevelopment should not occur rapidly.

The Act for International Development, passed in 1950, authorized money and technical assistance for poor countries. The first stage in US development assistance, from 1948-1960, has been characterized as a period of "Containment and Frontiersmanship."[4] It established a norm that US foreign aid was primarily intended to serve strategic political interests. Foreign aid was created as another weapon for winning the Cold War. In a period of boldly interventionist foreign policy, aid was used aggressively to counter any growth of Soviet influence in the developing world. Military and defensive aid was emphasized, and aid was freely given in return for military base rights to serve perceived geopolitical and strategic needs. Under the terms of the 1951 Mutual Security Act, military, technical and economic aid were brought together to provide the necessary economic underpinnings for militarization that accompanied the creation of a network of interlocking, anti-Communist alliances (NATO, SEATO, CENTO). Military aid climbed as a percentage of all aid from 24% in 1951 to 38% in 1952 and to 70% in 1956. Much of it went on a grant basis to political systems that were weak and economically risky, therefore inherently unstable.

During the period from 1961-1972, often referred to as the "Alliance for Progress" period, US foreign aid was less explicitly security-oriented than during the previous period. Indeed the rhetoric had a distinct aura of "manifest destiny" about it, trumpeting the benefits of American liberal/democratic values and institutions and trying to ensure their adoption by as wide a swath of Third World countries as could be induced to adopt them. But when persuasion failed, and US policy makers perceived a security threat in the form of a potential chink in the Cold War/Iron Curtain, they quickly returned to their previous containment stance, embracing not only military aid but also destabilization tactics to ensure the removal or the non-election of politicians regarded as security risks because of their "left leaning," radical stances. A conundrum of US aid during this stage was the fact that although an avowed purpose of aid was to spread democracy and the promotion of pluralism in developing countries, nevertheless, at the first sign of any "left leaning" tendencies on the part of aid recipients (no matter how mild) aid would be cut off and the recipient would be regarded as a dangerous security risk, a domino that might fall unless the US intervened to prevent such development! Such turnarounds led to questioning of the effectiveness of US aid programs which resulted in a switch from projects to "country programming" during the Johnson administration. The crisis of the Vietnam War and its domestic repercussions, effectively took the spotlight off foreign aid in the late 1960s and early 1970s, but the reexamination of US government and foreign policy that followed the conclusion of the war embraced a general examination of the US role in global affairs, including foreign aid.

The period from 1973 to 1980 is referred to as the period of "New Directions" in US foreign aid. The Foreign Assistance Act of 1973 recognized the extensive criticisms of the prior aid record. It targeted aid to the poor, seeking to avoid corrupt mechanisms that channelled aid to rich Third World elites. Based on an expressed concern for effective development, it had a distributional objective, and a program-budgeting mechanism. It favored grass roots, participant projects using local, simple, appropriate technology and import-substitution, without forgetting environmental concerns. This was such a radical departure from previous aid prescriptions that it took about a decade for these ideas to permeate the Agency for International Development (AID).[5]

In the meanwhile, another new era in US foreign aid had started when Ronald Reagan assumed the Presidency in 1981. Under Reagan, the most important thrust in foreign aid became the focus on private sector initiative in development, driven by security and private-sector concerns, but the major shift was the increasing percentage of foreign aid for security, as opposed to development purposes.

The trends in US foreign aid identified in the preceding paragraphs are clearly illustrated in Tables 7, 8 and 9. Table 7 presents the composition of foreign aid from 1946-1989 by program. This table dramatically represents the gradually diminishing amount of US foreign aid over the period, and the increasing significance of military and ESF/Security funds, compared with funds available for development and food programs.

> The share of the total foreign assistance budget going to development related programs (development, food and multilateral development bank support) has decreased from nearly 50% in the late 1970s to less than 40% today. Military assistance, which previously took 25% to 30% of the budget, increased to over 40%

in the mid 1980s and has been running at 36% of the budget during the past three years. ESF [Economic Support Fund] obligations have ranged between 20% and 25% of the budget.[6]

Table 7 U.S. foreign aid. 1946-89, by major program

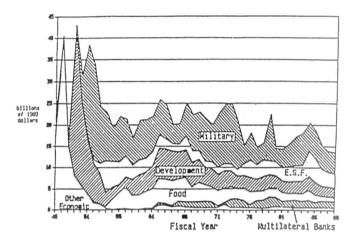

NOTE: THE DEVELOPMENT CATEGORY INCLUDES US VOLUNTARY CONTRIBUTIONS TO INTERNATIONAL DEVELOPMENT ORGANIZATIONS AND PROGRAMS.

Source: *Report of the Task Force on Foreign Assistance to the Committee on Foreign Affairs*, US House of Representatives. February 1989, page 9.

Tables 8 and 9 illustrate the changing regional composition of US aid. The early focus on Europe is graphically clear. Asia was the major recipient between 1945 and 1975. Prior to 1972, the Middle East received little US foreign assistance but has been the largest recipient since 1976-77, accounting for fully 47% of all US aid since 1977. Given the major infusions of aid to the Middle East following the Camp David Accords in 1979 and a special supplement in 1985-86, it is the case that Israel and Egypt alone have generally received over half of US bilateral aid since 1977 and those two countries plus Turkey, Pakistan, Spain, India and South Korea have received about 70% of all US bilateral foreign aid since 1977. The record shows that US foreign assistance is highly concentrated on a few strategically important countries, and is frequently received in return for base rights so that the aid virtually becomes rental payment for the bases.

Table 8 U.S. foreign aid, 1946-1989, by region

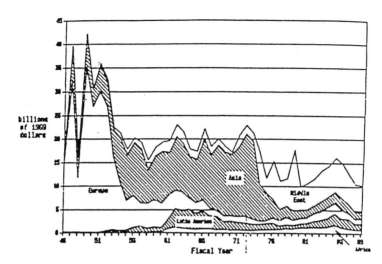

Source: Report of the Task Force on Foreign Assistance to the Committee on Foreign Affairs, US House of Representatives. February 1989, page 9.

The overall trend in volume of US aid in real terms has been ever-downward relative to the initial major infusions of Marshall Plan monies in the late 1940s and early 1950s, but it was in the 1960s that US aid to less developed countries peaked. During the period 1950-55, the United States contributed over 50% of all development assistance world-wide. The US has remained the largest single donor of development aid through 1988, but the US share in world development assistance has fallen from 46% in 1960-61 to 22% in 1983-84. In terms of aid as a percentage of GNP, the US peaked with an aid rate of 0.56% GNP in 1960-61, but since then has steadily declined and currently in terms of aid as percentage of GNP, the US ranks lowest among all DAC members at 0.21%. (Denmark, France, Netherlands, Norway and Sweden all exceed the OECD 0.7% GNP target.)

To give the flavour of current assessments of the policy objectives of US foreign-development assistance, we cannot do better than to present a few excerpts from the principal findings of the 1989 House of Representatives Task Force Review:

> The US foreign assistance program is an important element of US foreign policy. It serves US foreign policy objectives by promoting

29

Table 9 Major recipients of individual DAC members' aid (cont'd)

Gross disbursements		United States		*Percentage of total ODA*	
1960-1961		1970-1971		1982-1983	
India	10.0	India	13.9	Israel	2.2
Brazil	7.8	Viet Nam	10.5	Egypt	11.3
Korea, Rep.	6.1	Indonesia	7.8	Turkey	3.6
Pakistan	6.0	Pakistan	5.0	El Salvador	2.3
Turkey	4.3	Korea, Rep.	4.5	Bangladesh	2.3
Viet Nam	4.0	Brazil	3.6	Sudan	1.7
Iran	3.7	Turkey	3.6	P.I.T.T.*	1.7
Chile	3.6	Colombia	3.0	India	1.6
Yugoslavia	3.3	Israel	1.6	Pakistan	1.5
Taiwan	3.2	Laos	1.6	Costa Rica	1.4
Egypt	3.1	P.I.T.T.*	1.5	Indonesia	1.4
Mexico	3.0	Morocco	1.4	Jamaica	1.3
Morocco	2.6	Nigeria	1.3	Philippines	1.2
Tunisia	2.0	Tunisia	1.3	Peru	0.8
Colombia	1.9	Thailand	1.0	Honduras	0.8
Indonesia	1.7	Philippines	1.0	Kenya	0.8
Jordan	1.6	Dominican Rep.	0.9	Dominican Rep.	0.8
Israel	1.5	Chile	0.9	Liberia	0.7
Argentina	1.5	Jordan	0.7		
Laos	1.4	Bolivia	0.7		
Philippines	1.2	Ghana	0.7		
Greece	1.0				
Afghanistan	0.8				
Venezuela	0.8				

* P.I.T.T.: Pacific Islands Trust Territory

Total above	76.2	Total above	66.5	Total above	47.2
Multilateral ODA	7.6	Multilateral ODA	11.4	Multilateral ODA	33.8
Unallocated	6.4	Unallocated	11.3	Unallocated	7.8
Total ODA $million	3477.0	Total ODA $million	3328.0	Total ODA $million	8650.5

Source: OECD, *Twenty-five Years of Development Cooperation.*

the political and economic stability of nations important to US interests. It supports US national security by helping allies maintain adequate defense capabilities and stable economies. It serves US economic interests by stimulating economic reform and growth overseas. It promotes US long-term national interest by sustaining partnerships with other countries and enhancing their capacity to cooperate on issues of global importance. It responds to US humanitarian concerns by helping alleviate suffering from disasters and poverty and by helping to promote more equitable and just societies.

US leadership, expertise, and experience are of great value. Even with limited resources, the program still achieves significant results and contributes much to US development interests and to US relationships with recipient countries. The US foreign assistance program has a positive record of accomplishment, management, and expertise in development. AID's overseas missions are a unique asset.[7]

The theory behind the program has evolved. The program began with an emphasis on large resource transfers during the Marshall Plan, shifted toward technical assistance during Point Four, to infrastructure during the 1960s to basic human needs during the 1970s, and finally to the role of markets and policy reform during the 1980s ... US foreign assistance is highly concentrated on a few strategically important countries. The major strategic recipients, Israel, Egypt, Pakistan, Turkey, the Philippines, El Salvador, and Greece receive 72% of the $11 billion provided to countries for ESF, military, food, and development assistance. Israel and Egypt alone receive 50% of this total.

The focus of foreign assistance has changed. Over the past decade, the balance has shifted towards the Middle East, to military assistance, to grants rather than loans, and to bilateral rather than multilateral assistance. ESF is increasingly favored by the Executive branch because of its greater flexibility and faster disbursement.[8]

The program does not enjoy broad public support. US public support for helping poor people remains strong, but the public does not view the aid program as doing this effectively. The public has very little concept of the aid program as an instrument of foreign policy, used to advance US interests. There is evidence that the public would support development programs focused on key problems affecting the well-being of the United States.[9]

The Task Force recommended a new premise, framework and purpose for US foreign assistance with four goals—growth, environmental sustainability, poverty alleviation, and pluralism—with a clear distinction between development assistance and support for US political, economic and security interests, and separation of military assistance from the other types.[10]

III. Trade and Aid: The EEC

The European Economic Community (EEC) forms the single largest market and trading entity in the contemporary world. Individual member nation-states of the European Community (EC) were the major participants in the development of trade during the modern period of history; Portugal, Spain, Britain, France and the Netherlands all contributed significantly to exploration and to the establishment of trade—discovering the distribution of world resources, initiating trade and later creating colonial empires to further economic interests by assuring access to the raw materials necessary for industrialization. Although eighteenth- and nineteenth-century struggles for power between the European nation-states were settled by military means, the military and defensive capability depended on economic development and resources. While the industrialization of Western Europe was fairly consistent across the north, it was Britain, France and Germany that emerged as the major powers, both military and economic. In the nineteenth century, the British Empire became the preeminent trading entity in the global arena, but other current EC members continued to expand their trade and played significant roles in developing the global economy. In the twentieth century, two wars, both with their origins in Europe, escalated to world scale and disrupted trade.

World War II was particularly devastating for European economies because of the scale of industrial destruction achieved through aerial warfare. At the end of the war, European economies were virtually destroyed and in ruins. Reconstruction of postwar Western Europe was greatly affected by the Marshall Plan, the United States' first foreign aid experience. The Marshall Plan's requirement for cooperative and coordinated reconstruction planning by the Europeans certainly played a part in bringing about the creation of the European Community, although revulsion against war and its devastation, and determination that European national conflicts should never again embroil the world in such catastrophe, also played an important part.

Britain chose not to participate in the early stages of the European Community, unwilling to yield any sovereignty or to throw in its economic lot with the continental "losers" of the war. It was only with the success of the economies of the members during the 1960s, compared with the poor performance of the British economy, that Britain decided to join with the six original members (France, West Germany, Italy, Belgium, the Netherlands and Luxembourg). When it was eventually admitted in 1973, it joined along with Denmark and Ireland, bringing EC membership to nine. The current EC was completed with the admission of Greece in 1980 and of Spain and Portugal in 1986, bringing membership to twelve and total population to 320 million. In this form, the European Economic Community is a formidable player in world trade, accounting in 1986 for slightly over 50% of total global trade, compared with Canada's 6%.

Individually, several of the EC member states are equally as dependent on trade as Canada, in terms of ratio of trade to GNP: Belgium, the Netherlands, Luxembourg, Denmark, Germany, Ireland and Portugal all have a high degree (25% plus) of dependence on trade, although the EC total is only 21%. Although exports to LDCs are more significant for the EC (14%) than they are for Canada (7.75%), they are nowhere near as significant a component as for US trade (34%). The EC is a major importer of raw materials and an exporter of agricultural and manufactured goods, with a global diversity of trading connections arising from the different historic economic links of its twelve member states.

The European Community has been engaged collectively in development assistance since its creation.[11] The 1958 Treaty of Rome, which is the constitutional foundation for the EC, provided for the association of member states' overseas territories and dependencies. This arrangement was intended to maintain access to raw materials and established trade patterns, and to promote the economic development of the associates through links which included preferential access to the EC market and a European Development Fund for EC common investment in the associated areas (to supplement existing bilateral aid).

Despite the fact that many of the associates gained their independence during the period of the first Implementing Convention (1958-63), they wanted to continue the arrangement, and sought a new convention. Thus began EC involvement in development assistance, which has continued to the present largely under a series of conventions: Yaoundé I (1964-69), Yaoundé II (1970-74), Lomé I (1975-79), Lomé II (1980-85), and Lomé III (currently in effect, 1985-90). (Negotiations for Lomé IV (1990-95) are now taking place.) This series of conventions is the centerpiece of common EC development assistance, existing alongside programs for EC aid to non-associated areas, and, of course, the much larger amounts of bilateral and multilateral development assistance donated by the twelve EC member states individually. Each of the twelve member states has its own aid policies, and participates as well in the common EC programs. As it is beyond the scope of this paper to deal with the trends in member states' aid policies, we will focus on the overall picture for the EC.[12]

It is notable that, from the start, the EC package for development assistance combined both aid and trade provisions. Preferential access to the European market and stabilized export earnings for commodities and minerals (STABEX and SYSMIN) have been regarded as equally, if not more, significant than funds for development aid projects. In addition, the fact that this package has been renegotiated every five years by the "partners" has meant that a broad and sometimes acrimonious dialogue on development has taken place within the institutions that are a part of the treaty framework between the EC and the (now) 66 African, Caribbean and Pacific (ACP) nation-states that are signatories to the conventions.

Although the Lomé Conventions were initially hailed as a new partnership in development, the high hopes have not been realized. Despite the elements in the Lomé Conventions intended to assist the ACP countries in increasing their share of the EC market, their exports have *not* made major advances, and ACP trade balances with the EC have deteriorated, at the same time as EC investment in the ACPs has declined. The current negotiations for Lomé IV are permeated with an atmosphere of gloom related to global economic and trade problems; Third World debt, the declining position of Third World economies, and the falling percentage of developed countries' GNP being spent on aid are major topics of discussion. The major direction being taken by the EC is that the ACP's preferential access to the EC market will inevitably be eroded because it represents a derogation from the GSP. The EC, therefore, is concerned with stimulating Third World trade in general (to include the ACPs), but, with the degree of disillusionment relating to the effectiveness of aid, is telling the ACPs that they must take the responsibility for launching their own initiatives, using the private sector.

IV. Analysis

The picture that has been presented in the two preceding sections identifies Canada as a nation-state that is heavily dependent on trade for its well-being, but which is having a difficult time maintaining its position as a global trader. While Canada's dependence on world trade has increased, its position as a world trader has been eroded. The changing nature of the world economy has had a negative impact on Canada, and it is not clear whether Canada can successfully adapt to new global economic conditions. Canada's share in world trade has declined more than that of other industrialized countries.

Although the US has been a leading trade partner for Canada throughout this century, from 1945 to 1960 a significant proportion of Canadian trade, particularly exports, was with Great Britain. During the 1960s, Canada increased its dependence on US trade. When faced with the prospect of British membership in the European Community in the early 1970s, which might mean the loss of a significant market, Canadian policies attempted to diversify trade patterns to increase trade with the European Economic Community and Japan, in order not to become overly dependent on a single trade partner—the US. These efforts at diversification met with little success. In the late 1970s, Canadian identification with, and support for, Third World demands for a New International Economic Order to redress the inequities of the global trading system, though couched in terms of concern for the Third World, was equally intended to promote Canadian interests as a producer of raw materials vulnerable to US protectionist tendencies. In these multilateral debates, far from being a disinterested champion of Third World interests, Canada was in fact taking care of its own interests. Undoubtedly, Canada's willingness at that stage to channel increasing proportions of its development assistance through multilateral institutions was to some degree intended to enhance Canadian prestige in those quarters which were also the forums for decisions regarding global trade practices (the UN, GATT, World Bank). Canada hoped that its "good global citizen" behaviour would benefit Canadian interests.

Although not abandoning strategies for diversification of trade, these policies were largely superseded in the 1980s by a realistic acceptance of Canada's overwhelming trade involvement with the United States, leading the government of Canada to enter into free-trade negotiations with the US to obtain the best terms of trade for Canada, and to save Canada from the effects of any protectionist tendencies of the US. These efforts culminated in the US-Canada Free Trade Agreement which came into effect on

January 1, 1989. Canada has also made significant efforts in the 1980s to increase its exports to Pacific Rim countries.

What this narrative confirms is a fairly static picture: despite strenuous efforts, Canada has been essentially unable to change its trade pattern, which is concentrated in trade with the developed world and dominated by trade with the US. Only 8% of Canada's trade is with the less developed countries, and most of that trade is with the "NICs"—the newly industrialized countries—which are *not* the ones to which Canada has given development assistance. There has been a fairly significant shift in the composition of Canadian trade, from 8% manufactured exports in 1960 to 42% manufactured exports in 1984, but the destination of these manufactured exports continues, to a great extent, to be to other developed economies; indeed, the US is by far the major importer of all leading categories of Canadian exports (except for wheat), accounting for 64% of Canada's exports. The US is also the dominant exporter to Canada, leading in thirteen of the top fifteen commodity import categories for Canada (which account for 66% of all Canada's imports).

The 8% of trade with the Third World consists mainly of exports of motor vehicle and aircraft parts to Brazil, car parts to Venezuela, newsprint to Brazil and Venezuela, tractors to China, industrial machinery to India and wheat to China, Cuba, Brazil, Algeria, Egypt and Bangladesh. Imports from the Third World to Canada are comprised primarily of motor vehicle parts from Mexico; motor vehicles and chassis from South Korea; equipment, machinery and tools from Taiwan and South Korea; communications equipment from South Korea, Mexico, Taiwan and Hong Kong; crude petroleum from Nigeria, Venezuela, Iran, Saudi Arabia and Mexico; and textiles and apparel from Hong Kong, South Korea and Taiwan.

Looking at the same period, the picture of Canada as a provider of development assistance shows an early participant, giving rising amounts from 1948 to 1980. Canada's relative generosity, combined with a high volume of rhetoric on the subject, gained Canada an enviable reputation and a high profile, which has been gratifying for Canadian diplomats and has accorded them a degree of prestige in international circles which they might not otherwise have earned.[13] Major recipients of Canadian development assistance were initially former colonies of Great Britain in South Asia (India, Pakistan, Sri Lanka and later Bangladesh) and then later the Caribbean, and Anglophone followed by Francophone Africa. The destination and nature of early Canadian development assistance (1948-60) were determined within the framework of the British Commonwealth. There is no question that Canadian links with Britain—political, economic and cultural—played a major part in shaping those early aid policies. It is also quite clear that Canada resisted US pressure to provide development assistance to Latin America in the 1960s, not wanting the small Canadian contributions to be lost or overshadowed by the magnitude of the US contributions. This resistance also reflected continuing Canadian chagrin at US opposition to Canadian membership in the Pan-American Union, the forerunner of the Organization of American States. Canada's continuing non-membership in the OAS[14] reflects Canadian unwillingness to become involved in disputes between the US and Latin America.

British application, followed by its membership in the European Community, had a significant effect on Canadian thinking about both trade and aid: by joining the EEC and becoming part of the European Common Market, Britain was willing to see Canadian exports to Britain adversely affected by the EC's common external tariff (CET). This also applied to New Zealand and Australia. Britain had made a calculated decision to abandon Canada and the Commonwealth in favor of Europe. That being the case, Canada had to scramble for its own interests, and was no longer obliged to remain loyal to emotional "family-of-the-Commonwealth" ties. To pursue Canadian interests meant to pursue diversification of trade, not to lose Britain to the EC but to court trade with all the members of the EC. This implied more Canadian concern with the interests and sensibilities of other Europeans, not just the British. Coincidentally with diversifying trade, Canada could also mollify indignant domestic political interest by divorcing aid from its British Commonwealth roots and opening up aid opportunities with Francophone Africa. The diversification of aid destinations which occurred in the 1970s was certainly tied to hopes that this aid would lead to widespread opportunities for expanding Canadian exports to the Third World.

The late 1970s and early 1980s were a period of disillusionment: aid had not opened up trade and, worse, aid had not even led to development or alleviated poverty. The demands for effective aid were counterbalanced by demands from the business community for aid to be translated into trade expansion policies. Although the trade/aid link was frequently referred to, and has been used as, a promotional tool for gaining support among the business community for development assistance in Canada, various studies that have been carried out have demonstrated that only the most tenuous links exist. Aside from two possible exceptions, there is no sign that Canadian development assistance has led to the establishment of export markets for Canadian goods. India was an early and ongoing recipient of Canadian aid that did in 1986 receive 1.3% of Canada's exports of industrial machinery. While this could indicate that trade has indeed followed aid, it

37

is much more likely that what this represents is a tied-aid export, which is the other exception. Until 1970, direct government-to-government aid was fully tied to procurement in Canada. Since 1970, 80% of Canada's bilateral country program development assistance budget has been tied to Canadian procurement, while the overall split of Canadian official development assistance is 60% untied and 40% tied, making Canada one of the least flexible donors in the DAC group. What this means is that the value of tied-aid shows up as exports to Third World countries, when in fact these figures reflect the expenditure on Canadian products of Canadian development assistance monies rather than increased trade.

As was pointed out previously, Canada's most significant Third World trade partners for exports are Venezuela, Brazil, South Korea, Taiwan, China, India, Iraq, Cuba, Algeria, Bangladesh, and Egypt. Of these, only India and Bangladesh have been long-term, major recipients of Canadian aid. Canada's major Third World trade partners for imports are Mexico, South Korea, Taiwan, Hong Kong, Pakistan, Nigeria, Venezuela, Iran, Saudi Arabia, and Jamaica, of which only Pakistan, Nigeria and Jamaica have been major recipients of Canadian development assistance.

Despite the increasingly shrill demands of the business community in the 1980s for development assistance to be used to support trade expansion, and government assurances to that effect, there has been an almost complete lack of coordination between those promoting and administering trade policies and those promoting and administering development assistance policies. As Canadian provinces have increasingly seized the initiative in trade promotion, there have been significant tensions between the federal and provincial levels of government regarding trade, and the provinces have been increasingly critical of federal policies and practices relating to development assistance.

In contrast to the Canadian situation, there is much more linkage between US trade and aid. In part this is simply a reflection of the much greater volume of US aid and the much higher level of US engagement in trade with LDCs (35% of a much larger volume of trade against Canada's 8%). Since the large amount of US aid is directed at relatively few countries (compared with Canada's small volume of aid spread over small projects in more than 100 countries) it makes its mark. The major beneficiaries of US aid almost inevitably become trade partners of the US. The fact that the major beneficiaries of US aid have not been the least developed countries is also of significance: major recipients of US aid have generally been those countries with the most potential for development. With massive infusions of US aid they have been able to launch themselves as NICs into the global market place. Once this is accomplished they no longer need aid. The most spectacular examples of this are Taiwan, South Korea and Brazil. Turkey and Spain are other examples of major recipients of US aid that could hardly be regarded as least developed countries. Indeed, the whole of Western Europe, as recipient of Marshall Plan aid, became the major trading partner of the US.

Another element of US trade that is related to aid is arms exports: the US is a major arms exporter. Many LDCs have received large amounts of military and security assistance from the US, which shows up as trade in the US arms exports figures. Pakistan, Israel, Egypt, South Korea and Turkey have all been the beneficiaries of US military aid and arms exports. US bases overseas, many of them located in LDCs, are also the source of much demand for US goods that show up in the export trade figures. Canada has virtually no comparable categories of military aid induced trade.

The European Community picture is more similar to that of Canada than that of the US. Yet only 14% of the huge volume of EC trade (over 50% of world trade) is with LDCs, and most of this trade is in the form of LDC exports of raw materials or of tropical agricultural products (sugar and bananas) to Europe. European industry's dependence on the Third World for raw materials is in stark contrast to the Canadian situation. Since LDCs are able to export their raw materials to the EC, they earn credit there and, not surprisingly, spend their credit on European manufactured goods. Although these trade linkages are based on historic colonial patterns which preceded development assistance and aid policies, they have been perpetuated in the association arrangements combining trade and aid measures. The statistics for the EC, however, demonstrate that aid is not generating trade. In fact, those LDCs that receive aid and preferential access to the EC market under the Lomé provisions are actually declining in their market share, and doing less well in the EC market than LDCs not receiving aid and preferential access.[15] Again the explanation seems to lie in the relative development and prosperity of the markets concerned. It is the NICs among the LDCs that are increasing their market shares, while the LLDCs (which make up a majority of the ACP countries) are losing out. Since the very small amount of combined EC development assistance is distributed amongst so many recipients, the amounts each country receives are small, too small to have a significant impact upon their production capacity.

V. Conclusions

Of the three cases we have considered, the Canadian case exhibits the least linkage between trade and aid. This arises partly from the very nature of Canada's economy, which mainly produces raw materials that LDCs, who are the recipients of aid, do not want. Another partial explanation is that Canada has not had a long-term dependence on LDCs to provide raw materials, a linkage which has served as the foundation for a formalized trade/aid relationship for the European Community with Africa, the Caribbean and the Pacific. Canada's lack of involvement in military and security aid also accounts in part for absence of the aid/trade linkage. While Canadians claim that the purpose of aid is the eradication of poverty and accordingly direct their assistance to the poorest sectors of the population in the poorest countries, virtually everyone in the US regards aid as a tool to advance foreign policy goals, emphasizing strategic concerns and accordingly concentrating massive amounts of aid in strategically located LDCs, which have often then become important export markets for US goods. The EC experience only serves to underline the Canadian one— focusing aid on a large number of LDCs does not result in trade returns to the donor.

The overall import of our study relative to Canadian aid is to illustrate further that Canadian aid, as it has been distributed, does not lead to significant trade. Humanitarian aid directed at the poorest sectors of the population in LDCs is unlikely to generate any significant trade potential and should not be expected to do so. Trade and aid policies should be kept distinct: although there is the potential for Canada to increase its trade with the Third World, particularly with the NICs, aid is not the vehicle for the realization of this potential. The means to increasing trade with LDCs is probably through import stimulation, thereby creating credit balances for the purchase of exports. Balanced trade is the goal of most contemporary nation-states, and the best hope for economic growth is through increased trade resulting from the elimination of protectionist trade barriers. Canada's interests once again will be best served through multilateral initiatives such as the GATT rounds, which seek to free trade from existing constraints, and UN initiatives, which seek to make global trade fairer.

Notes

1. V. Corko and O. Havrylyshyn, *Canada's Trade Relations with Developing Countries* (Ottawa: Economic Council of Canada 1980), 7.

2. Government of Canada, *Competitiveness and Security, Direction for Canada's International Relations* (Ottawa: Ministry of Supply and Services 1985), 9.

3. The chronological descriptive narrative of Canadian Development Assistance draws heavily on information provided in a number of sources including several landmark government documents: Government of Canada, *Competitiveness and Security: Directions for Canada's International Relations* (Ottawa: Department of External Affairs 1985); *Foreign Policy for Canadians: International Development* (Ottawa: Department of External Affairs 1970); *Strategy for International Development Cooperation 1975-1980* (Ottawa: CIDA 1975); *Elements of Canada's Official Development Assistance Strategy 1984* (Ottawa: CIDA 1984); *Canada's International Relations: Response of the Government of Canada to the Report of the Special Joint Committee of the Senate and the House of Commons* (Ottawa: Department of External Affairs 1986); *For Whose Benefit? Report of the Standing Committee on External Affairs and International Trade on Canada's Official Development Assistance Policies and Program* (Ottawa: House of Commons, May 1987): OECD, *Twenty Five Years of Development Cooperation: A Review* (Paris: OECD 1985; North-South Institute, *In the Canadian Interest? Third World Development in the 1980s* (Ottawa: North-South Institute 1980); Richard Swift and Robert Clarke (eds.), *Ties That Bind: Canada and the Third World* (Toronto: Between the Lines 1982).

4. The descriptive narrative of US Development Assistance draws on information provided in a number of sources including several government documents: US House of Representatives, "Trends in Foreign Aid, 1977-1986," (Select Committee on Hunger, 1986); "Report of the Task Force on Foreign Assistance," (Committee on Foreign Affairs, 1989); "Background Materials on Foreign Assistance," (Committee on Foreign Affairs, 1989); United States Senate, "International Security and Development Cooperation Act of 1987," (Committee on Foreign Relations, 1987): United States Agency for International Development, *Development and the National Interest: US Economic Assistance into the 21st Century* (Washington, DC: AID 1989); OECD, *Twenty Five Years of Development Cooperation* (Paris: OECD 1985); George M. Guess, *The Politics of United States Foreign Aid* (New York: St. Martin's Press 1987); Elliot R. Morss and Victoria A. Morss, *U.S. Foreign Aid: An Assessment of New and Traditional Development Strategies* (Boulder, Colorado: Westview Press 1982); Frances Moor Lappe et. al., *Betraying the National Interest* (New York: Grove Press 1987).

5. Guess, *The Politics of United States Foreign Aid*, p. 24.

6. ESF is the fastest growing part of the US foreign aid budget over the last ten years, whose objectives are "to support US economic, political and security interests and the advancement of US foreign policy objectives." US House of Representatives, "Report of the Task Force on Foreign Assistance," p. 8.

7. Ibid., p. 24.

8. Loc. cit.

9. US House of Representatives, "Report to the Task Force on Foreign Assistance," p. 26.

10. Ibid., pp. 29-31.

11. The descriptive analysis of European Community aid draws upon research conducted by the author for publication of Diddy R.M. Hitchins, "The European Community and Africa, Caribbean and the Pacific," Chapter 13 in Juliet Lodge, *The European Community* (London: Frances Pinter 1983) with updated information from Commission of the European Communities, *Official Development Assistance from the European Community and its Member States* (Brussels: Europe Information 1988).

12. But to give perspective, in 1986 the members of the European Community gave a total of $11.7 billion in development aid combining all programs (bilateral, multilateral and through the EEC) of all 12 member states: of that total, $1.9 billion represented EEC aid, which corresponded to 4.3% of world official development assistance and 12% of total aid donated by the member states to all aid programs.

13. Kim Richard Nossal, "Mixed Motives Revisited: Canada's Interest in Development Assistance," *Canadian Journal of Political Science*, XXI:I (March 1988), 35-56.
14. In November 1989 Canada eventually joined the OAS.
15. Commission of the European Community "Change and Continuity Commission Policy on the new ACP-EEC Convention," *The Courier*, No. 109 (May/June 1988).

Martin Thunert

The Canadian Charter of Rights and Freedoms and the Political Tradition of Canada: A Changing Concept of Political Community?

Abstract

This paper focuses on the role of the Canadian Charter of Rights and Freedoms in moulding the self-perception of Canada as a political community. The Charter is understood both as a governmental response to centrifugal trends in the political tradition of Canada, and as an expression of multiple cleavage patterns salient in contemporary Canadian society which are the result of demographic, social and cultural changes in postwar Canada. A look at recent developments in constitutional politics, at public attitudes towards charter rights, at court decicions, and at political discourse supports the thesis that, while the Charter has been a successful tool to nationalize political discourse, it must not be interpreted as a national consensus on substantive issues, nor as an adequate instrument to centralize government.

Résumé

Cet article examine le rôle de la Charte canadienne des droits et libertés dans le façonnement de la perception que le Canada a de lui-même en tant que communauté politique. La Charte est conçue à la fois comme une réponse du gouvernement aux tendances centrifuges qu'on trouve dans la tradition politique du Canada et comme l'expression des divers types de clivage caractéristiques de la société canadienne contemporaine, qui sont le résultat de l'évolution démographique, sociale et culturelle du Canada d'après-guerre. L'examen de l'évolution récente des politiques constitutionnelles, des attitudes de l'opinion publique vis-à-vis des chartes des droits, des décisions des tribunaux et des discours politiques accrédite la thèse selon laquelle la Charte s'est avérée un instrument efficace pour nationaliser le discours politique, mais ne doit pas être interprétée comme un consensus national sur les questions de fond ou un outil de centralisation pour le gouvernement.

Now, why am I such an opponent of separatism? I guess I just feel that the challenge of the age is to live together with people who don't have all the same values as yourself. I believe in pluralistic societies. I believe that the way of progress is through the free exchange of ideas and confrontation of values. Separatism is really an ethnocentric-based society which says that all the French must live together, and all the Scottish, and all the Welsh . . . and there should be no intercommunication between them except at the official level of the state . . . . And the challenge is to have all these values challenge each other in terms of excellence . . .

—Pierre Elliott Trudeau[1]

Introduction

A Charter of Rights was not entrenched into Canada's patriated constitution in 1982 to mark an end to a period of tyranny. A discourse about rights and their constitutional status came to Canada, notwithstanding her excellent historical record in the protection of human rights when compared not to utopian visions but to the dismal records of many other nations. Inevitably, one has to ask why this discourse became so important in postwar Canada.

The causes for this phenomenon are—as always—manifold. Undoubtedly international legal developments, such as the Universal Declaration of Human Rights or the general trend towards the "constitutionalization of the world," are indispensable explanatory variables for an understanding of the Canadian constitutional experiment. But this very experiment— including its most recent stage; the Meech Lake Accord—teaches us that constitutional questions have always been political and social issues, too important to be left to lawyers and legal scholars alone. Hence, this paper will focus on constitutional developments within the framework of intergovernmental and state-society relations, thereby running the risk of excluding legal aspects to an extent that cannot be sufficiently justified.[2] It concentrates on the role of the Charter in moulding the self-perception of Canada as a political community, under the premise that its foreseeable impact cannot be understood without extensive references to the Charter's place in the Canadian political tradition and to important changes in state-society relations of advanced industrial democracies since 1945.

Conceptions of community are understood as a complex of attitudes and identifications which define for a person his or her political community.

Political community includes the set of people with whom one feels common citizenship and obligation (see Elkins & Simeon 1979, xiii). Political institutions and policies such as the Charter of Rights are nothing less than embodiments of such conceptions, while at the same time they contribute to modify political identities. Political community also entails questions of scale and of purpose: what are the social and territorial boundaries of one's foremost political loyalties, and what is the purpose behind this "imagined community"? Contrary to what studies about the political loyalties of Canadians have suggested in particular, citizens of advanced industrial democracies are hardly faced with either/or decisions as far as political loyalties are concerned. Most of us have multiple spatial and functional political loyalties, ranging from interest group, municipality, state or province, nation, class, ethnicity and gender, to the hemisphere, political alliances or the universe as such. All of these sentiments have their political expression. Which forms of political community are dominant institutionally, and the way the constituents of such communities, that is, the people, see themselves are the politically decisive factors.

The evolutionary inclusion of a Charter of Rights and Freedoms into Canada's "power map"—the constitution—has been frequently interpreted as an underpinning for the development of a national political community in Canada, as an act of institutional centralization and an important victory for the federal government in the never-ending intergovernmental dispute with the provinces, which are limited only by the emergency exit of the notorious "notwithstanding clause." Nothing in this paper will refute this thesis, but the main argument will show that the "nation-building approach" is too narrow in scope. Beyond its impact on national identity formation, the Charter of Rights is understood by and large as an adequate attempt to recognize the legitimacy of multiple competing political identities: spatial, functional, sociological or ethnical. Therefore, the entrenchment of a bill of rights in the Canadian constitution was a necessary reform of a constitution which simultaneously reflects and moulds a variety of perceptions of political community in a society undergoing profound transformation.

I. The Backgrounds of the Canadian Charter of Rights and Freedoms

1. *The Governmental Dimension: the Charter of Rights and Changing State-Society Relations since the Second World War in Comparative Perspective*

In terms of state-society relations, the common experience of most Western liberal democracies has been the politicization of society since the end of World War II. In the Western societies of "embedded states" (Cairns 1985), legal norms penetrated and politicized communicatively structured areas of civil society in an unprecedented fashion: nothing from health care, schooling, and pensions to family relationships was to be left to chance or to traditional modes of regulation. To be sure, the concentration of regulatory power in the welfare state was seen as a freedom-guaranteeing process intended to rival the concentration of private power in the economic sector. The democratic welfare state enhanced freedom and expanded the life chances of its citizens because it bridled a powerful economic system in the same way the constitutional state of the nineteenth century expanded freedoms for the bourgeoisie when it bridled the administrative system of absolutist regimes (see Habermas 1987, II:357-61).

The political, geographical and ideological unit within which the welfare-state ideal typically unfolded its regulatory potential was the nation-state. In Western Europe, the democratic welfare state was considered the driving force that created a modern nation where premodern regional, ethnic, and even religious, cleavages lost some of their importance, relative to cross-cutting cleavages based on class and economic sectors that then prevailed.[3] In a nation with a federal tradition such as the United States, a sense of national and political citizenship has been cultivated since the 1930s to support the extended involvements of centralized government and national economic institutions which had developed as part of the New Deal. The nation replaced the neighbourhood, the small town and even the city and the state as the unit of public policy and economic activity (see Sandel 1984). In social theory, the inevitable process of modernization was expected to entail increasing nationalization, centralization and integration. Lines of political conflict and cleavages would be organized around functional lines such as class or gender, replacing the vertical lines of territory or ethnicity.

2. *The Case of Canada*

In Canada, a combination of structural factors and constitutional arrangements made it increasingly difficult for the welfare state to unfold its nationalizing potential. More than in any other Western capitalist democracy, it became clear in Canada that modernization could not be paired with centralization, and that the modernization of society through welfare politics did not lead to the erosion of traditional regional loyalties and to a close attachment of the citizen to the nation state. The welfare state never fully completed the nation-building project because its centralizing impact was too short-lived. Political scientists like Donald Smiley have been analyzing "the attenuation of federal power" ever since the early 1960s (Smiley 1968). The literature mentions two different kinds of explanations for this development: one institutional, the other sociological.

i. Institutional dualism

Centralizing and decentralizing tensions are built into the Canadian constitution. Many welfare policies like Medicare, regional development, pension plans, and so on were commissioned by the federal government as a national policy, while other key welfare areas such as education, social policy, and health care remained under provincial jurisdiction or were administered by local or provincial authorities, although funding could come from Ottawa. As Richard Simeon writes:

> Throughout the period (of the development of the welfare state) provincial and local spending increased considerably faster than at the federal level; hence the federal share of revenues and expenditures declined. Provincial governments became larger, more confident, more assertive, more anxious to see themselves as agents of economic growth . . . (Simeon 1986, 370)

The welfare modernization of Canada did not result in the nationalization of politics, but developed the concept of "province building". Province building—which is variably placed in the period between the late 1950s and the 1970s—was not limited to the creation of provincial welfare policies, but soon reached the constitutional level, when the demands of the provinces for increased jurisdictional power challenged the federal power and urged the Trudeau government to react on precisely this level.

ii. Societal fragmentation

The Canadian welfare state did not fulfil its role as a natural ally to the project of national community building. In Canadian political life, collective identities revolved around the federal or the provincial state rather than around class. To remedy this situation, one had to address the question of whether the regional or provincial communities as beneficiaries of province building had an authentic sociological base. The answer in Canadian political science is—as always—highly ambivalent. Empirical research by Simeon and Elkins carried out in the 1970s (1979, Chapters I and II especially) has identified distinguishable political subcultures in both English Canada and Quebec. Their findings seemed to confirm Livingston's sociology-based explanation of Canadian federalism,[4] which holds that regional political subcultures and loyalties are constitutive of the political boundaries of Canadian federalism. Provincial variations in attitudes towards political trust and political efficacy could no longer be explained as functions of other variables like class, educational level or party identification. Regionalism withstood the test of these controlling variables.

The persistence of differences within all categories of the control variables strengthens our confidence that, independent of these other social and economic forces, there are indeed differences between the provinces which may be called cultural, which are rooted in the matrix of historical and sociological factors unique to each province (Simeon & Elkins 1974, 433).

What were the consequences of these cultural differences between the provinces for the process of political community formation? If the orientations of citizens shaped the character of institutions and political visions in a one-way manner, if culture was seen as prior to politics, the Charter of Rights would be a futile attempt to transcend a deeply rooted, dominantly provincially fragmented concept of community. But cultural research also suggests that the causation is mutual and the sociology-based explanation by itself is insufficient. Even Elkins and Simeon found a striking affinity between certain attitudinal patterns and the policy styles of different provinces. Where policy had been personalistic or patronage-oriented, as in rural Quebec and the Maritimes, patterns of distrust in politics and lack of political efficacy prevailed (Elkins & Simeon 1979, 71).

The foremost challenger of the society-centred explanation of federalism in Canada, Alan Cairns, states that "the national and provincial communities are increasingly the products of the policy output of the two levels of government" (in Banting & Simeon, eds. 1985, 60). A century after Confederation, one finds in Canada "governmentalized societies, both federal and provincial, interwoven with each other in relations of competitive interdependence" (Cairns 1979, 108). If this interpretation of Canadian federalism and regionalism as a product of institutional arrangements and policy rather than of society is correct, it was a plausible step for the federal government to develop a policy promoting the creation of a national political community despite and against a continuing trend toward economic and political decentralization.

iii. The Charter of Rights and Freedoms as a federal policy instrument

While Canadian welfare policies resulted in a more decentralized state and failed to remedy the regional fragmentation of community, the entrenchment of a distinctively Canadian Charter of Rights was seen as the next best hope of the federal government to fight the forces of political centrifugalism and as an integrative tool to modernize democracy on a national scale.

If democratic politics was to be effectively located on the level of the nation, it was not only necessary to redesign structures and reform institutions, but to recast the meaning of democratic citizenship on a new scale by means of political education and socialization. Despite various regional identities, two linguistic communities, and diverse cultural heritages, Canada had to develop a common idea of citizenship; a genuine Canadian personality had to be discovered, as the federal government pointed out in its 1968 brochure *Federalism for the Future*:

> But Canada is more than a collection of communities, heritages and traditions. There is a Canadian personality. We are not carbon-copy Englishmen, carbon-copy European nor carbon-copy Frenchmen . . . (page 12)

Historically, institutions like Parliament, nationwide banks, a national railway and airline as well as a national media are embodiments of the attempt to create such a national political community, at least on a symbolic level. But on the level of political process, the party system has "performed well below the optimum level" (Meisel 1976, 34) in its function to develop and foster a national political culture.

As an instrument of national community building, a proposed Charter of Human Rights emerged on the federal agenda of constitutional politics after "the increased salience of linguistic divisions, in response to economic and social change in Quebec, was the trigger for major constitutional discussions beginning in the 1960s" (Banting & Simeon 1985, 11). Again, a Charter proposal was at the heart of a federal constitutional reform initiative, after province building had reached its apex in Quebec in 1976, and when "shifts in the economic balance between the resources and the manufacturing regions of the country accounted for a new set of constitutionally based demands in the 1970s" (Banting & Simeon 1985, 11). As Donald Smiley convincingly demonstrated (1987, 178), the proposed Charter of Rights became an important second pillar of the Trudeau government's "Third National Policy" in 1980, accompanying economic policies such as the National Energy Program and the Western Development Fund. As a policy initiative, the basic rationale for Trudeau's Charter strategy was to urge these centrifugal forces into a constitutional debate about national citizenship—a discussion that had little to do with the province's own federal-provincial division of powers agenda.

In this light, the Charter policy was not primarily a strategy to centralize government, but an attempt to nationalize politics and political discourse in Canada.[5] The result of this attempt, it shall be argued, is neither the creation of a national consensus about substantive issues (e.g., about what is distinctively Canadian) nor the establishment of a truly national political community of shared purposes. Instead, the Charter represents the notion of the "neutral state" and of a political community characterized not by shared purposes, but by fair procedures to ensure nationwide equality of opportunity in the life-chances of the individual citizen.

3. The Socio-Political Dimension: the Charter as an Expression of Multiple Cleavage Patterns and as Response to Demographic and Cultural Change in Postwar Canada[6]

As much as it was a bargaining chip in the power struggles between the two orders of government, the Charter was also a result of three important sociological developments salient in postwar Canadian society: the demographic de-Britanization of Canada caused by vigorous "third force" immigration after World War II; the new assertiveness of French Canadians after 1960; and the so-called "self-consciousness explosion" since the late 1960s. From this perspective, the Charter represents the culmination of a growing consciousness of rights in Canada and elsewhere triggered by the experience of the holocaust, European totalitarianism and home-made violations of civil liberties against Japanese Canadians during the war and under the Duplessis regime in Quebec. A feeling grew among political and intellectual elites that the British approach to protect rights in a low key fashion through statutes, the common law and a liberal consensus was no longer true to the reality of a country where the British proportion of the population was rapidly declining. This sentiment was best expressed in Eugene Forsey's submission to the 1950 Special Committee of the Senate on Human Rights and Fundamental Freedoms. Arguing in favour of an entrenched Bill of Rights, Forsey held that:

> Canada is a land of many peoples and many traditions. This enriches our national life. But it gives prejudice extra targets and it means that the British tradition is only one among many, some of them much less tolerant or much less alert to the dangers of

intolerance . . . the British tradition itself, in the matter of civil
liberties, is a good deal less robust here, even among people of
British origin, than it is in Britain. (Senate of Canada 1950, No. 10,
page 79)

Nothing in the literature suggests that these considerations or subsequent
legal reforms such as the enactment of the 1960 Bill of Rights—a federal
statute—contributed to the development of some kind of social movement
for an entrenched catalogue of rights. The spark that was needed to set off
a broader public debate about citizens' rights was the self-consciousness
wave of the late 1960s and early 1970s, when women, lifestyle groups, and
ethnic and "third force" Canadians claimed recognition for their newly
developed political identities and for their demands about access to abortion, non-discrimination, public funding for parochial schools, etc.

While most politicians and academic advisers emphasized the institutional
reform of federalism, Trudeau could be assured of widespread public
support and media coverage when he sold the Charter as a "people's
package" to create a counterweight to the dull song of repeated provincial
demands for more jurisdictional power. Despite its popularity in the media
and in opinion polls, the Charter proposal remained pure government
policy until 1980 when "the bargaining forum shifted from intergovernmental conferences to debate within Parliament and its committees" (Banting
& Simeon 1985, 17). In the public hearings held in the winter of 1980/81,
the Charter was overwhelmingly accepted by interest groups, social movements and rights-conscious individuals as a "citizen's constitution" (Alan
Cairns), because its legitimacy resided in its capacity to give constitutional
recognition to identities beyond territory and region.

From the perspective of political psychology, the Charter debates around
and following the 1980/81 parliamentary hearings mark an important
change in the constitutional culture of Canada. For the first time in constitutional politics, the political demands of women, native people, ethnic
and third-force Canadians, the handicapped and others were phrased as
constitutional rights competing for recognition and consideration with the
long-established rights of French- and English-language groups and both
levels of government.

II. Main Currents of Criticism against the Charter

A look at the political and academic debates preceding entrenchment and at the content of the Charter itself proves that its vision of Canadian citizenship had to confront a variety of objections raised by representatives of major currents of the Canadian political tradition.

On an institutional, level the Charter proposals had to survive the grindings of executive federal-provincial negotiations, where fears of centralizing impacts were phrased in the disguise of arguments about the merits of British legislative supremacy. Section 33 of the Charter—the notorious "notwithstanding clause"—proves that the Charter did not pass through this purgatory unharmed.

The intellectually most serious arguments against entrenchment were raised in scholarly debates on an ideological-political level: in contrast to the United States, where social reform trickled down from the federal level to the states, partly by adjudication, Canada was perceived as a country in which the provinces had been the pacemakers of social progress. Therefore, a federal Charter, based on the lowest common denominator of political elites, and adjudicated and administered by a conservative and federally appointed judiciary, had the potential of becoming an instrument of rigidity and social stagnation, where flexibility was demanded. Some of these fears are expressed in section 1 of the Charter, in which the primacy of democratic politics is reaffirmed. Yet it is up to the Supreme Court to decide whether the primacy of collective democratic decisions over narrowly interpreted individual rights will still be respected in Charterland.

While the above argument was mainly brought up by provincial-rights supporters, the socialist left was suspicious of the Charter on more fundamental grounds: based on negative experiences of legalization of labour disputes, the "juridicalization" of political conflicts under the Charter was rejected because of its supposedly destructive impact on the mobilization of workers and the disadvantaged. Court litigation, it was argued, individualizes collective conflicts, abstracts struggles from their settings in history and class and disguises structural inequalities between capital and labour by applying seemingly neutral judicial standards.[7] Courts were simply not seen as arenas of collective struggle where social movements had anything to gain.

Another current of criticism revolves around the tension between the values of liberty, as expressed by entrenched rights on the one hand, and the values of authority and community on the other. While the right-wing variant of this type of criticism primarily anticipates and fears an erosion of law and order and predicts ungovernability of an increasingly rights-seeking entitlement society, the left-wing or communitarian version laments the loss of community attachment and increasing alienation in a society where negative liberty triumphs over participatory rights and important policy questions are litigated in terms of rights instead of being discussed as questions of substantive justice (see Taylor 1985). The content of the Charter is not unresponsive to such concerns, as sections 1 and 33 and minority language education rights and the affirmative action provision of section 15(2) well illustrate.

III. The Impact of the Charter of Rights and Freedoms on the Perception of Political Community

How can we assess the changes the Charter has brought to Canadian political life nearly eight years after its entrenchment? Has the Charter been a successful tool to change the constitutional balance of power, has an erosion of community values "Americanized" Canadian politics, and has the discourse of federalism-regionalism been replaced by the political language of class, gender, lifestyle or ethnicity? A look at recent developments in constitutional politics, public attitudes towards rights-related values, and beliefs of Canadians in court decisions and political discourse will attempt to give some preliminary answers to these important questions.

1. Constitutional Politics: the "De-governmentalization" of Canada?

Despite being rooted in the Canadian political tradition, the underlying philosophy of the Charter reflects a refashioned concept of political community: Canadians receive constitutional recognition as members of a national community and partly as members of sociologically defined communities based on mother tongue, gender, ethnicity, first-nation Canadian and so on, irrespective of the rights of their provincial governments. Endowing the individual citizen and groups, defined by other than regional standards, with upgraded constitutional status has integrated "people" as new participants into the power game of constitutional politics, both on a symbolic and a judicial-political level. In its role as what Alan Cairns has called a "citizen's constitution," the Charter is clearly at odds with those forces in constitutional politics that conceive of Canada mainly as a compact of regions and their governments.

The Charter permits citizens and interest groups especially to bypass the federal-provincial policy process and to address their grievances directly to the courts. In particular, groups such as the women's movement, for whom the constitutional process in 1980/81 became a collective experience of identity formation, have adopted these strategies. While the Charter remained a document bearing a strong provincial imprint in substantive matters (e.g., section 33 and the limitation of mobility rights), the most significant changes occurred on the procedural level: "from this vantage point the constitutional process produced more constitutional change than appears in formal amendments" (Cairns 1984, 103; see also Russell 1988, 389-91).

While the Quebec referendum, televised parliamentary hearings, inter-governmental conferences, and the lobbying efforts of women and native people called into question the legitimacy of constitutional politics as an exclusive domain of executive federalism, the Meech Lake Accord is a perfect example of the salience of tensions between old and new approaches to constitutional politics. It is a traditional Canadian compromise between governments and, therefore, by expressing the old compact vision of political community, Meech Lake has—until recently—generally been approved of by the majority of Canada's political elite, while encountering strong criticism and open rejection by new "Charter" beneficiaries and supporters of the 1982 constitutional reform package who consider the accord a threat to their status as equal partners in the constitutional process.

The opening up of constitutional politics through the Charter has been seen as a mixed blessing. On the one hand, a number of authors share Peter Russell's sceptical assessment of the Meech Lake example, that, because of the stimulus given to interest groups to participate in public hearings, "Canadians may prove to be incapable of reaching a constitutional accord in a more democratic fashion" (Russell 1988, 391). Others share Alan Cairns' hope that the democratization of constitutional politics around the Charter will not remain an "ephemeral aberration from the elitism characteristic of Canadian politics" (Cairns 1984, 113).

2. Changes in Canadian Political Culture: "Americanization" and "Homogenization"

The most detailed survey of public attitudes toward the Charter and civil liberties to date was conducted by a research team in Toronto in 1987.[8] Some of their results, taken from polls among the general public and decision-makers, will contribute to modify theories about Canadian political culture that revolve around the "counter-revolution" thesis of Seymour Martin Lipset and the "regional political cultures" thesis of Elkins and Simeon.[9]

According to Stanford sociologist Lipset, the value systems of Canada and the United States still display fundamental differences, despite the gradual disappearance of structural differences between the two neighbouring countries (see Lipset 1986). The subfield of legal culture may serve as an example to illustrate Lipset's point: here a different frontier experience still explains different approaches to law and order in both societies. While the US has always been following a "due process" model of emphasizing the rights of the accused, the Canadian approach to criminal law favours "crime control"; it prefers the rights of the community over the rights of the individual if they are in conflict. In general, Lipset concludes, Canadians are more inclined to show deference toward police and authority than Americans.

Although the survey on the Charter does not completely refute Lipset's thesis, it throws an interesting light on some of its implications. When Canadians were asked how far they were prepared to go in tolerating views and behaviour of fellow citizens with a quite opposite view of the world, political and legal elites were prepared to grant more liberty of expression to dissenters than was the general public. While Sniderman and his colleagues consistently found deep cleavages between elites and the masses in support of civil liberties, they could find no marked differences between the responses of English and French Canadians. Moreover, the cleavage pattern between elites and the public is consistent with American surveys on attitudes toward fundamental freedoms (see McClosky *et al.* 1983).

Another result, however, seems to confirm the often-mentioned "state-bias" of Canadian political culture which is at the heart of Lipset's writings. The same elites who showed a high degree of support for dissenting views and manifestations were also more inclined to accept the rights of governments to interfere in the private sphere of citizens (wiretapping, etc.) than the general public, who was less inclined to accept the reason of state as an excuse for such measures. Yet even this result is compatible with American findings.

The real question behind the Charter and its impact on political culture is how much entrenched rights would strengthen the value of liberty and weaken values of community and authority. The empirical findings of Sniderman *et al.* indicate that the contemporary Canadian perception of this tension between liberty, on the one hand, and community and authority, on the other, again contains elements of continuity and change. Canadians —both elites and the public—seem to respect both liberty and a sense of community. They choose, so it seems, to live with a built-in tension between the rights of the citizen to a maximum of personal freedom and the rights of governments to uphold an orderly society. The research data does not allow us to conclude that Canadian political culture has yet embarked on a path of worshipping unrestrained individualism. With respect to the Anglophone-Francophone cleavage, the points of similarity in the attitudes of members of the two language groups by far outweigh those of difference. Regarding basic political attitudes, the authors conclude that "the notion of Quebec as a distinct society does not fit the results of our study" (Sniderman *et al.* 1988, 15). There are, however, significant differences among elites with respect to government rights—differences that largely depend on ideology and occupation. Members and supporters of the Conservative Party, Tories, Socreds and executive elites are more willing to accept state interference in civil liberties than members of the NDP or persons in the legal professions.

In conclusion, the survey on the Charter shows that community is still an important and salient value in forming the opinion of Canadians on individual and government rights. On the other hand, American and Canadian as well as French- and English-Canadian attitudes seem to converge into a more North American political culture: in both countries and all regions the value differences underlying many political issues are at the centre of political discussion.

3. *Judicial Interpretation: a Canadian Approach or American-style Judicial Review?*

The vast majority of Charter cases decided between 1983 and 1988 belonged to the field of criminal justice (see Morton 1987 and Monahan 1987). A high success rate[10] of Charter-based claims seemed to indicate that the traditional emphasis on crime control as the basic rationale of the criminal justice system is yielding to the due process approach (see Morton 1987 and Lipset 1986).

The two fears raised before entrenchment by different lobby groups have so far been proven wrong by Supreme Court rulings. Neither did the court use the Charter to strike down mainly provincial legislation nor did the justices continue to treat the Charter as a toothless tiger in the tradition of the statutory Bill of Rights. There seems to be a consensus in the Court that the justices have an explicit constitutional mandate to strike down any legislation that violates the Charter.

Although this is not a consensus about judicial activism, the broad application of the Charter has inevitably brought on a debate about the nature of judicial review in Canada. The reality of the Charter as a third pillar of the Constitution has shifted the academic and political debate away from the discussion of judicial review as such to the conflict between judicial activism or self-restraint. This debate appears partly in the disguise of institutional reform proposals to change the appointment process, and partly as a debate between an "American" as opposed to a "distinctively Canadian" approach to judicial review. While the Canadian Bar Association, advisers of provincial governments, and some academics emphasize institutional reform, a growing number of younger constitutional lawyers have directed their attention primarily to the underlying philosophy of recent Charter decisions. Authors such as Monahan and Petter are rather suspicious of an activist Supreme Court which—according to their reading—has already embarked on a primarily individualistic interpretation at the expense of developing an approach that is more in tune with the "community" traditions of Canadian politics. Such a Canadian approach would take into account the creative tension between negative and positive liberty, i.e. between the rights of the individual and the entitlements of sociologically defined groups as manifested in the Charter (see Monahan 1987).

The most important arena of debate on judicial review is the bench itself; the "demonstration" clause of section 1 compels the justices to indulge in such an internal debate. In the landmark section 1 case, *Regina v. Oakes*, the Supreme Court sent a clear message to the political arena that the burden of proof to demonstrate the reasonableness of legislation in conflict with the Charter is on the government rather than on the plaintiff.

4. *Political Discourse: Towards a Plurality of Political Languages?*

In terms of political discourse or agenda setting the advent of the Charter marked a very special kind of change. The Canadian welfare state had been unsuccessful—as we mentioned a while ago—in establishing a dominant cleavage pattern, such as class, that cuts across regional fragmentation. The Charter, by raising to the national forum mainly questions concerning conflicting values such as freedom of expression, language policy, the right to privacy or the rights of the unborn, which might or might not have a particular regional or contextual origin, seems to centre a good deal of political debate around single issues and ideological questions. This tendency has led Gibbins and others to believe that the Charter, combined with the agenda of the ruling Conservative Party, "has the potential to contribute to reorientation of Canadian political discourse away from its traditional emphasis on territorialism and toward a more explicit emphasis on ideology" (Gibbins & Knopff 1985, 166; see also Knopff & Morton 1985).

If ideological polarization cuts across traditional regional cleavages, then the nation-building potential of the Charter depends on the way in which federalist issues are approached by both levels of government. If the federal government manages to appease the provinces, Charter disputes of an ideological rather than territorial nature will dominate the constitutional agenda. Since a considerable number of political issues become constitutional issues under the Charter, this document—like the Bill of Rights in the United States—will rise to the top of the political agenda.

Should the intergovernmental climate become characterized by confrontation, section 33 would be invoked and weaken the Charter's position. Then, citizenship questions would remain—at least on a symbolic level—core elements of a constitutional counter-agenda, as they were from 1968 to 1982.

The Charter does not seem to replace the dominant political discourse of regionalism and federalism with a single other dominant discourse. While it derogates region as the dominant variable in Canada's political system, it accounts for a plurality of political languages expressing cleavage patterns that are prominent in modern complex societies such as Canada.

IV. Conclusion: the Multiple Political Functions of the Charter

1. *A Mirror of Political Tradition*

As a legal institution the Charter reflects continuity and change in Canada's political tradition. It is "congealed politics" (*geronnene Politik*), since its content is an expression of the political conflicts which determined its making.

The federal government's agenda is reflected by classical individual rights as well as manifested through mobility and language rights, both of which are constitutive of Canadian citizenship. Regional fragmentation and the British institutional heritage are reflected in the opting-out provision of section 33 and the limitation clause of section 1. Multiple identities of Canadians are represented by section 15(2), which allows for programs of reverse discrimination in favour of minorities and women; the non-discrimination clause of 15(1); and the recognition of gender equality, native rights and Canada's multicultural heritage.

The Charter enhances the legitimacy of the Canadian state, because it gives constitutional recognition to multiple reinforcing and cross-cutting cleavage patterns salient in the contemporary Canadian political community. Citizenship questions are as important as division of power disputes. The Charter, as the business card of Canadian citizenship, performs some essential political functions on a judicial level. It integrates classes, regions, ethnic groups, lifestyles, generations and sexes into one domestic political community.

2. The Charter as a Medium Moulding Canadian Society

As part of the supreme law of the land, the Charter is a medium moulding a political community with a fragile consensus. It is, however, a mistaken point of view or simply rhetorical to conceive of charter law as a national consensus on substantive issues. Quoting legal philosopher Ronald Dworkin, who holds that "the concept of rights against the government has its most natural uses when a political society is divided, and appeals to cooperation or a common goal are pointless" (1977, 184), Donald Smiley rightly rejects the perception that the Charter represents a national consensus. The document rather identifies ". . . a set of preferred claims that one group of citizens can express against another group of citizens" (Smiley 1986, 189).

The Charter is, nonetheless, a procedural consensus—section 33 notwithstanding—that the place to decide on the legitimacy of such claims are the courts rather than the political arena of parliaments and executive meetings. Since many of these claims refer to substantive policy issues like abortion, store closing hours, affirmative action programs, language legislation, parochial school funding, mandatory retirement, etc., a good deal of responsibility is transferred to the Supreme Court of Canada. It depends on one's perspective whether this shift of responsibility is seen as a relief in workload or as a loss of power for the political process. In an age of media politics when politicians are reluctant to make unpopular decisions, the Canadian Supreme Court has forced politicians on both levels of government to deal with electoral no-win issues like abortion and language legislation in Quebec.

To be sure, as a government policy the Charter was designed under the assumption that constitutional law is an effective and adequate mechanism for changing situations and actors and thereby lowering the threshold of acceptance within the citizenry for other controversial policy initiatives, such as in the fields of language, school funding, criminal law, and even energy. Today the "crisis of the welfare state" has partly undermined the belief in the superior regulatory potential of the law in complex societies.[11]

Thus, constitutional law and Charter litigation should not be expected to perform the role of a medium "managing" or even resolving contextually defined ad hoc disputes within civil society or between individuals and the state in subfields like family law, school law or labour law. Instead, a catalogue of entrenched rights is a medium influencing the standards by which belief systems are shaped and by which the courts and the public assess and judge individual behaviour and public institutions. "Legal regulation is appropriate for programmes and issues of medium-range complexity, that is, for events that do not change very rapidly" (Offe 1984, 280).

Designed as an instrument to improve the protection of individual and specifically Canadian rights and to counterbalance centrifugal regional forces, the Charter's performance as an instrument of political socialization will be measured by its ability to integrate a variety of divisions in Canadian society which the Charter itself recognizes and sometimes intensifies.

Notes

1. Television interview, *Gallery*, New Zealand Broadcasting Commission, Wellington, NZ, 14 May 1970.
2. The literature on the legal origins and the legal implications of the Charter has become legion. For a chronological overview, see Edward McWhinney (1979 and 1982); for a case by case analysis, see Russell, Knopff, Morton (1989).
3. "The development toward a democratic welfare state can in fact be understood as the institutionalizing in legal form of a social power relation anchored in class structure" (Habermas 1987, II:361).
4. For the society-centred explanation of Canadian federalism and regionalism, see Livingston (1956). For a classic case of the policy-centred approach, see Cairns (1979). A somewhat mediating position is taken by Herman Bakvis:
   > Institutions may not be the product of societies, but they do need to strike a responsive chord in their societies in order to survive and flourish. They must be attractive to elites as vehicles for promoting their interests as well as those of their constituents. In short, there has to be some sense of community, of a political society, in which leaders, citizens and institutions play a role. (1981, 15)
5. In this section, I am much influenced by the debate between communitarians and liberals about justice and citizenship, especially by Michael Sandel (1984).
6. The following section is heavily dependent on the writings of Professors Alan C. Cairns and Cynthia Williams. See Cairns (1984) and Cairns & Williams (1985).

7. For a comprehensive, but orthodox, socialist critique of the Charter and constitutional rights in general, see the special edition on the Constitution of the journal *Socialist Studies*, 1984, and Michael Mandel's recent study (1989).
8. The survey research project, *Attitudes toward Civil Liberties and the Canadian Charter of Rights* was conducted by the Institute for Social Research of York University for Paul M. Sniderman (Stanford), Joseph F. Fletcher (Toronto), Peter Russell (Toronto) and Philip E. Tetlock (Berkeley).
9. Lipset has modified his thesis several times over the past 25 years. For his most recent account on comparative US-Canadian political culture, see Lipset (1986). For details on the "regional political cultures" argument, see Elkins & Simeon (1979) and Bell & Tepperman (1979).
10. During the first three years (1982-85) in Charterland, nine out of fifteen, or 60% of cases were decided in favour of Charter rights.
11. For a more detailed account of doubts about the regulatory potential of law in modern welfare states, see Claus Offe (1984, 279ff). The following lines summarize the essence of his considerations on the role of law.

Bibliography

Bakvis, Herman (1981) *Federalism and the Organization of Political Life: Canada in Comparative Perspective*. Kingston, Ont.: Institute of Inter-governmental Relations.

Banting, Keith and Simeon, Richard (eds, 1985) *Redesigning the State: The Politics of Constitutional Change*. Toronto: University of Toronto Press.

Bell, David and Lorne Tepperman (1979) *The Roots of Disunity: A Look at Canadian Political Culture*. Toronto: McClelland & Stewart.

Cairns, Alan C. (1984) "The Canadian Constitutional Experiment: Constitution, Community and Identity." *Dalhousie Law Journal*, 9, 87-114.

———, (1979) "The Governments and Societies of Canadian Federalism." *Canadian Journal of Political Science*, 10:4, 695-725.

Cairns, Alan & Williams, Cynthia (1985) *Constitutionalism, Citizenship and Society in Canada*. MacDonald Commission Vol. 33. Toronto: University of Toronto Press.

Canada (1984) *Constitution of Canada, Official Consolidation, 1867-1982*. Ottawa: Supply and Services.

Corry, J.A. (1958) "Constitutional Trends and Federalism." In *Evolving Canadian Federalism*. Edited by A.R.M. Lower. Durham, NC: Duke University Press, 92-125.

Dworkin, Ronald (1977) *Taking Rights Seriously*. Cambridge, MA: MIT Press.

Elkins, David and Richard Simeon (1980) *Small Worlds: Provinces and Parties in Canadian Political Life*. Toronto: Methuen.

Gibbins, Roger and Knopff, Rainer (1985) "Canadian Federalism, The Charter of Rights and the 1984 Election." *Publius: The Journal of Federalism*, 15 (Summer), 155ff.

Habermas, Jürgen (1987) *The Theory of Communicative Action*. Volume II. Boston: Beacon Press.

Knopff, Rainer & Morton, F.L. (1985) "Nation-Building and the Canadian Charter of Rights and Freedoms." In Cairns & Williams (1985), 133ff.

Lipset, Seymour Martin (1986) "Historical Traditions and National Characteristics: A Comparative Analysis of Canada and the United States." *Canadian Journal of Sociology*, 11:2, 113-55.

Livingstone, W.S. (1956) *Federalism and Constitutional Change*. Oxford: Clarendon Press.

Mann, Michael (1989) *The Charter of Rights and the Legalization of Politics in Canada*. Toronto: Wall & Thompson.

McClosky, Herbert and Brill, A. (1983) *Dimensions of Tolerance: What Americans Think about Civil Liberties*. New York: Russell Sage.

McWhinney, Edward (1979) *Quebec and the Constitution 1960-1978*. Toronto: University of Toronto Press.

————, (1982) *Canada and the Constitution 1979-82: Patriation and the Charter of Rights*. Toronto: University of Toronto Press.

Meisel, John (1976) "Recent Changes in Canadian Parties." In *Party Politics in Canada*. 3rd edition. Edited by H.G. Thorburn. Scarborough, Ont.: Prentice-Hall.

Monahan, Patrick (1987) *Politics and the Constitution: the Charter, Federalism and the Supreme Court of Canada*. Toronto: Carswell.

Morton, F.L. (1987) "The Political Impact of the Canadian Charter of Rights." *Canadian Journal of Political Science*, 20:2, 31-55.

Offe, Claus (1984) *Contradictions of the Welfare State*. Cambridge, MA: MIT Press.

Russell, Peter H. (1983) "The Political Purposes of the Canadian Charter of Rights and Freedoms." *Canadian Bar Review* 61, 30-54.

————, (1985) "The First Three Years in Charterland." *Canadian Public Administration* 28, 367-96.

————, (1988) "Canada's Charter of Rights and Freedoms: A Political Report." *Public Law* (Autumn), 385-401.

Russell, Peter, R. Knopff & T. Morton (1989) *Federalism and the Charter: Leading Constitutional Decisions*. Ottawa: Carleton University Press.

Sandel, Michael (1984) "The Procedural Republic and the Unencumbered Self." *Political Theory*, 12:1 (February), 81-96.

Senate of Canada (1950) *Proceedings of the Special Committee on Human Rights and Fundamental Freedoms*. Document No. 10. Ottawa: Queen's Printer.

Simeon, Richard (1986) "Considerations on Centralization and Decentralization." *Canadian Public Administration*, 29, 445-64.

Simeon, Richard and Elkins, David J. (1974) "Regional Political Cultures in Canada." *Canadian Journal of Political Science*, 7:3 (September), 397ff.

Smiley, Donald V. (1968) *The Canadian Political Nationality*. Toronto: Methuen.

————, (1986) "The Three Pillars of the Canadian Constitutional Order." *Canadian Public Policy*, 12th Supplement (February), 103-21.

————, (1987) *The Federal Condition in Canada*, Toronto: McGraw-Hill.

Sniderman, P., Fletcher, J., Russell, P. and Tetlock, P. (1988) "Liberty, Authority and Community: Civil Liberties and the Canadian Political

Culture." Paper presented at the Annual Meetings of the CPSA and CLSA, Windsor, June.

Taylor, Charles (1985) "Alternative Futures." In Cairns & Williams (1985), 183ff.

Trudeau, Pierre Elliot (1968) *Federalism and the French Canadians.* Toronto: Macmillan.

José Woehrling

Les oppositions à l'Accord du lac Meech et la Charte canadienne des droits et libertés

Résumé

L'Accord du lac Meech a été conclu en 1987 par le chef du gouvernement fédéral et les dix premiers ministres provinciaux pour apporter certaines modifications à la Constitution du Canada, dans le but de satisfaire les revendications du Québec. Parmi les changements prévus, figure la reconnaissance de la dualité linguistique du Canada et du caractère distinct de la société québécoise. Ces dispositions alimentent une vive controverse, certains groupes considérant qu'elles menacent les droits qui leur sont garantis par la Charte canadienne des droits et libertés. L'auteur tente d'élucider la signification des dispositions en cause, en faisant l'historique des concepts de «dualité» et de «société distincte» et en examinant leurs éléments constitutifs. Il en conclut que si la reconnaissance de la dualité vise à protéger les minorités de langue officielle, la protection et la promotion du caractère distinct du Québec ont pour objet le maintien et le développement du caractère francophone de la société québécoise; en cas de conflit entre ces deux objectifs, il faudra tenir compte du fait que l'accord constitutionnel reconnaît une nette primauté à la dualité canadienne. L'auteur examine ensuite l'impact éventuel de l'Accord du lac Meech sur les droits garantis par la Constitution aux groupes qui s'opposent à son adoption: les minorités francophones hors Québec, la minorité anglo-québécoise, les groupes culturels et ethniques autres que les minorités de langue officielle, les peuples autochtones et, enfin, certains groupes de femmes.

Abstract

In 1987, the head of the federal government and the ten provincial first ministers worked out the Lake Meech Accord—an agreement designed to effect certain changes in the Canadian constitution which would satisfy the claims of Quebec. Among the changes proposed were recognition of Canada's linguistic duality and recognition of the distinct character of Quebec society. Both these issues have been responsible for considerable controversy—certain groups consider that the proposed changes threaten rights guaranteed to them by the Canadian Charter of Rights and Freedoms. The author attempts to elucidate the meaning of the proposed changes, tracing the history of notions of "duality" and "distinct society," and examin-

José Woehrling

ing their constitutive elements. He concludes that, while recognition of duality is designed to protect the official-language minorities, the protection and promotion of the distinct character of Quebec is designed to maintain and develop the Francophone character of Quebec society. In the case of a conflict between these two objectives, it should be remembered that, within the constitutional agreement, recognition of Canadian duality has been granted precedence. The author then examines the impact the Accord could have on rights guaranteed by the Constitution to groups opposed to its adoption; that is, to Francophone minorities outside Quebec, to the Anglophone minority in Quebec, to ethnic and cultural groups outside of the two official-language groups, to native peoples, and to some women's groups.

Introduction

Au terme de presque deux ans de négociations, les dix premiers ministres provinciaux et le chef du gouvernement fédéral ont conclu, le 3 juin 1987, un *accord constitutionnel* (l'Accord du lac Meech) en vertu duquel ils conviennent d'apporter certaines modifications à la Constitution du Canada, dans le but de satisfaire les conditions posées par le gouvernement du Québec pour son adhésion à la *Loi constitutionnelle de 1982*. Pour entrer en vigueur, l'accord devra être ratifié par le Parlement fédéral et chacune des dix législatures provinciales avant le 23 juin 1990.

À l'article 1er de l'Accord du lac Meech figurent certaines dispositions relatives à la reconnaissance de la dualité linguistique du Canada et du caractère distinct de la société québécoise. Ces dispositions alimentent, depuis plus de deux ans, une vive controverse. Certains considèrent que les concepts utilisés sont trop ambigus, d'autres que leur inclusion dans la Constitution entraînerait des résultats indésirables en affaiblissant la *Charte canadienne des droits et libertés*[1]. Cinq groupes entretiennent des craintes particulières en considérant que leurs droits et libertés sont spécialement menacés. Il s'agit: 1. des francophones hors Québec; 2. des anglophones du Québec; 3. des minorités culturelles et ethniques qui n'appartiennent pas aux deux collectivités linguistiques principales (les «tiers groupes linguistiques»); 4. des peuples autochtones; et, enfin, 5. de certains groupes de femmes. Dans mon exposé je tenterai d'évaluer l'impact, sur les droits de ces groupes et sur la *Charte* en général, des dispositions de l'accord relatives à la dualité et à la reconnaissance du caractère distinct du Québec. Cet impact dépend évidemment de la signification que les tribunaux donneront à ces dispositions. Or il existe à ce sujet un désaccord considérable entre les partisans et les adversaires de l'Accord du lac Meech. C'est pourquoi il est nécessaire, pour commencer, d'éclairer le sens et la portée juridique des dispositions relatives à la dualité et au caractère distinct du Québec.

I. Signification et portée juridique des dispositions relatives à la dualité et au caractère distinct du Québec

L'article 1er de l'accord constitutionnel se lit comme suit:

1. La *Loi constitutionnelle de 1867* est modifiée par insertion, après l'article 1, de ce qui suit:

2(1) Toute interprétation de la Constitution du Canada doit concorder avec:
a) la reconnaissance de ce que l'existence de Canadiens d'expression française, concentrés au Québec mais présents aussi dans le reste du pays, et de Canadiens d'expression anglaise, concentrés dans le reste du pays mais aussi présents au Québec, constitue une caractéristique fondamentale du Canada;
b) la reconnaissance de ce que le Québec forme au sein du Canada une société distincte.

(2) Le Parlement du Canada et les législatures des provinces ont le rôle de protéger la caractéristique fondamentale du Canada visée à l'alinéa (1) a).

(3) La législature et le gouvernement du Québec ont le rôle de protéger et de promouvoir le caractère distinct du Québec visé à l'alinéa (1) b).

(4) Le présent article n'a pas pour effet de déroger aux pouvoirs, droits ou privilèges du Parlement ou du gouvernement du Canada, ou des législatures ou des gouvernements des provinces, y compris à leurs pouvoirs, droits ou privilèges en matière de langue.

Comme on le constate, une fois la modification constitutionnelle entrée en vigueur, les dispositions en cause figureront à l'article 2 de la *Loi constitutionnelle de 1867*[2]. Pour saisir véritablement leur signification et leur portée, il est nécessaire de tenir également compte de l'article 16 de l'Accord du lac Meech, qui énonce:

16. L'article 2 de la *Loi constitutionnelle de 1867* n'a pas pour effet de porter atteinte aux articles 25 ou 27 de la *Charte canadienne des droits et libertés*, à l'article 35 de la *Loi constitutionnelle de 1982* ou au point 24 de l'article 91 de la *Loi constitutionnelle de 1867*.

En combinant les articles 1 et 16 de l'Accord du lac Meech, on y trouve en premier lieu la «reconnaissance» solennelle de deux réalités sociolinguistiques — la dualité linguistique du Canada et le caractère distinct du Québec, ensuite certaines dispositions destinées à conférer à cette reconnaissance une portée juridique et, enfin, deux «clauses de sauvegarde» destinées, au contraire, à limiter les effets juridiques susceptibles d'en découler.

1. *La dualité linguistique du Canada*

En ce qui concerne la dualité, l'Accord du lac Meech stipule que «l'existence de Canadiens d'expression française, concentrés au Québec mais présents aussi dans le reste du pays, et de Canadiens d'expression anglaise, concentrés dans le reste du pays mais aussi présents au Québec, constitue une caractéristique fondamentale du Canada». La réalité sociologique visée par cette formulation est l'existence de groupes linguistiques *minoritaires*, de langue française au Canada anglais et de langue anglaise au Québec. Du point de vue juridique, cette reconnaissance doit au moins signifier que l'existence des minorités est constitutionnellement consacrée et protégée. L'*étendue* exacte de cette protection découle des autres dispositions de l'accord constitutionnel, comme on le verra plus loin.

2. *Le caractère distinct du Québec*

Dans l'Accord du lac Meech, le caractère distinct du Québec ne fait l'objet d'aucune définition explicite. Aussi la notion donne-t-elle matière à controverse, la question étant de savoir si le Québec est normativement défini comme société *française*, ou au contraire comme société *bilingue et multiculturelle*.

Selon une première interprétation, le caractère distinct du Québec tiendrait à la coexistence, sur le territoire de la province, d'une majorité francophone, d'une minorité anglophone et de tiers groupes d'autres cultures et d'autres langues. Dès lors, la protection et la promotion du caractère distinct du Québec devraient logiquement viser le maintien du bilinguisme et du multiculturalisme de la société québécoise. Je pense que cette première interprétation du «caractère distinct du Québec» doit être rejetée, et ceci pour trois raisons.

En premier lieu, la coexistence au Québec d'une majorité francophone et d'une minorité anglophone est déjà constitutionnellement consacrée par le biais de la reconnaissance de la *dualité*, laquelle vise précisément la protection des droits des minorités. La reconnaissance du caractère distinct du Québec doit donc logiquement renvoyer à autre chose que la présence au Québec d'une minorité anglophone.

On peut ajouter à cela que dans un système fédéral, toutes les entités constituantes sont en quelque sorte «distinctes». En effet, c'est précisément le caractère distinct des États-membres et, surtout, le fait qu'ils désirent conserver cette spécificité, qui expliquent le choix de la forme fédérative, de préférence à l'État unitaire. Par conséquent, l'affirmation expresse du caractère distinct du Québec — et seulement de cette province — signifie qu'il existe une différence de nature entre la spécificité québécoise et celle de chacune des autres provinces. À mon avis, cette différence tient au fait que *le rapport démographique qui prévaut dans toutes les autres parties du Canada se trouve renversé au Québec*, où vit la seule majorité francophone.

Enfin, il faut donner un sens au fait que la dualité est seulement *protégée*, alors que le caractère distinct du Québec peut faire l'objet d'une *protection* et d'une *promotion*. Or au Québec, c'est le fait francophone majoritaire qui nécessite d'être promu, et non seulement protégé, à cause de sa fragilité. En effet, toute majoritaire qu'elle soit au niveau provincial, la langue française est minoritaire partout ailleurs au Canada et en Amérique du Nord. À mon avis, l'Accord du lac Meech reconnaît donc de façon implicite que la majorité francophone du Québec est une majorité «menacée», qui doit défendre sa langue.

En conclusion, si le caractère distinct du Québec tient au fait que celui-ci est la seule province canadienne dont la majorité est de langue et de culture françaises, il faut conclure que sa protection et sa promotion visent logiquement le maintien et le développement du caractère francophone et français de la société québécoise, dans le respect il est vrai du principe de la dualité.

3. *La primauté de la dualité linguistique du Canada sur le caractère distinct du Québec*

Le texte de l'Accord du lac Meech affirme à deux reprises que la dualité linguistique constitue «une caractéristique fondamentale du Canada»; quant au caractère distinct du Québec, son existence est simplement reconnue, sans qu'il soit pareillement qualifié de «caractéristique fondamentale». S'il surgit un conflit entre la nécessité de protéger la dualité et celle de protéger ou de promouvoir le caractère distinct du Québec, les tribunaux devront par conséquent tenir compte de la hiérarchie qui est ainsi expressément établie.

Il faut donc conclure que le rôle du Québec à l'égard de son caractère distinct doit être, lui aussi, subordonné à son rôle de protéger la dualité: autrement dit, la protection et la promotion du fait francophone ne peuvent aller jusqu'à remettre en cause la protection de la minorité anglophone du Québec.

II. L'impact général de l'accord constitutionnel sur la Charte canadienne des droits et libertés

Après un certain nombre de remarques concernant les rapports entre la *Charte* et l'accord constitutionnel, il y aura lieu de voir quels sont les effets que les dispositions relatives à la dualité et au caractère distinct du Québec sont susceptibles de produire, d'une part sur la *définition* des droits garantis par la *Charte*, d'autre part sur leur *limitation*.

1. *Les rapports entre la Charte et l'accord constitutionnel*

Une première constatation s'impose: les dispositions de l'Accord du lac Meech, une fois celui-ci entré en vigueur, s'appliqueront à la *Charte*. En effet, elles feront alors partie de la Constitution au même titre que la *Charte* et l'on sait que tous les éléments d'un texte constitutionnel doivent s'interpréter et s'appliquer les uns par rapport aux autres. En outre, l'article 1er de l'accord constitutionnel dispose que «[t]oute interprétation de la Constitution» doit concorder avec la reconnaissance de la dualité et du caractère distinct du Québec; or la *Charte* est contenue dans la *Loi constitutionnelle de 1982*, laquelle fait évidemment partie de la «Constitution du Canada».

À cette première constatation s'en ajoute une seconde: la *Charte* s'appliquera elle-même aux dispositions de l'accord, notamment celles qui ont trait à la reconnaissance de la dualité et du caractère distinct du Québec. Autrement dit, ces dispositions n'écartent pas la *Charte*, pas plus qu'elles ne la supplantent. La raison en est d'abord, comme je l'ai déjà mentionné, que la *Charte* et l'accord feront partie du même texte constitutionnel et, dans cette mesure, s'appliqueront concurremment. Ensuite, les dispositions relatives à la dualité et au caractère distinct du Québec n'étant qu'interprétatives, elles ne peuvent avoir d'effet autrement qu'en venant se combiner avec les dispositions de fond de la Constitution, dont celles de la *Charte* en particulier.

Par conséquent, dans la mesure où la *Charte* s'applique aux dispositions relatives à la dualité et à la reconnaissance du caractère distinct du Québec, elle devra être pleinement respectée par les lois et autres mesures adoptées pour protéger la dualité, ainsi que par celles qui ont pour but de protéger ou de promouvoir le caractère distinct. Cela signifie que ces mesures devront, soit ne restreindre aucun des droits et libertés garanti par la *Charte*, soit les restreindre uniquement dans la mesure permise par l'article 1er de celle-ci, c'est à dire d'une façon «raisonnable» et «dont la justification puisse se démontrer dans le cadre d'une société libre et démocratique». C'est à ce double point de vue, de la *portée* des droits et libertés et de leur *limitation*, que les dispositions de l'accord constitutionnel sont susceptibles d'avoir un impact sur la *Charte*.

2. L'effet des dispositions relatives à la dualité et à la reconnaissance du caractère distinct du Québec sur la définition et sur la limitation des droits garantis par la Charte

En ce qui concerne tout d'abord l'interprétation du *contenu* des droits et libertés, les dispositions de la Constitution les plus susceptibles d'être affectées sont celles qui portent sur les droits linguistiques des minorités, c'est-à-dire l'article 133 de la *Loi constitutionnelle de 1867*, l'article 23 de la *Loi de 1870 sur le Manitoba*[3] et les articles 16 à 20 et 23 de la *Charte* elle-même. Ainsi que nous le verrons plus en détail en examinant l'impact de l'accord sur les droits des francophones hors Québec et des anglo-Québécois, la reconnaissance de la dualité pourrait justifier une interprétation des droits des minorités *plus large et plus libérale* que celle qui leur a été donnée dernièrement par la Cour suprême du Canada.

Par ailleurs, l'article 1er de la *Charte* prévoit que les droits et libertés «peuvent être restreints [...] dans des limites qui soient raisonnables et dont la justification puisse se démontrer dans le cadre d'une société libre et démocratique». Si on les combine avec cet article 1er, les dispositions relatives à la dualité et au caractère distinct du Québec pourront donc être invoquées afin de justifier les restrictions aux droits et libertés considérées comme nécessaires pour protéger la dualité ou le caractère distinct du Québec, ou pour promouvoir celui-ci. C'est précisément ce que craignent certains des groupes qui s'opposent à l'adoption de l'accord constitution-nel, notamment les anglo-Québécois et les groupes de femmes, et c'est la raison pour laquelle ils exigent une modification de l'accord, afin de conférer clairement une primauté à la *Charte* sur les dispositions relatives à la dualité et au caractère distinct du Québec. Le gouvernement du Québec quant à lui s'oppose fermement à ces demandes, et cela avec raison d'après moi. En effet, il est facile de démontrer que la reconnaissance du caractère distinct n'aura aucun impact sur le partage des compétences entre le Québec et le fédéral, à cause de la clause de sauvegarde qui figure au paragraphe 2(4) de l'accord constitutionnel[4]. Si la *Charte* était également soustraite à l'application des dispositions relatives à la reconnaissance du caractère distinct du Québec, celles-ci seraient dépouillées de toute portée juridique véritable et n'auraient plus qu'une portée purement symbolique.

En fait, les craintes des groupes qui s'opposent à l'accord constitutionnel semblent largement exagérées. Il faut en effet rappeler que la Cour suprême a fait découler de l'article 1er de la *Charte* des conditions extrêmement exigeantes pour justifier les restrictions aux droits et libertés. Une mesure limitant un droit ou une liberté doit poursuivre un *objectif* social «suffisamment important pour justifier la suppression d'un droit ou d'une liberté garantis par la Constitution» et les *moyens* choisis pour atteindre cet objectif doivent satisfaire une sorte de critère de proportionnalité.

Concernant la première exigence, il va de soi que la protection de la dualité ainsi que la protection et la promotion du caractère distinct du Québec devront être considérées comme des *objectifs* importants lorsque l'accord constitutionnel sera entré en vigueur. Cependant il ne fait pas de doute que ces deux finalités peuvent dès aujourd'hui être considérées comme suffisantes pour justifier une restriction aux droits et libertés, indépendamment de l'accord constitutionnel. C'est ce que la Cour suprême du Canada a reconnu dans son récent jugement *Ford c. P. G. Québec* du 15 décembre 1988, à propos de l'objectif de protection et de promotion de la langue française qui est inscrit dans le préambule de la *Charte de la langue française* du Québec[5].

Mais le «test» de l'article 1er de la *Charte* comporte un deuxième volet: les *moyens* choisis pour atteindre les objectifs poursuivis doivent être raisonnables, c'est-à-dire qu'ils doivent satisfaire une sorte de critère de proportionnalité. D'après la Cour ce critère de proportionnalité comporte trois éléments:

– premièrement, les mesures adoptées doivent avoir un lien rationnel avec l'objectif en question;

– deuxièmement, même à supposer qu'il y ait un tel lien rationnel, le moyen choisi doit être de nature à porter «le moins possible» atteinte au droit ou à la liberté en question;
– troisièmement, il doit y avoir proportionnalité entre les *effets* des mesures restreignant un droit ou une liberté garantis par la Charte et l'objectif reconnu comme «suffisamment important»[6].

On peut sans doute considérer que le recours aux dispositions de l'Accord du lac Meech exigera des tribunaux qu'ils *abaissent* le seuil de difficulté de ce «test» de proportionnalité dans l'application de l'article 1er de la *Charte*. Cependant, il demeurera toujours très difficile de justifier les restrictions aux droits et libertés, fussent-elles fondées sur la protection de la dualité ou du caractère distinct du Québec. C'est ce que nous constaterons en examinant l'impact de l'Accord du lac Meech sur les droits spécifiques de chacun des groupes qui s'opposent à son adoption.

III. L'impact des dispositions relatives à la dualité et au caractère distinct du Québec sur les droits des divers groupes qui s'opposent à l'accord constitutionnel

Je rappellerai rapidement, pour chacun des groupes en cause, les craintes et les griefs qu'il entretient à l'égard de l'Accord du lac Meech, pour ensuite tenter d'évaluer leur bien-fondé.

Dans cette double démarche, je tiendrai compte aussi bien de la situation strictement *juridique* des groupes concernés que de leur statut *politico-constitutionnel*. En effet, il faut souligner qu'au Canada les questions constitutionnelles sont devenues, depuis l'adoption de la *Charte canadienne des droits et libertés* en 1982, l'enjeu d'une véritable course au «positionnement symbolique», les groupes ethniques et les diverses catégories sociologiques cherchant à obtenir dans l'ordonnancement constitutionnel un «créneau» privilégié. Il est même devenu possible de parler, en termes imagés, du «constitutional pecking order». Cela tient au fait que la Constitution, et la *Charte* en particulier, ont pour fonction à la fois de protéger juridiquement les droits et libertés et de conférer une reconnaissance symbolique aux divers groupes qui composent la société canadienne.

L'Accord du lac Meech rehausse évidemment la position symbolique des deux collectivités de langue officielle et, davantage encore, celle de la majorité francophone du Québec. Il était inévitable que tous les autres groupes qui ne sont pas mentionnés dans l'accord considèrent celui-ci comme rabaissant, de façon relative, leur propre position. Par ailleurs, les francophones hors Québec et les anglophones du Québec sont également au nombre des groupes qui s'opposent à l'accord constitutionnel, alors que leur position est pourtant reconnue dans celui-ci, par le biais de la dualité. Cependant, cette reconnaissance leur paraît insuffisante. Je commencerai par examiner la situation de ces deux groupes.

1. *Les francophones hors Québec*

Les francophones hors Québec adressent essentiellement deux reproches à l'accord constitutionnel: d'une part, il ne bonifie pas les droits qui leur sont *déjà* reconnus par la Constitution à l'heure actuelle et, d'autre part, il ne leur permet pas davantage de réclamer des droits additionnels dans l'avenir. À mon avis, si la deuxième critique est bien fondée, ce n'est pas le cas de la première.

En effet, la reconnaissance de la dualité comme «caractéristique fonda-mentale du Canada» consacre l'existence des minorités francophones hors Québec et de la minorité anglo-québécoise et devrait donc, en toute logique, amener les tribunaux à donner aux droits que la Constitution leur reconnaît déjà l'interprétation la plus large, la plus libérale et la plus extensive possible.

Or, certaines garanties constitutionnelles relatives à l'usage du français et de l'anglais dans les procédures judiciaires ont reçu de la Cour suprême du Canada, dans les années récentes, une interprétation fort restrictive. En effet, celle-ci a décidé dans les affaires *MacDonald* et *Bilodeau* (1986)[7] que le droit du justiciable de choisir — entre l'anglais et le français — la langue dans laquelle il veut plaider devant les tribunaux n'entraîne pas que le tribunal doive s'adresser à lui dans la langue de son choix, ou encore de façon bilingue. Ainsi donc, un justiciable anglophone du Québec peut voir sa cause jugée dans une décision rédigée uniquement en français (et inversement). Dans l'affaire *Société des Acadiens* (1986)[8], une majorité de la Cour est allée jusqu'à décider que le même droit du justiciable ne lui donne pas le droit d'être compris par le tribunal auquel il s'adresse. Elle a justifié cette surprenante décision en soulignant que les droits linguistiques enchâssés dans la Charte sont fondés sur un «compromis politique» et que les tribunaux doivent, pour cette raison, hésiter à leur donner une interprétation trop large.

Si les problèmes posés dans ces jugements sont à nouveau soulevés dans l'avenir et que l'accord constitutionnel est entré en vigueur, la Cour suprême devrait logiquement être portée à décider d'une façon plus favorable aux minorités qui sont les bénéficiaires des droits en cause. Par conséquent, de ce point de vue, l'accord constitutionnel peut être considéré comme venant *bonifier* quelque peu la situation des minorités linguistiques. Il est vrai que l'avantage ainsi acquis reste hypothétique tant que les tribunaux n'auront pas démontré qu'ils entendent effectivement tirer de la reconnaissance de la dualité le mandat de donner une interprétation plus généreuse aux droits des minorités.

La deuxième critique que les francophones hors Québec élèvent contre l'accord constitutionnel consiste à souligner que celui-ci ne leur permettra pas, dans l'avenir, de revendiquer des droits *nouveaux* du fédéral et des provinces. Ceci me paraît tout à fait exact et résulte principalement de deux modifications à l'accord qui ont été demandées par le Québec. La première consistait à transformer l'«engagement» du Parlement fédéral et des dix législatures de protéger la dualité en un simple «rôle», qui n'entraîne aucun effet véritablement contraignant. La seconde modification a consisté à ajouter aux dispositions relatives à la dualité et au caractère distinct du Québec une clause de sauvegarde en vertu de laquelle ces dispositions n'ont pas «pour effet de déroger aux pouvoirs, droits ou privilèges du Parlement ou du gouvernement du Canada, ou des législatures ou des gouvernements des provinces, y compris à leurs pouvoirs, droits ou privilèges en matière de langue». Selon moi, cette clause indique clairement que la reconnaissance de la dualité et du caractère distinct du Québec n'a pour effet, ni de modifier le partage des compétences entre le fédéral et les provinces, ni de conférer aux minorités des droits additionnels à ceux que la Constitution leur reconnaissait avant l'entrée en vigueur de l'accord constitutionnel. En effet, toute reconnaissance d'un droit nouveau ou d'une nouvelle liberté aurait pour effet de déroger aux compétences existantes du fédéral ou des provinces, puisque les droits des citoyens entraînent toujours des obligations ou des limitations correspondantes pour l'État.

Cette clause de sauvegarde a surtout été réclamée par le Québec afin de faire en sorte que la minorité anglophone ne puisse pas s'appuyer sur le principe de la dualité pour obtenir des tribunaux qu'ils imposent de nouvelles obligations linguistiques au Québec. Cependant, la minorité anglaise bénéficie d'ores et déjà de droits linguistiques fort importants et le fait qu'elle ne puisse en réclamer l'augmentation sur la base du principe de dualité n'est donc pas dramatique pour elle. De son point de vue, l'essentiel est que ses droits actuels soient à l'abri d'une diminution, ce en quoi l'accord constitutionnel lui donne satisfaction, comme on le verra plus loin. La situation des minorités francophones hors Québec est bien différente; les plus favorisées d'entre elles, au Nouveau-Brunswick et en Ontario, sont encore bien loin de bénéficier d'une situation aussi favorable que celle des anglo-Québécois. Dans leur cas, ce qui s'impose, c'est une amélioration de leur statut. Elles auraient possiblement pu revendiquer une telle amélioration en se fondant sur le principe de la dualité si la clause de sauvegarde ne les en empêchait, dans la mesure où elle dispense les provinces anglophones de leur consentir quelque droit ou bénéfice supplémentaire.

En fait, le caractère *asymétrique* de la situation des anglo-Québécois et des francophones hors Québec aurait justifié que des dispositions différentes leur soient appliquées dans l'accord constitutionnel, la situation des minorités francophones exigeant une *promotion* de leurs droits, alors que celle de la minorité anglo-québécoise n'appelle qu'une simple *protection*. Pour sauvegarder la fiction de l'égalité, on leur a cependant appliqué des dispositions entièrement symétriques; voilà qui explique les faiblesses que reprochent à l'accord les minorités francophones.

2. *Les anglophones du Québec*

En examinant la situation des francophones hors Québec, nous avons été amenés à analyser également celle des anglo-Québécois. En effet, la minorité anglophone tire de l'accord constitutionnel les mêmes avantages limités que les minorités francophones, c'est-à-dire une interprétation possiblement plus large des droits linguistiques qui sont déjà garantis par la Constitution à l'heure actuelle. En ce qui concerne la revendication de nouveaux droits, elle est soumise aux mêmes restrictions découlant de la clause de sauvegarde du paragraphe 2(4). Comme je viens de le noter, ces limitations n'ont cependant pas la même signification concrète pour les anglo-Québécois que pour les minorités francophones des autres provinces.

L'organisme représentatif des anglo-Québécois, *Alliance-Québec*, exige certaines modifications à l'accord constitutionnel, dont la plus importante est l'addition d'une clause affirmant la suprématie de la *Charte* tout entière sur l'Accord du lac Meech. Ainsi que je l'ai déjà indiqué, le Québec ne peut accepter pareil amendement, dans la mesure où celui-ci dépouillerait de toute portée juridique véritable les dispositions portant sur la dualité et le caractère distinct du Québec. Au surplus, une telle précaution est inutile: dans la mesure où l'accord constitutionnel subordonne clairement le caractère distinct du Québec à la dualité linguistique du Canada, la protection et la promotion du fait francophone majoritaire ne pourront pas être invoquées pour diminuer les droits linguistiques de la minorité anglophone du Québec. Afin de le démontrer, il suffit d'examiner l'impact éventuel de l'accord sur la récente décision de la Cour suprême, dans l'affaire *Ford c. P. G. Québec*.

Dans cette affaire, la Cour suprême a reconnu que la liberté d'expression, qui est garantie par l'alinéa 2)*b* de la *Charte*, comprend le droit de s'exprimer dans la langue de son choix, du moins dans le domaine des relations privées. Elle a ensuite déclaré inopérants les articles 58 et 69 de la *Charte de la langue française* dans la mesure où ils prohibent l'usage d'une langue autre que le français pour les affiches, la publicité commerciale et les raisons sociales. La Cour a considéré que cette restriction de la liberté d'expression n'est pas justifiable en vertu de l'article 1er de la *Charte*, car l'interdiction des langues autres que le français ne constitue pas, selon elle, un moyen *nécessaire et proportionné* d'atteindre l'objectif légitime de la loi, qui est de préserver le «visage linguistique» français du Québec.

La Cour suprême aurait-elle jugé différemment si l'Accord du lac Meech avait été en vigueur au moment de la décision? Je pense qu'il n'en est rien. En effet, la Cour aurait alors dû tenir également compte du principe de la dualité canadienne et du rôle attribué au Québec de protéger celle-ci. Et il serait très étonnant qu'elle considère un tel rôle comme compatible avec la prohibition complète de l'usage de l'anglais dans l'affichage public, la publicité commerciale et les raisons sociales.

3. *Les minorités culturelles et ethniques*

En troisième lieu, il faut analyser la situation des groupes culturels et ethniques autres que les minorités de langue officielle (les «tiers groupes culturels»). Il convient de distinguer leurs craintes à l'égard des conséquences *juridiques* de l'accord constitutionnel et leurs doléances à l'égard de la signification *politique* de celui-ci.

La seule disposition de la *Charte* spécifiquement consacrée aux droits *culturels* des minorités est l'article 27, qui dispose que «[t]oute interprétation de la présente charte doit concorder avec l'objectif de promouvoir le maintien et la valorisation du patrimoine multiculturel des Canadiens». Étant donné qu'il s'agit d'une disposition interprétative, elle ne confère de par son seul effet immédiat aucun droit supplémentaire. C'est en combinant l'article 27 avec d'autres dispositions de la *Charte* que les tribunaux pourront éventuellement lui faire jouer un certain rôle. Par ailleurs, comme la langue et la culture sont intimement liées, l'article 27 est susceptible d'avoir également une certaine portée sur les droits *linguistiques* des minorités, même s'il ne fait référence expressément qu'à la culture[9].

Il faut également rappeler le texte de l'article 16 de l'accord constitutionnel du 3 juin 1987:

> L'article 2 de la *Loi constitutionnelle de 1867* n'a pas pour effet de porter atteinte aux articles 25 ou 27 de la *Charte canadienne des droits et libertés*, à l'article 35 de la *Loi constitutionnelle de 1982* ou au point 24 de l'article 91 de la *Loi constitutionnelle de 1867*.

La seule fonction de l'article 16 semble être d'empêcher que les dispositions de l'Accord du lac Meech puissent être interprétées comme modifiant, de quelque façon, la portée actuelle de l'article 27 de la *Charte*, ou des autres articles constitutionnels mentionnés. Ce point de vue s'accorde parfaitement avec la lettre de l'article 16 et correspond à ce que l'on sait de la genèse de cette disposition, qui a été adoptée sur les instances du premier ministre de l'Ontario pour calmer les craintes des communautés culturelles de cette province. Si l'article 16 préserve la portée *actuelle* de l'article 27 de la *Charte,* l'Accord du lac Meech ne menace d'aucune manière les droits qui pourraient découler de cette disposition pour les minorités culturelles et ethniques.

Si les dispositions relatives à la dualité et au caractère distinct du Québec ne menacent donc nullement les droits *juridiques* des minorités culturelles et ethniques, elles viennent par contre diminuer l'importance relative de leur statut constitutionnel «symbolique», lequel est d'acquisition récente.

En effet, alors que la Constitution canadienne réserve depuis 1867 une place particulière aux deux «groupes fondateurs» du pays, les anglophones et les francophones, la reconnaissance du «multiculturalisme» ne date que de 1982. En outre, cette reconnaissance n'a pris la forme que d'une simple règle d'interprétation, contenue dans l'article 27 de la *Charte*, alors que les minorités de langue officielle se voient reconnaître des droits confessionnels et linguistiques substantiels par les articles 93 et 133 de la *Loi constitutionnelle de 1867* et par les articles 16 à 20 et 23 de la *Charte*. Du moins l'adoption, en 1982, de l'article 27 avait-elle apporté une certaine satisfaction aux minorités culturelles en assurant pour la première fois leur insertion dans l'ordonnancement symbolique de la Constitution, même si c'est à un rang inférieur à celui des minorités de langue officielle. Dans la mesure où l'accord constitutionnel de 1987 reconnaît la dualité anglophonie-francophonie comme «la caractéristique fondamentale du Canada», sans en faire de même pour le multiculturalisme, les «tiers groupes» culturels ont le sentiment très net que l'on rabaisse le statut qui leur a été octroyé dans la *Charte*. Aussi voudraient-ils faire modifier l'accord de façon à ce que le multiculturalisme soit également reconnu comme une «caractéristique fondamentale du Canada». En fait, il semble que l'Accord du lac Meech soit devenu l'occasion pour les «tiers groupes» de réclamer une égalité de statut avec les deux «peuples fondateurs».

4. *Les peuples autochtones*

La situation des autochtones, face à l'accord constitutionnel, ressemble à celle des minorités culturelles que nous venons d'analyser. Sur le plan *juridique*, elle n'est menacée d'aucune façon par les dispositions relatives à la dualité et au caractère distinct du Québec, étant donné que la clause de sauvegarde de l'article 16 empêche que celles-ci puissent porter atteinte aux droits qui sont reconnus aux peuples autochtones par l'article 25 de la *Charte* et l'article 35 de la *Loi constitutionnelle de 1982*.

Les griefs des autochtones à l'égard de l'accord se situent donc sur le plan de la symbolique constitutionnelle, et ils sont bien plus graves encore que ceux des minorités culturelles. En effet, de tous les groupes opposés à l'accord, les autochtones constituent le seul qui revendique, lui aussi, d'être reconnu comme une «société distincte», parce qu'il est le seul, avec le Québec, à avoir des ambitions «nationales» ou, du moins, certaines revendications en matière d'autonomie gouvernementale. La reconnaissance des autochtones comme «société distincte» favoriserait ces revendications sur un plan politique.

En outre, contrairement aux «tiers groupes» culturels, les peuples autochtones peuvent invoquer une légitimité historique non seulement égale, mais grandement supérieure à celle des deux «peuples fondateurs». En fait, ils se considèrent à juste titre comme les vrais peuples fondateurs du Canada. Pourtant, leur existence n'a pas été reconnue comme une «caractéristique fondamentale» dans l'accord constitutionnel, ni ailleurs dans la Constitution.

5. *Les groupes de femmes*

Les griefs des groupes de femmes, en ce qui concerne la portée *symbolique* de l'accord constitutionnel, ne sont évidemment pas les mêmes que ceux des peuples autochtones et des minorités culturelles. En effet, dans la mesure où les femmes ne constituent pas une collectivité culturelle ou ethnique, elles n'entrent pas, en tant que groupe, en concurrence avec les minorités de langue officielle, ou avec la collectivité majoritaire du Québec; aussi ne réclament-elles pas que l'accord constitutionnel reconnaisse leur «caractère distinct», ou consacre leur existence comme une «caractéristique fondamentale du Canada».

Les craintes véritables des groupes de femmes à l'égard de l'accord concernent l'impact que les dispositions relatives à la dualité et au caractère distinct du Québec sont susceptibles d'avoir sur leurs droits *juridiques*, principalement le droit à l'égalité. À cet égard, la principale inquiétude des groupes de femmes concerne la possibilité de combiner l'article 1er de la *Charte* avec les dispositions relatives à la dualité et au caractère distinct du Québec pour tenter de justifier d'éventuelles atteintes à l'égalité sexuelle.

La question fondamentale qui se pose alors est de savoir s'il existe véritablement des possibilités de conflit entre l'égalité sexuelle, d'une part, la dualité et le caractère distinct du Québec, d'autre part. Beaucoup de ceux qui se sont penchés sur la question pensent qu'une telle éventualité est radicalement exclue, dans la mesure où le sexe n'a rien à voir avec la langue et la culture auxquelles réfèrent les dispositions relatives à la dualité et au caractère distinct. C'est d'ailleurs en adoptant ce point de vue que les associations féministes québécoises se sont désolidarisées des critiques soulevées contre l'Accord du lac Meech par les groupes de femmes du Canada anglais.

On peut cependant souligner que le partage des rôles sociaux entre les deux sexes et le statut de la femme font partie des structures fondamentales qui organisent les diverses cultures et les distinguent les unes des autres. Or dans la plupart des cultures existantes — voire dans toutes — il existe un partage des rôles sociaux qui désavantage les femmes ou qui, du moins, ne correspond pas à l'idéal contemporain d'égalité des sexes. Dès lors, il n'est pas complètement absurde de prétendre que la conservation d'une culture traditionnelle pourrait être considérée comme exigeant, dans certains cas, le maintien des rôles sexuels existants et, par là, celui d'une certaine inégalité des femmes. Si le caractère distinct de la société québécoise, ou l'existence de la dualité, était considéré comme relié à un certain statut traditionnel des femmes, celui-ci pourrait donc être éventuellement légitimé à partir des dispositions de l'accord constitutionnel.

À mon avis, une pareille inquiétude repose sur des assises fort ténues. Il serait cependant erroné et injuste de la rejeter comme dénuée de tout fondement. En effet, elle s'appuie sur une certaine expérience historique acquise par les femmes canadiennes à l'occasion du débat sur l'article 12(1)*b* de la *Loi sur les Indiens*, dans l'affaire *Lavell c. P. G. Canada* (1974)[10]. Dans cette affaire la Cour suprême a précisément semblé admettre que la protection d'une culture minoritaire menacée, celle des autochtones en l'occurrence, peut justifier le maintien de certaines inégalités sexuelles. Si l'on analyse de cette façon le jugement *Lavell*, il est tentant de faire le rapprochement avec les situations où il s'agirait de défendre le caractère distinct du Québec ou la dualité linguistique.

Il existe donc une possibilité très réduite que les dispositions de l'Accord du lac Meech relatives à la dualité et au caractère distinct du Québec puissent entraîner des effets négatifs sur les droits de certaines femmes. Cela justifie-t-il que l'on reprenne les négociations pour modifier l'accord afin d'exclure de son application les dispositions de la *Charte* qui ont pour objet de garantir l'égalité sexuelle? Étant donné les difficultés qu'il faudrait surmonter pour arriver à un nouveau compromis, la réouverture de l'accord constitutionnel semble devoir être évitée. Par ailleurs, une fois l'accord entré en vigueur, le fédéral et les provinces pourraient assez facilement s'entendre sur un amendement à la *Charte* disposant que l'accord n'a pas pour effet de porter atteinte à l'égalité sexuelle garantie par celle-ci. Il suffirait, pour adopter une telle modification constitutionnelle, de l'accord de sept provinces et des deux chambres fédérales.

Conclusion

Pour conclure, je tenterai de dégager quelques éléments de réflexion axés sur le thème du congrès: Canada: traditions et révolutions.

Traditionnellement, la politique constitutionnelle au Canada s'est articulée autour de trois grands axes: la souveraineté du Parlement, le fédéralisme et la dualité canadienne. En 1867, en s'abstenant d'adopter un *Bill of Rights* comme celui qui existait aux États-Unis, les Pères de la Confédération ont choisi d'appliquer au Canada le principe britannique de la souveraineté du Parlement, c'est-à-dire de laisser le dernier mot concernant les choix politiques et sociaux aux élus du peuple, plutôt qu'aux tribunaux. Ils ont en outre opté pour le système fédéral plutôt que pour l'État unitaire, en grande partie d'ailleurs pour satisfaire les demandes des francophones du Québec. Jusqu'en 1949, le Comité judiciaire du Conseil privé a interprété les dispositions relatives au partage des compétences de façon à favoriser les provinces, ce qui a entraîné une nette augmentation des pouvoirs de celles-ci et fait du fédéralisme canadien un des plus décentralisés du monde. Enfin, la Constitution de 1867 reconnaît implicitement la dualité canadienne, dans la mesure où elle garantit certains droits collectifs aux minorités francophones et anglophone pour faciliter la coexistence des deux «peuples fondateurs» du pays.

L'adoption, en 1982, de la *Charte canadienne des droits et libertés* constitue une véritable révolution par rapport à cette tradition constitutionnelle, dans la mesure où les troix axes décrits ci-dessus sont abandonnés ou, du moins, modifiés. En effet, les tribunaux se voient reconnaître le pouvoir de vérifier la constitutionnalité des lois sur la base de la *Charte*. Les droits et libertés garantis par celle-ci n'étant pas définis de façon précise, les juges y infusent inévitablement leurs propres conceptions politiques et philosophiques et substituent donc leurs choix de société à ceux du Parlement. On passe ainsi de la souveraineté des élus du peuple au «gouvernement des juges». Par ailleurs, l'application de la *Charte* par le biais d'une hiérarchie judiciaire extrêmement centralisée, qui utilise une approche «nationale» uniforme pour appliquer les standards constitutionnels, met en branle une dynamique d'uniformisation du droit provincial qui risque, à long terme, de vider l'autonomie des provinces d'une partie de sa signification concrète. Enfin, la *Charte* donne nettement le primat aux droits individuels, ce qui risque d'affaiblir les droits collectifs traditionnellement reconnus aux communautés linguistiques; elle consacre également le principe du multiculturalisme, qui entre en concurrence avec celui de la dualité.

Dans ce contexte, l'Accord du lac Meech renoue avec la tradition constitutionnelle d'avant 1982; on pourrait dire qu'il constitue une sorte de «contre-révolution» par rapport à la *Loi constitutionnelle de 1982*. En effet, l'accord atténue le caractère centralisateur et uniformisateur de la *Charte* puisqu'il permet aux tribunaux d'abandonner, si nécessaire, l'interprétation uniforme de celle-ci pour l'appliquer de façon à tenir compte de la situation particulière de chaque province en matière linguistique et, surtout, de manière à respecter le caractère distinct du Québec. On a souligné à juste titre que le principe du fédéralisme justifie déjà, à lui seul, une certaine «régionalisation» dans l'application de la *Charte*, dans la mesure où le fédéralisme légitime l'existence d'une certaine diversité dans les droits provinciaux et, même, dans l'application du droit fédéral aux diverses parties du pays. Par conséquent, les dispositions de l'Accord du lac Meech relatives à la dualité et au caractère distinct du Québec confirment et renforcent en quelque sorte l'impact «diversificateur» du principe fédéral sur la *Charte*. L'accord réaffirme également l'importance de certaines valeurs collectives par rapport aux droits individuels. Enfin, il consacre une certaine hiérarchie des symboles constitutionnels, en établissant la primauté de la dualité linguistique du Canada et du caractère distinct du Québec sur le multiculturalisme.

Par ailleurs, l'Accord du lac Meech ne diminue nullement l'influence des tribunaux; au contraire, en ajoutant au texte de la Constitution d'autres concepts flous et de nouvelles règles d'interprétation, il augmente encore leur pouvoir, déjà formidable, de participer aux choix politiques qui définiront à l'avenir la nature de la société canadienne et québécoise.

Notes

1. La *Charte canadienne des droits et libertés* est la Partie I (articles 1 à 34) de la *Loi constitutionnelle de 1982*, Annexe B de la *Loi de 1982 sur le Canada* (R.-U.), 1982, c. 11.

2. *Loi constitutionnelle de 1867*, 30 & 31 Vict., R.-U., c. 3.

3. S.R.C. 1970, app. II. Le contenu de l'article 23 de la *Loi de 1870 sur le Manitoba* est semblable à celui de l'article 133 de la *Loi constitutionnelle de 1867*.

4. Sur cette question, voir: J. Woehrling, «La modification constitutionnelle de 1987, la reconnaissance du Québec comme société distincte et la dualité linguistique du Canada», *Cahiers de Droit* 1:29 (1988), 25-7; J. Woehrling, «La reconnaissance du Québec comme société distincte et la dualité linguistique du Canada: conséquences juridiques et constitutionnelles», dans *The Meech Lake Accord — L'Accord du Lac Meech*, numéro spécial de *Canadian Public Policy/Analyse de Politiques* 43 (septembre 1988), 50.

5. *Ford c. P. G. Québec*, [1988] 2 R.C.S. 712, pp. 777-9.

6. *R. c. Oakes*, [1986] 1 R.C.S. 103, p. 139.

7. *MacDonald c. Ville de Montréal*, [1986] 1 R.C.S. 460; *Bilodeau c. P.G Manitoba*, [1986] 1 R.C.S. 449. Dans ces deux affaires, la Cour a justifié sa solution par les termes exprès des articles 133 de la *Loi constitutionnelle de 1867* et 23 de la *Loi de 1870 sur le Manitoba*, lesquels, il est vrai, semblent conférer le libre choix entre l'anglais et le français, non seulement aux particuliers qui plaident devant les tribunaux, mais également au personnel judiciaire et aux fonctionnaires des tribunaux. Nous préférons cependant, quant à nous, nous rallier à l'opinion dissidente du juge Wilson dans l'affaire *MacDonald* (p. 504 s.), selon laquelle le droit conféré à un justiciable d'utiliser sa propre langue au cours des procédures judiciaires impose une obligation correspondante à l'État de respecter ce droit et d'y donner suite. Pour remplir cette obligation, l'État doit traiter avec un justiciable dans la langue que celui-ci comprend.

   Dans l'affaire *P.G. Québec c. Blaikie*, [1979] 2 R.C.S. 1016, p. 1030, la Cour suprême a laissé entendre que les termes de l'article 133 habilitent les juges visés par cette disposition à rendre des jugements unilingues. Ainsi, un citoyen québécois pourrait constitutionnellement voir sa cause décidée par un tribunal du Québec en anglais seulement. La dissidence du juge Wilson dans *MacDonald* nous semble tout aussi pertinente dans ce cas.

8. *Société des Acadiens c. Association of Parents*, [1986] 1 R.C.S. 549. La Cour a cependant décidé que le droit à un procès équitable, qui est également garanti par la *Charte*, inclut le droit des parties, quelle que soit leur langue, de comprendre ce qui se passe dans le prétoire et d'y être comprises (par l'intermédiaire d'un interprète).

9. Sur l'article 27 de la *Charte*, voir: J. Woehrling, "Minority Cultural and Linguistic Rights and Equality Rights in the Canadian Charter of Rights and Freedoms", *McGill Law Journal* 31 (1985), 50; J. Woehrling, «La Constitution canadienne et la protection des minorités ethniques», *Cahiers de Droit* 27 (1986), 171.

10. *P. G. Canada c. Lavell; Isaac c. Bédard*, [1974] R.C.S. 1349.

Jean McNulty

The Internationalization of Broadcasting and its Implications for Canadian Policy[1]

Abstract

This paper looks at the current trend towards internationalization of broadcasting and argues that the changes are less dramatic than at first sight, particularly in their effects on Canadian broadcasting policy for domestic services. The author argues that internationalization in the forms of transborder transmissions or programming sales are not new phenomena for Canada, although they have reached a new stage in Western Europe. The paper also argues that the national constraints on Canadian policy making for broadcasting have not been changed by events in Western Europe, although there could be new opportunities there for sales by Canadian television programming producers.

Résumé

Cet article porte sur les tendances contemporaines vers l'internationalisation de la radio-télédiffusion et soutient que les changements qui ont eu lieu sont moins importants que l'on pensait à première vue, et ce particulièrement dans le domaine des effets de l'internationalisation sur la politique canadienne de radio-télédiffusion concernant les services domestiques. L'auteure soutient que l'internationalisation des formes de transmissions trans-frontalières ou des ventes de programmations ne sont pas de nouveaux phénomènes au Canada même s'ils ont atteint un nouveau stade en Europe. Finalement, cet article soutient que les contraintes nationales sur le processus de décision politique en matière de communications au Canada ne sont pas affectées par les événements en Europe de l'Ouest, bien qu'il se pourrait que de nouvelles perspectives pour la vente de productions télévisuelles canadiennes aient été créées.

Jean McNulty

Introduction

The theme of the 1989 International Conference in Canadian Studies is "Canada: Traditions and Revolutions," and I believe this fits very well with the perennial condition of broadcasting policy in Canada. The broadcasting industry, as in any modern communications sector, is continually in a state of technological revolution, and the framework of policy making seeks to accommodate these changes within the context of Canadian cultural traditions.

A good indication of the resistance to change can be seen in the progress of new broadcasting legislation. Since around 1978, the Parliament of Canada has considered a number of broadcasting or communications bills that would have changed in various ways the broadcasting policy framework for Canada put in place in 1968. Despite the urgency for change, as presented by successive federal Minsters of Communications, none of these bills has been passed into law. The reasons for seeking legislative change have been largely focused on the rapid technological changes and on the need to respond to the perceived internationalization of broadcasting (see, e.g., DOC 1983; Canada 1986).

Revolutions in communications technologies change not only the techniques of electronic transmission and storage of information; obviously, they also have major effects on the balance of economic, political, and social power in society and on how a society creates its own cultural life. Thus, it is not surprising if the successive revolutions are looked upon with some awe, as well as dread, by those likely to be affected by them.

One of the ways in which the current technological revolution is being described is as the "internationalization" of broadcasting. This label appears to cover two separate, not necessarily related, trends in the provision for broadcasting services. First of all, it means the increased opportunities for broadcasting signals to be received across national boundaries, primarily due to the use of satellite systems to distribute broadcasting signals over very large areas. (Although satellite systems distribute radio as well as television signals, the greater attention from entrepreneurs and policy-makers has gone to television.)

The second trend towards internationalization is the increased tendency for television programming packages to be coproduced, bought and sold between national markets. The reasons for the increased binational or multinational transactions are varied, some are related to the rapidly rising costs of popular entertainment productions and to increased market fragmentation and competition for audiences due to satellite distribution, mainly in the United States and Western Europe. From these activities, there is the gradual evolution of an increasingly large transnational market in programming for television broadcasting.

Essentially, the trends towards increased internationalization of broadcasting are focused almost entirely on television, not radio. This paper, therefore, will confine most of its discussion to television broadcasting. To summarize what the paper is concerned with, the argument is that the internationalization of television broadcasting services:

a) is not a new phenomenon in terms of transborder transmissions or in programming sales, but has been present from the beginning of domestic broadcasting systems[2] in almost all countries;

b) has not reached a dramatically new or different stage for Canada in recent years, although it may have for other developed countries, especially in Western Europe;

c) does not change the national constraints under which Canadian broadcasting policy must be developed.

The following discussion seeks to provide an elaboration of this argument.

Transborder Broadcasting and the Nation-State

It is a truism that broadcasting signals do not stop at political boundaries; therefore, it can be said that transnational broadcasting has occurred from the start of radio transmission. Yet, the management of broadcasting is based entirely on the sovereign power of nation-states. Through international agreement, achieved through the International Telecommunications Union (ITU), the use of radio frequencies has been managed more or less in harmony throughout the world. Within one country, however, the national government retains total authority to decide who will use the assigned frequencies and for what purpose.

It has been customary for writers to discuss domestic broadcasting on a nation-state basis, as though the broadcasting services involved were only receivable in that one country and no foreign signals could be received at all. While that may have been technically true in a country such as Australia or New Zealand, it is rarely the case in other counties. However, there have been many effective barriers to broadcasting signal reception across national borders other than simple distance or inhospitable geography—barriers that are politically, economically and culturally motivated.

For example, some countries have selected technical distribution standards that are incompatible with those of neighbouring countries, thus seeking to ensure that the national audience is tied to domestic reception. Other countries have engaged in electronic interference (i.e., "jamming") with foreign transmissions. Neither of these solutions was politically viable for Canada—and some have argued that the Canadian state deliberately ensured that the American broadcasting signals would be easily receivable in Canada (e.g., Smythe 1981).

Some of the barriers to transborder reception have not been created by government decisions but are due to audience preferences. One of the major barriers of this type is language. Another less obvious barrier is a difference, perceived by the audience, in the cultural values presented through broadcasting. (Of course, this cultural difference can work against a national broadcaster when its usual audience finds programming on a foreign service more to its liking.) Beyond reasons of language and culture, audiences may prefer to receive broadcasting from their own country because the content relates more to their daily lives. This is especially the case in informational programming and news.

In Canada, barriers to transborder reception from the United States have been due either to physical distance, in the case of Northerners (although this has been overcome by satellites) or to language, in the case of French Canadians, primarily in Quebec. Thus, it is not surprising that the English-Canadian research literature inevitably spends much time and effort in trying to describe and analyze the direct and indirect influences of the American broadcasting system on Canadian broadcasters and audiences (e.g., Wier 1965; Peers 1969, 1979).

Broadcasting policy has changed considerably in most developed countries within the past few years.[3] In one country after another, public broadcasting has been under strong pressure to change or has been swept aside in the tide of "privatization" or commercialization of television services. The customary justification of the need for public ownership of broadcasting systems loses further ground when it becomes apparent that the supposed scarcity of broadcasting transmission frequencies need no longer exist through the development of cable television and satellite systems. If there is no scarcity of channels to carry broadcasting services, then, the argument goes, the private market will be able to meet all consumer demands for services and can specialize in the provision of particular kinds of programming to those who are willing to pay for it. The alternative argument, that not all audience interests in programming can be met by consumer markets, is being swept aside or forgotten.

The Canadian Experience

From the Canadian point of view, internationalization of broadcasting distribution is not new, nor is the transnational trade in broadcasting programming content. In terms of signal distribution, Canada has been in the position of being able—and willing—to receive foreign broadcasting signals from the beginning. Anyone at all conversant with the history of broadcasting in Canada will know that radio stations in the United States were able to have significant influence on the creation of the Canadian audience in the 1920s, before the Canadian broadcasting system had really got started in the early 1930s.

This was even more the case in television, which the Canadian government hesitated about introducing because of the high expense. To a considerable degree, the timing of its introduction in the early 1950s was pushed forward by the fact that American broadcasters were busy installing border TV stations that easily reached many Canadian cities with programming and advertising. When cable television technology was developed, also in the 1950s, Canadian viewers welcomed it mainly because it would allow for the clear reception of numerous American TV signals. The rapid growth of Canadian cable systems attests to the popularity of this idea. At present, around 70% of all Canadian households subscribe to cable; the subscription levels are about 80% in the cities. Canada is the second most cabled country in the world, after Belgium, although the population density in Canada is much lower.

In the case of the most recent major revolution in distribution, satellite communications systems have been used in Canada since 1972 and in the United States since 1975. Because of overlaps between Canadian and American satellite footprints, the satellite-fed services in each country have been receivable in the other, although the transnational reception has been almost entirely one-way, from the US to Canada. At present, Canadian households are not reached by the broadcasting signals of any other country.[4] This makes Canada's situation very different from that of Western European countries where satellite footprints have recently enabled broadcasters to reach many countries simultaneously.

As far as television programming markets are concerned, Canada has always been in the habit of buying foreign programs in considerable quantities—though the sale of Canadian products abroad has been much more difficult to achieve. Actually, "internationalization" may be too grand a term for what is essentially a process of economic domination of the television programming market worldwide by a handful of the larger film and video production companies, primarily in the United States, Britain, France and Japan (and, to a lesser extent, West Germany, Brazil and Hong Kong).

No one seriously imagines that sales of television programming by producers in emerging African nations such as Tanzania, in smaller Western nations such as Norway or Canada, or even in Eastern European countries such as Poland, are making any significant economic impact on the transnational domination of the worldwide sales of film and video products by countries such as the United States and Britain in the English-speaking nations or by France in "la francophonie." Some observers of the Canadian policy field suggest it is about time that the requirements of international marketing for Canadian cultural products received more attention than they customarily have been receiving in Canadian policy making (Acheson and Maule 1988).

So, what is new about the present situation of Canadian broadcasting? From the Canadian perspective, the principal new factor in the ongoing pressures for transnational markets is the use of satellite technology in Europe to distribute national and transnational television services within Western Europe. Perhaps for the first time since the 1930s, Canadians are paying serious attention to broadcasting developments outside North America. The launch of "Sky Television" by Rupert Murdoch, and the numerous commercial television and radio services in the offing from BSB and others, look as though they will seriously challenge, for the first time, the national sovereignty systems in Western Europe.

The Recent Experience in Western Europe

The dramatic changes in Western European television may not ultimately have as extreme an effect within any one country as they appear capable of at present. The balance of power between broadcasters, politicians, and the bureaucracy may remain essentially the same, despite apparently drastic changes to the broadcasting system (see e.g., Kuhn 1985). Nevertheless, there has been a significant shift of political opinion against the monopolies previously held by public broadcasters. Greater opportunity is being given to private broadcasters as the means to provide more choices to television audiences—presumably at little expense to the taxpayers.

A major element in the trend towards private-sector provision of broadcasting services in Europe has been the recent introduction of satellite-fed television services across much of the continent. The start of "Sky Television" has been a shock to the traditional terrestrial broadcasters, one that they feel must be responded to, either by imitating the type of content carried—primarily American entertainment and sports—or by launching similar types of services themselves.

The economic effects of introducing these new services can be predicted from Canadian experience: an increase in the fragmentation of the audience between available channels, an increase in the importance of advertising as a source of revenue to pay for the television programming, and an increase in the cost of acquired programming because of bidding wars between the broadcasters. All of these factors will affect both public and private broadcasters. Again, if Canadian experience is any guide, the political effects of these changes will be a continual erosion in the cultural and social importance of public broadcasters and increasing difficulty in raising the necessary funds for their programming services.

It is not yet clear whether the satellite TV services can find sufficient advertising revenues in order to survive in the longer term. In particular, the mirage of a trans-European audience, and of a single huge advertising market able to reach 320 million people at once, may remain a mirage. The linguistic and cultural differences have not disappeared and are not likely to in the next decade. It is more probable that several regional advertising markets will evolve within Western Europe (Heads 1988).

A second question that is also important is how these transnational services will affect the production and sale of video and film productions between European nationals and from those outside Europe. The imminent arrival of the 1992 deadline, when most of the trade barriers within the European Common Market are to come down, could lead one to imagine that there will be more frequent coproductions between broadcasters and independent production companies based in different countries of the European community. If this is so, the effects on coproduction activity with other countries such as Canada may be detrimental.

During 1989, Canadian producers were greatly concerned that they could be excluded from any participation in coproductions with Europeans because of new European quotas in broadcasting content. Significant efforts were made to impress upon European governments, particularly the French government, the importance of Canadian coproduction treaties. By the end of 1989, it appeared that the coproduction work would be able to continue and would probably qualify as European content, by some means or other. Whether the same quantity of Canada-Europe coproductions will continue remains unclear.

On the other hand, coproductions between American and European corporations are likely to increase. As new TV services distributed by satellite and cable in the US have developed, their demand for television programming has increased apace. It has become commoner for US cable networks such as the Arts and Entertainment (A&E) channel to look for coproductions rather than acquisitions as a means to improve their appeal to viewers. For obvious reasons, British broadcasters and independent producers are of primary interest to the Americans; for example, A&E has developed strong links with BBC Enterprises (Friedman 1989, 23).

Not all the attention is going from the US towards Britain; some of it goes the other way. As the future of the ITV private broadcasters in Britain becomes more uncertain, they are looking to the American market as the means to develop other activities and, thus, to become less dependent on their franchise revenue. One sign of this is the recent purchase of MTM Enterprises by TVS Entertainment, the owner of an ITV broadcasting franchise. Other US production companies may be bought by Europeans in the near future (Pearce 1988).

Both France and Quebec are concerned that proliferating European television services are overwhelmingly English-language. One response has been the creation of TV5, a cable/satellite service containing primarily French, Swiss, Belgium and Québécois TV programming: one evening each week is devoted to showing programs from Quebec. The service began satellite distribution across Canada in September 1988 (although not many cable systems outside Quebec are carrying it). Unfortunately, audiences for TV5 in Canada and Western Europe are very small. Also, access to air-time on TV5 still does not necessarily give Quebec producers any better sales to television networks in France, the key francophone market.

In summary, Canadians are interested in these developments for at least three reasons: (1) to see how European systems, which have emphasized public service broadcasting much more than has Canada in recent years, are changed to meet the economic challenges raised by satellite broadcasting; (2) to explore the new commercial opportunities that may arise for

Canadian film and video products within a new trans-European television marketplace; (3) to consider investing in the distribution technologies—such as cable TV systems and small satellite dishes—that will be used to sell new television services to European consumers. However, in my view, none of the three interests mentioned above appears likely to affect significantly how Canadian broadcasting policy making is now carried out. This is because the policy framework is constrained by a number of factors, most of which are not primarily economic in nature but rather are political, social, and cultural.

National Constraints on Canadian Broadcasting Policy

Although the constraints under which Canadian policy-makers work are well known, they are worth summarizing here. First and foremost, sparse settlement over much of a vast territory combined with about 60% of the total population gathered into a handful of cities, with different immigration settlement patterns and different regional economies, means that national policies that suit all regions equally are virtually impossible to devise. Second, in the political evolution of the nation, there has been the firm entrenchment of the need to accommodate the two major linguistic groups in providing broadcasting services across the country. Third, the contemporary idea of the "cultural mosaic" has raised the service expectations among numerous ethnocultural groups; increasingly, these groups are vocal in demanding broadcasting programming relevant to their particular cultural and social needs.

The fourth constant concerns the federal government's responsibility for policies affecting the lives of the aboriginal peoples; this responsibility remains significant and there has been a strong acknowledgement that special provisions must be made to create and support broadcast programming by and for native peoples in their own languages, at least in Northern Canada. Fifth, there is the political tension between the two levels of government in a federal state; even though broadcasting has been declared judicially to be an exclusively federal matter for law making and regulation, the interests of provinces (especially Quebec) in social and cultural policy inhibit the federal government's total occupation of the regulatory field.

Sixth—and, some would say, most significantly—there is the constraint of the economic dominance of the United States' cultural production industries, especially in English Canada. This dominance is long-established and pervades a number of related industries: audio and video music recording, feature film and video production, book publishing, and magazine publishing. The dominance is not, of course, limited to cultural products but exists in many areas of the Canadian economy.

Concluding Comments

The above discussion has sought to outline some of the changes currently taking place in broadcasting internationally that are of interest to Canadian policy-makers. In my view, the dramatic shift towards internationalization of broadcasting, particularly television, is less dramatic on closer examination. In terms of distribution reach, transnational broadcasting is certainly not new and has been a pervasive factor in Canadian policy making from the beginning of regular broadcasts, first in radio and then in television.

One new element may be the permanent downgrading of public broadcasters in Europe within their national policy frameworks. However, it is by no means clear that private broadcasters are going to become as dominant as they are in the United States or as significant as they are in the provision of broadcasting services in Canada.

Currently, the most significant new element in the transnational broadcasting environment is the increasing coproduction activity between American and European (particularly British) television broadcasters and programming producers. This makes it all the more necessary for Canadian programming producers and broadcasting policy-makers to make a serious, concerted effort to ensure that Canadian television content has greater access to the video and film marketplaces outside North America, particularly in Western Europe.

From the perspective of Canadian policy, however, the national constraints on policy-makers will remain the same. These constraints will continue to determine what are the priorities for development of broadcasting services within Canada for Canadian audiences.

Notes

1. The opinions expressed in this paper are the personal view of the author and do not necessarily represent the policy positions held by the Ontario Ministry of Culture and Communications.

2. Domestic broadcasting systems refer to those radio or television systems intended to serve all or part of a national audience, although the signals transmitted may spill over into other countries. The other type of broadcasting, which is intended to reach a global or continental audience, is short-wave radio broadcasting; examples of these systems are Radio Canada International, the Voice of America, the BBC World Service and Radio Moscow.

3. Excluded from discussion throughout this paper are potential changes in the broadcasting systems of Eastern European countries, which were just beginning their transformation after the political upheavals of 1989.

4. Although Russian broadcasting satellite signals are technically receivable, their incompatibility to North American systems have made reception difficult.

Bibliography

Acheson, Keith and Christopher Maule (1988) "The Carrot and the Stick: A Review of Canadian Broadcasting Policy." *Cinema Canada* (September 1988), 17-19.

Canada (1970) Parliament of Canada. *Broadcasting Act.* Revised Statutes of Canada, 1970, chapter B-11.

Canada (1986) *Report.* Task Force on Broadcasting Policy (Caplan-Sauvageau, co-chairpersons). Ottawa: Minister of Supply and Services Canada.

DOC (1983) Department of Communications (Canada) *Towards a New National Broadcasting Policy.* Ottawa: Minister of Supply and Services Canada.

Friedman, Wayne (1989) "Going Behind the Camera in Multi-national Co-ventures." *Cablevision* (February 13, 1989), 23-30.

Heads, Barrie *et al.* (1988) "1992: New Rules of the Game in Europe." *Television Business International* (October), 52-60.

Kuhn, R. (1985) "France: The End of the Government Monopoly." *The Politics of Broadcasting.* Edited by R. Kuhn. London: Croom Helm.

Pearce, Kevin *et al.* (1988) "Target: Hollywood." *Television Business International* (September), 6-8.

Peers, Frank W. (1969) *The Politics of Canadian Broadcasting 1920-1951.* Toronto: University of Toronto Press.

Peers, Frank W. (1979) *The Public Eye: Television and the Politics of Canadian Broadcasting, 1952-1968.* Toronto: University of Toronto Press.

Smythe, Dallas (1981) *Dependency Road: Communications, Capitalism, Consciousness and Canada.* Norwood, N.J.: Ablex Publishing Corporation.

Weir, E. Austin (1965) *The Struggle for National Broadcasting in Canada.* Toronto: McClelland and Stewart.

Roy Turner

Modernity and Cultural Identity: Is There an Alternative to the "Loose Confederation of Shopping Malls"?*

Abstract

It is argued that Trudeau's dictum—"The stakes are whether Canada will be a strong united nation or a loose confederation of shopping malls"—is best interpreted as a manifestation of that modernity which Grant feared as the source of "homogenization." Cultural identity is examined as a phenomenon which requires collective imagination; this is related to the fact that modernity finds imagination in the political realm suspect as no more than "rhetoric." It is suggested that contemporary conceptions of cultural identity have much in common with the notion of lifestyle, which itself is an avoidance of the strong purpose and commitment that a "united nation" needs.

Résumé

L'auteur soutient que les propos de P.E. Trudeau affirmant que l'enjeu majeur au Canada se situait entre une vision d'un pays fort et unifié et une vision d'une vague fédération de centres d'achats, sont interprétés comme une manifestation de cette modernité que George Grant considérait comme la source de l'homogénisation progressive des sociétés. L'identité culturelle est examinée en tant que phénomène qui requiert une imagination collective; ceci est relié au fait que du point de vue de la modernité, l'imagination en politique est vue comme étant quelque chose de suspect et qui donne lieu à pure rhétorique. L'auteur suggère que les conceptions modernes de l'identité culturelle ont plus en commun avec la notion de «style de vie», qui elle aussi tend à éviter l'engagement requis de ses citoyens par une «nation forte et unie».

"Nearly all Canadians," George Grant tells us, "think that modernity is good." This is bad news for Canada, according to Grant, since "modern civilization makes all local cultural anachronistic," and hence modernity manifests itself as "homogenization."[1] Thus Canadians are preoccupied with the distinctiveness of their cultural identity just when that identity is jeopardized by something that most Canadians think is good. Yet Pierre

Trudeau seems to take a more open view of Canada's situation, arguing that "The stakes are whether Canada will be a strong united nation or a loose confederation of shopping malls." While it is true that the "loose confederation of shopping malls" speaks of modernity and homogenization, Trudeau nevertheless seems to offer the possibility that Canada can choose, that there is an alternative.[2] That alternative is "a strong united nation": strong, despite the vulnerability which seems to belong to a child of Europe and neighbour to the United States; and united, despite an internal condition perhaps closer to Siamese twins than two solitudes.

There is a tension here in need of exploration: while Trudeau seems to offer Canadians a choice between sharply posed alternatives, the very suggestion that there *is* a choice might itself be considered a manifestation of the modernity which, for Grant, constitutes the threat to Canada. If this is true, then there is a curious resemblance between the idea that grounds Trudeau's dictum—the idea that we are free to choose a future and a form of communal life—and the lesser of the alternatives that it names, i.e. the possible preference for those shopping malls—the very emblems of preference and choice—that represent a turning away from strength and unity. This suggests that Trudeau's words are not spoken from a secure place outside of the framework of modernity, but that they are committed to its belief in the optional character of communal futures: Trudeau is not so much positioning himself vis-à-vis the question of choice as making a recommendation which presupposes that that question has been answered.

Whether or not one shares Grant's lament, there remains his reminder of the need to reflect upon contemporary representations of cultural identity and its "problems." In effect, Grant treats the contemporary discourse on cultural identity as the play of representation or manifestations of some deeper phenomenon (modernity) yet to be disclosed; he shifts the focus of attention from adjudicating between competing accounts to asking what it is that they variously seek to represent. Grant will not call for a check-list of attributes which may or may not seem to describe the Canadian character, but will urge us to ask what cultural identity could signify from within the perspective of modernity. Grant tells us then, that to understand Canada it is first necessary to understand modernity, to ask what is the dream of modernity which gives rise to various contemporary versions of a culture's identity. Alternatively, Grant calls on us to turn away from the vocabulary in which cultural identity now appears in the community's reflections and self-descriptions and to seek a language adequate to the dreaming which motivates such representations.[3]

To do this, to conceive of cultural identity as a phenomenon whose intelligibility requires us to turn our attention to modernity, since it is modernity which supplies the grounds of the argument, will commit us to resisting the contemporary terms of the discourse on cultural identity. To resist is not, of course, to ignore. Much of what follows will pay close attention to just such discourse, in the interests of delineating the phenomenon it addresses.

Tradition and Change

Grant glances backward at what he thinks Canada has lost or is losing. Trudeau speaks to Canadians posed for a future yet to materialise, and hence perhaps open to influence. Together they remind us that, since every community is embedded in history, it needs to look both backward and forward in order to understand and shape its present; but they also bring to our attention the empirical possibility that the community may be ambivalent or anxious about undertaking such self-reflection. In modernist discourse, "tradition" as a topic invokes the urge to severely limit the influence of the past, or else to describe its continued presence as a threat —a threat to progress, to freedom, to democracy. "Revolution," on the other hand, makes reference to modernity's belief in the future as a *tabula rasa,* the place where the injustices of the past will be wiped out and its failures rectified, according to the will of the present.

Modernity thus prefers to throw in its lot with the future, since this is where the good will appear, and seeks to disassociate itself from its own history which, if it cannot be forgotten, serves only as a constant reminder of the possibility of injustice and failure. In effect modernity treats any other kind of interest or valuation of the past—such as the presently disputed notion of the canon—as metaphysical: the past is dead, and has no reality (as modernity understands reality). What modernity is supremely confident of, however, is the reality of both the future and its own technological powers to inscribe that future.

Yet this orientation to temporality is also a source of anxiety, insofar as the pastness of the past raises the possibility that we may have lost what we once possessed, and the empirical absence of the future postpones the satisfaction of what has not yet come into being. How this anxiety is reflected in a concern with cultural identity is well expressed by Craig Boydell et al.:

> The concern over Canadian identity is chronic rather than new. Current concern is expressed primarily in terms of the danger of Canada losing or not maintaining her identity, her sense of being

an entity that is separate, special, and independent of other national entities. Another view, not quite so widely held, is that Canada has been having difficulty in actually developing an identity of her own.[4]

What I have tried to argue so far is that the current widespread ambivalence and concern over Canada's cultural identity is not so much a simple reflection of Canada's external conditions and circumstances as it is a way of reading those conditions through the lens of modernity. One can begin to trace a healthier view of the place of history and its influence on the present, and hence the possibility of a quite different version of cultural identity, through Gadamer, who writes:

> Even the most genuine and solid tradition does not persist by nature because of the inertia of what once existed. It needs to be affirmed, embraced, cultivated. It is, essentially, preservation, such as is active in all historical change . . . preservation is as much a freely-chosen action as revolution and renewal.[5]

Gadamer here denies the view of the survival of tradition widespread in contemporary political and social thought which often pictures history as dead, and thus can only explain the persistence of tradition as indeed a kind of inertia. Gadamer shows us that what this image reveals is not tradition, but modernity. Thus Gadamer does not deny the current hostility to tradition, but offers a better grip on its meaning by showing that such notions as inertia are not simply descriptive but are the product of the specific work of modernity aimed at a purification of the present. The contemporary negative attitude toward tradition is not then the necessary expression of tradition's natural status as a ghostly object, but is rather the expression of modernity's investment in a certain (peculiar) understanding of the future, i.e. of the future as the place of freedom.

Gadamer thus makes it possible to distinguish between a community which embraces and affirms its traditions and a community which tries to ignore or discard them (this itself, like repression, is a form of preservation). The relevance of this distinction is clear: a community shows what it is through the way it cultivates (or fails to cultivate) its history and its traditions. Thus, cultural identity is not the mere emanation of conditions, not a simple empirical outcome of history or circumstances, but in part the product of the kind of work a community is willing to do in reflecting on its own status as a temporal phenomenon. We might call the work that is called for, "imagination."[6] Since imagination befriends difference rather than sameness, it would appear to have something to offer to a community that understands identity as distinctiveness from neighbours (to mention a Canadian preoccupation). Yet, paradoxically, modernity is reluctant to give imagination a prominent place in public life, fearing that it will subvert social equality, which modernity understands (and fosters) as sameness.

Thus the threat of homogenization then arises not from simple contiguity, the influence of neighbours, but from modernity's distaste for the exercise of imagination. Hence one must look for the roots of this homogenization in scepticism concerning imagination, allied with a belief in sameness as the proper standard for a democratic society. The paradox of modernity, in short, is that it nurtures sameness while it yearns for difference. Its difficulty is that it cannot imagine a source of difference that is not at the same time a source of ideological distortion or elitism.

Modernity's Reluctance to be Imaginative

Lawren Harris once wrote that "An Art must grow and flower in the land before the country will be a real home for its people."[7] A generous interpretation of Harris will hear this as making a vital distinction between mere geography—"the country"—and something that can be made of a country through acts of imagination, namely, "a real home." A "real" home, this tells us, is not a simple, natural phenomenon but an artful and imaginative creation; more than a place for survival and maintenance, it is a place where an identity is cultivated; thus it is also the place that represents the local and particular that modernity threatens, according to Grant. A community that is a real home, that is, takes pride in its particularities not just as outcroppings of circumstances but as the result of its cultivating and affirming the accidental. It is in this sense that we speak of "making a home" out of what might initially be no more than a chance assemblage of possessions and possibilities: to make a home *is* to affirm and develop what one has, however one comes to have it.[8]

Harris provides something that is missing in Boydell's doleful words, to the effect that Canada inhabits a hiatus: uncertain of what it has lost, equally uncertain of what it can hope for. Above all, in Boydell's view, since the past is irretrievable, the best Canada can do is to wait, to see what will emerge as contingencies come and go and the future materialises as the present. What Harris makes clear—echoing Gadamer—is that a genuine and strong cultural identity is not something that merely reflects its immediate circumstances, as though by analogy with the laws of physics, but requires art and imagination, i.e., cultivation and affirmation. If one hears Trudeau's remark as ironic, one might hear him as saying that if Canadians follow their mundane sense of their social world—that is, if they are unimaginative—they will find themselves in a country whose self-realization is to be found only in what its shopping malls stand for. A strong nation, on the contrary, can only arise from the work of affirmation and cultivation, and this will only be undertaken by a community that affirms such work as *itself* valuable and desirable.

What is common to Gadamer and Harris, and lacking in Boydell, is the imaginative ability to envisage something worthwhile, something other than what sheerly occurs or is provided by conditions. To say this is again to expose modernity's unwillingness to trust art and imagination, its readiness to collect them as "rhetoric," with implications of tyranny and deceit.[9] What is wrong with art and imagination, according to modernity, is that they depart from the empirical and the descriptive as the standard, and hence run the risk of arbitrariness. In that they are not grounded in and governed by the facts of the everyday world, visible to all, they show themselves to be irresponsible because not consensual.

Harris and Gadamer, on the contrary, argue the position that strength is at home precisely where risks are taken so that something "flowers" and is worth the positive action of preservation. They thus deny that if circumstances are poor, or unhelpful, no cultural identity—at least no worthwhile cultural identity—can or will appear. What Harris reminds us is that cultural identity, like art, just is the kind of thing that is produced *in the face of* circumstances. Thus, to succeed in creating either art or character is not the same as to be fortunate, to have favourable conditions. To succeed in these instances is to be able to orient to a standard of excellence, whatever the circumstances in which the work is undertaken: it is to make visible the distinction between the materials and the knowledge of how to make something of those materials, something that does not merely express their "natural" attributes. This surely is what Hannah Arendt addresses when she says that through speech and action "men distinguish themselves instead of being merely distinct."[10] I take it that she means by this that such phenomena as art and identity are not to be understood by the way they are descriptively available; cultural identity is not, for example, a kind of residue of history in the way that rocks and fossils are a residue of geological time. For Arendt, art and identity are ways whereby human beings show their concern for and their knowledge of what is good and worth achieving. Art and identity are scarcely accidental possessions, things which render us merely distinct. Arendt plays on the double sense of "distinguish," which allows us to speak not only of what is discernably different but also of what is accomplished as valuable. This needs to be developed.

Life and Lifestyle

What makes Trudeau's *bon mot* memorable is that it seems to hit a certain mark in the centre. But what is that mark? A facile answer would invoke the idea of a consumer society, one more attached to shopping malls than to the more austere and less tangible goods of public life. Yet public life and politics themselves possess many of the hallmarks of consumer society, and hence there is no genuine opposition here. Nevertheless, there is an invocation of the distinction between public and private life, and the tension between them—of which the strong nation and the loose confederation are emblematic—merits discussion.

A first observation is that the idea of the shopping mall itself seems to spring from a particular understanding of the public world. Initially it might seem that nothing speaks more directly to the private self, to the individual composed of interests and dreaming of their fulfilment, than the shopping mall, the supplier of props and costumes necessary for playing out lifestyles. Shopping is after all a transaction between the self and the identity it longs for. On a practical level the shopping mall is eminently public—it is a public place interactionally speaking, to be distinguished from the strong sense of public developed by Hannah Arendt (which I shall return to shortly). As a public place, the shopping mall offers neither sociability nor dialogue but gregariousness, the coming together of many engaged in their private searches for the materials of an identity, a feature well described by John Brinckerhoff Jackson: "it offers a spatial experience shared by a heterogeneous public which will sooner or later go its separate ways."[11] Jackson distinguishes this from the public square as a truly "political landscape," where "It is assumed that those who come there are *already* aware that they are all members of the community, responsible citizens, and that on occasion they will participate in public discussions and take action on behalf of the community."[12] Jackson is following a long tradition from Aristotle, who should be heard as speaking metaphorically rather than literally when he says of the agora, the public space, that "Nothing here . . . may be bought or sold."

What one learns from Jackson is that the public space neither creates nor defines the strong nation. This is not to deny the importance of contemporary concerns with the design and use of "effective" public spaces, but to remind ourselves that the very conception of such spaces manifests a community's sense of what constitutes public life. The fear is, after all, that the shopping mall perfectly expresses a powerful conception of what contemporary life ought to look like: the congregation of individuals in search of the consummation of private interests. Jackson claims that a strong nation is capable of creating its public space anywhere, since "public," for the strong community, refers less—if at all—to assembling and co-presence than to the conceptual space which Arendt draws to our attention as the locus where the political community has its life.

For Arendt, the public world is the space "between," the space where people appear to one another. But to appear does not signify to show up in our lifestyle trappings and to enact the part they proclaim our attachment to. "Betweenness" is only possible and meaningful because the public realm "gathers us together," simultaneously separating and relating us, and thus making the life of politics both possible and necessary. Hence to appear in this realm is to be present at the scene of action, according to Arendt, the place where greatness can show itself. Here the self is required to adopt an attitude that makes conversation rather than gesture possible. This self is not attached to the semiotic display of lifestyle but to the dialogic possibilities of the world: its security is not in what it initially portrays but in its confidence that the conversation is worthwhile.[13]

This invocation of alternative understandings of public and private raises the question of the individual's relation to community. One can imagine two sharply distinct possibilities. The first is that the individual derives strength and identity from the community, so that for him or her the community is something in which to take pride and turn to as a resource. The second possibility is a community which is no more than the collection of lives and identities which its members happen to possess and display, hence a community with an uneasy relation to the idea of cultural identity. The uneasiness stems from the fact that such a community can only be seen for what it is, i.e., a community which is unable to take pride in or identify with any particular way of life lived by its diverse members, which it understands as lifestyles, because it regards them as primitives, as atoms and origins beyond question. Like the shopping mall, such a community's chief concern is with what it thinks of as freedom or choice—multiple choice, in fact, where every selection is equally available and acceptable.

As it relates to the ambivalences and anxieties of cultural identity then, modernity can be understood as a denial of the possibility that the individual may find strength in membership, since this would betray an attachment to history and tradition and would acknowledge that the individual needs to respect something other than his or her own inclinations. Following the second possibility, modernity in effect conceives of the community as though it were itself a shopping mall; in other words, it tells the individual that the community is a repertoire of opportunities, a gallery of options, a cornucopia of futures and identities.[14] The contemporary way of expressing this sense of what it means to live within a society is in fact precisely conveyed by the idea of *lifestyle*; it can be argued that it is this commitment which threatens any community that comes to maturity under modernity.

But what is it about the idea of lifestyle that crystallises the uneasy relation between the shape of individual lives and the identity which distinguishes the community? Lifestyle is best understood in opposition to an alternative that perhaps has no better name than a purposeful life. Precisely what is lacking from lifestyle is any serious idea of purpose, and this is true because one who is committed to living out a purposeful life will necessarily learn that the life that results from the collaboration of purpose with circumstances[15] cannot insist on its shape, its scenes, its props, its effects—in a word, its *appearance*. To have a purpose is just to be ready to act on behalf of some conception of the good life and to act in ways that take circumstances into account as the medium for the realization of that good. This, of course, is the kind of thing one would expect of a strong and unified nation—namely that it will neither know, nor dwell upon, what it will look like as it moves into a future (i.e. moves into the orbit of fresh contingencies and changing circumstance), but it will know that whatever materializes as the scene of action it will act steadfastly to achieve outcomes in accordance with the standard by which it lives.

It is clear then that a strong and united nation cannot be selected as a lifestyle, because it lacks exactly what is essential to the idea of lifestyle: a ready image or set of images of what the lived future will look like *to other* (and hence to self)—the popular word "scenario" does justice to this— since knowing this, knowing the semiotic value of appearances, knowing what one will consume and be seen and understood to consume, is at the heart of the idea of lifestyle. There is, of course, a version of identity here. One will *be* what one appears to be, and hence the things one *can* be—the range of identities available—will depend upon the current semiotic vocabulary.[16] The lifestylist cannot risk the dialectic of a committed life, because there is no telling ahead of time what will eventuate and hence of how he or she will appear.

Conclusion

So far I have not raised the question of how cultural identity becomes problematic, of what makes it a significant phenomenon in the first place. Cultural identity can be reflected upon in two modes, which correspond to the distinction I have tried to make between a purposeful life and a lifestyle.

One way, certainly, of raising the question of identity has to do with a concern for the community's place in the community of communities—what being Canadian means to others, the reputation of being Canadian as opposed say to American or European. It is this version of cultural identity that can be likened to the idea of lifestyle, in that it seems to propose that we learn who and what we are by way of contrast with others with different identities (a kind of Saussurean conception of identity). What we are is consumed by others, so to speak, and we desire to be the thing that they are understood to consume. Just as the lifestylist needs to see himself or herself as choosing from an array (for it is only the array and the choice that make the substance of the life intelligible and consumable within the lifestyle perspective), so the one who approaches cultural identity in this frame of mind is required, figuratively speaking, to go abroad to find out an identity when at home.

But the alternative mood for reflecting upon cultural identity addresses the way one can think of a cultural identity as a resource rather than an emblem. A strong cultural identity would then nurture the self, enter into the formation of the citizen and foster pride and loyalty. Pride and loyalty, it seems, are things about which we are ambivalent with the mode of self-understanding promulgated by modernity. They smack of the particular, of the limited, and thus—it is said—of ideology. In its thrust for universality, as promised by the Enlightenment, modernity is suspicious of that it thinks of as the sheerly negative position it terms "conservative," which in this context must signify something like being contented with one's origins. Within modernity, contentment is suspect, since it speaks of failure to appreciate the gap between what we are and what technology (in Grant's sense) promises we can become.

This is the dilemma for cultural identity. A modern community that yearns for cultural identity either has in mind nothing more than the collective equivalent of a lifestyle, or else it is caught in the trap that modernity does not seem to possess. What Trudeau brings to our attention in speaking of the alternatives—a strong and united nation or a loose confederation of shopping malls—is that, prior to any notion that there is a choice, it is necessary to reflect upon those aspects of modernity which underpin our very conceptions of choice. I have suggested that to undertake this reflection is to discover that the prospect of a strong and united nation depends upon our ability to resist modernity. But, as I said earlier, to resist fact is not to ignore it. Canada will have to work out its cultural fate in a world where modernity rules. Strength comes from working out the life that this entails—not in itself something that can be scripted or tried on like a garment—rather than from the assumption that a desired identity must first

be designed, then implemented. Resisting modernity is all together different from the nihilism that would say the good and the worthwhile is no
longer possible, as though our circumstances are such that they could be
met with no distinguished response. To think this would be precisely to
forget that the task of collective, as well as individual, life is to work with
what is given, and to work with it to some purpose.

Notes

*   I began to think about the matters discussed here in response to a reading of Alan Blum
     and Peter McHugh's article, "The risk of theorizing and the good of place: a reformula-
     tion of Canadian nationalism," *Canadian Journal of Sociology* 3:3 (1978), 321-47; though
     I reach other conclusions, my discussion is deeply influenced by Blum and McHugh.

1.   George Grant, *Lament for a Nation* (Toronto: McClelland and Stewart 1965), 54.
2.   What Trudeau actually said was "shopping centres," but I have taken the liberty of
     substituting the term that is now current.
3.   I have borrowed the language of the dream in connection with discourse from Stanley
     Rosen, *The Limits of Analysis* (New Haven, Conn.: Yale University Press 1980), 120-1.
4.   Craig Boydell *et al* (eds.), *Critical Issues in Canadian Society* (Toronto: Holt, Rinehart
     1971), p. 357.
5.   H.G. Gadamer, *Truth and Method* (New York: Crossroad 1986), 250.
6.   In thinking about the sociological import of imagination, I have learned much from
     Stephen Karatheodoris and Stanley Raffel, "The Law, Conditions, and the Need for
     Imagination: The Case of the Apostle Paul," *Maieutics*, 2 (Winter 1981), 1-26.
7.   John Herd Thompson with Allen Seager, *Canada 1922-39* (Toronto: McClelland and
     Stewart 1985), 182. In this section I have been much influenced by Joan Allen's
     stimulating essay, "Imitation: Awe or Influence," *Maieutics*, 1:1 (Spring 1980).
8.   Cf. Michael Walzer, speaking of the moral world we inhabit: "No design procedure has
     governed its design, and the result no doubt is disorganized and uncertain. It is also very
     dense: the moral world has a lived-in quality, like a home occupied by a single family
     over many generations, with unplanned additions here and there, and all the available
     space filled with memory-laden objects and artefacts." Michael Walzer, *Interpretation
     and Social Criticism* (Cambridge, MA: Harvard University Press 1987), 19-20. See also
     Blum and McHugh, "The risk of theorizing," 339-40.
9.   For a thoughtful treatment of modernist conceptions of rhetoric, see Leslie Miller, "The
     Alienation of Influence: The Emergence of Liberalism as a Form of Discourse," Ph.D.
     dissertation, York University, 1984.
10. Hannah Arendt, *The Human Condition* (Chicago: University of Chicago Press 1958),
     176.
11. John Brinckerhoff Jackson, *Discovering the Vernacular Landscape* (New Haven, Conn.:
     Yale University Press 1984), 17.
12. Ibid.
13. Arendt, *The Human Condition*, 52
14. As Grant says, "when we represent technology to ourselves through its own common
     sense we think of ourselves as picking and choosing in a supermarket." George Grant,
     "Thinking About Technology," in Grant, *Technology and Justice* (Toronto: Anansi
     1986), 32.

15. An idea I borrowed from Karatheodoris and Raffel, "The Law, Conditions, and the Need for Imagination."
16. Cf. Jean Genet's play *The Balcony*.

Hans Hauge

George Grant's Critique of Modernity: Canadian Refractions of Continental Ideas

Abstract

Was George Grant's diagnosis of modernity adequate or was it simply wrong? This essay attempts to answer this question. Grant diagnosed modernity as the will to mastery. He arrived at his conclusion partly as a Canadian living north of the spearhead of modernity (the USA) and partly through his reading of Nietzsche and Heidegger. Grant's philosophy is, therefore, a Canadian refraction of certain European ideas. Today, however, both Nietzsche's and Heidegger's philosophies are being questioned by leading German philosophers. How will this questioning affect future assessments of Grant's work?

Résumé

Est-ce que le diagnostic de George Grant sur la modernité est adéquat ou est-il tout simplement erroné? Grant a analysé la modernité comme étant la volonté de maîtriser. Il est arrivé à cette conclusion en partie en tant que Canadien vivant juste au nord du fer de lance de la modernité (les États-Unis), et en partie à travers une lecture de Nietzsche et Heidegger. Il s'ensuit que la philosophie de Grant est un point de vue canadien issu d'idées européennes. Mais maintenant que les idées de Nietzsche et Heidegger sont remises en question par d'éminents philosophes allemands, il faut se demander comment l'oeuvre de Grant sera interprétée dans le futur.

I'm not quite sure that there is such a thing as a subject.

—Northrop Frye in an interview with John Ayre, *Acta Victoriana*, 94 (1970).

Die zeitgenossischen Dekonstruktivisten und Postmodernisten haben, in Neitzsches und Heideggers Nachfolge, die Ausbildung des Gedankens der Individualitat als den vorerst letzten und entscheidenen Ausdruck der Machtergreifung von Subjektivitat (ubers "Sein", uber die "Differenz", ubers "Nicht-identische" ober uber die "Alteritat") beschrieben.

(Contemporary deconstructionists and postmodernists have described—following Nietzsche and Heidegger—the formation of the idea of individuality as the most recent, last and final expression of subjectivity's seizure of power over "Being," "difference," the "non-identical," or "alterity.")

—Manfred Frank, "Subjekt, Person, Individuum," in Frank *et al.* (eds), *Die Frage nach dem Subjekt* (Frankfurt am Main: Suhrkamp 1988).

... the conception of time as history is not one in which I think life can be lived properly. It is not a conception we are fitted for. Therefore I turn away from Nietzsche and in so turning express my suspicion of the assumptions of the modern project.

—George Grant, *Time as History*.

I. Grant's Diagnosis of Modernity

George Grant's diagnosis of modernity derives partly from his experience as a Canadian living north of the spearhead of modernity, the United States, and partly from his reading of Nietzsche and Heidegger. His recent death has meant, apart from a loss to Canadian intellectual life, that a new assessment of his work can be made. The fundamental question is whether Grant's diagnosis of modernity was adequate or whether it was it was simply wrong? It was Grant's basic contention that man, although the creator of the modern project, is not equipped to live in modernity. According to Grant, we find ourselves in a situation where, having diagnosed the discontents of modernity and having experienced a sense of the deprivation modernity has produced, we are yet unable to find a cure. We are defenceless. As Grant put it in his essay, "A Platitude," in *Technology and Empire*:

the drive to the planetary technical future is in any case *inevitable*; but those who try to divert, to limit, or even simply stand in fear before some of its applications find themselves defenceless, because of *the disappearance of any speech* by which the continual changes involved in that drive could ever be thought of as deprivals (my emphasis).[1]

Grant here echoes what he also stated in *Lament for a Nation*:

> to many modern men, the assumptions of this age appear inevitable, as being the expression of the highest wisdom that the race has distilled. The assumptions appear so inevitable that to entertain the possibility of their falsity may seem to be the work of a madman.[2]

The disappearance of what Grant calls "any speech" and "the disappearance of Canada"[3] are intimately related. The speech or the language that would have made resistance to the American empire, or to the universal state, possible was the language of nationalism. Yet both the political language of nationalism and the existential language of deprival have disappeared. If the drive of modernity and the coming of the universal state are inevitable, and if we are forever deprived of any speech in which a critique of modernity could be formulated, we shouldn't wonder why Grant has been called a pessimist. It seems to me, however, that he means to say that modernity cannot be reflected upon or criticized from the outside.

Now, if Grant neither wants to divert, limit, nor stand in fear before modernity, and if he really means that he is defenceless and utterly deprived of an alternative language, what has he been doing all along in book after book? How does he *know* that we are not equipped to live in modernity, how does he *know* we have been deprived of something, and how does he *know* that we have lost the language of what belongs to man as man? He knows because, as he says in *Lament for a Nation*, "ancient philosophy gives alternative answers to modern man."[4] But he has realized that such answers cannot be given, and one of the reasons why they cannot is that they belong to what he calls "metaphysical assertions" rather than to the *genre* of political philosophy. Such assertions are about an eternal order and, while they could be made, they could never be heard nor believed. And this is the reason why he doesn't make them. Reference to an eternal order has become impossible because the concept of history or, to be more precise, historicism is at the heart of the modern project. This is what he means by the phrase "time as history." The phrase, however, also contains an unstated alternative. If one says that time is conceived of as history, the implication is that time could also be conceived of in another way. What that alternative description of time would be Grant does not say, and by now we realize why. It would again take us into metaphysical assertions.

We have now reached the following conclusion: modernization is inevitable. Resistance to it is impossible. Modernity undoes all differences. The undoing of the difference between the United States and Canada is merely one example. Modernity has demythologized what Robertson Davies once called the Canadian "Myth of Difference."[5] Grant seems to be in full agreement with Northrop Frye that neither Canada, nor any other country in the world, is being Americanized. Americanization is just another word for modernization, and we call it Americanization because the Americans are the first to be modernized, since America is the spearhead of modernity. Frye has also developed a thesis, similar to Grant's, on the disappearance of Canada by claiming that Canadians live in a post-Canadian world.

II. The Canadian Refraction

I began by claiming that Grant's diagnosis of the modern project derived partly from his experience as a Canadian and partly from his reading of certain European thinkers—Nietzsche and Heidegger.

Lament for a Nation relies neither on Nietzsche nor on Heidegger. Although it is true that it does depend rather heavily on Leo Strauss, it is nevertheless fair to say that *Lament for a Nation* derives its analysis of the modern age from Grant's experience as a Canadian nationalist. If this is true, we will have to ask whether the statement that Canada has disappeared is an empirical statement; in other words, did he *experience* this disappearance of Canada and can such a phenomenon be experienced at all?

In an article entitled "Religion and the Quest for a National Identity," John Webster Grant, the church historian, notes what he calls "the collapse of the nineteenth-century Christian programme for Canada." He continues by saying that this collapse is "so recent that even now we are too much under its shadow to be able to sift out what is significant in the contemporary reaction to it."[6] When George Grant lamented the disappearance of Canada, was he then not in fact thinking about the collapse of the so-called Christian program for Canada? If this foundation of a Canadian national identity has been lost, what can replace it, asks John Webster Grant. Although he cannot provide an answer, he is aware that national identities are never given; they have to be *created*.[7] This, however, is a modernist conclusion that George Grant would never draw. For if a national identity is merely created, it ceases to be true. With Nietzsche, George Grant places historical sense at the core of modernity. Historical sense teaches us "that all horizons are simply the creations of men" and shows that

> these horizons are not what they claimed to be; they are not true statements about actuality. They are man-made perspectives by which the charismatic impose their will to power. The historical sense teaches us that horizons are not discoveries about the nature of things; they express the values which our tortured instincts will to create.[8]

The same universally accepted historical sense will likewise teach us that nations are like horizons. Nationhood is incompatible with historical sense because that sense shows us the fictional character of nations. And as soon as one realizes that nationality is an invention why should one pay any allegiance to it?

III. The Magi of the North and the Disappearance of Canada

The formulation of this idea of the disappearance of Canada was made prior to Grant's reading of Nietzsche and Heidegger. After formulating the idea he began referring to himself as a North American or simply as a speaker of the English language. There are, of course, practical people who would deny that Canada has disappeared and would say instead that Canada has merely been transformed (Eli Mandel) or reconstructed (Robert Malcolm Campbell).[9] It is probably true that the majority of Canadians see no reason to lament the passing away and the collapse of the Christian program for Canada referred to by John Webster Grant.

Northrop Frye comments as follows on the disappearance of Canada:

> Nationalism suggests something aggressive, but culture in itself seeks only its own identity, not an enemy. . . . Politically, economically and technologically, the world is uniting; Canada is in the American orbit and will remain so for the foreseeable future. Canadians could not resist that even if they wanted to, and not many of them want to. *Culturally, both nations should run their own show. Things go wrong when cultural developments are hitched on to economic or technological ones* (my emphasis).[10]

Here we see a fundamental difference between Frye and Grant. Frye makes a sharp distinction between culture and nationalism. Frye's concept of culture is meant to replace nationalism. While John Webster Grant failed to see any alternative to the old national identity based upon the church's one foundation, Frye's concept of culture provides such an alternative. Robertson Davies seems in agreement with Frye; "people who look deeper into our national predicament desire more durable evidences of identity. *They seek it in the arts* . . . it is in poetry and fiction that the questers repose their greatest hopes (my emphasis)."[11] One could never imagine George Grant reposing his greatest hopes either in culture or in fiction, for one of his basic Heideggerian insights is that the phenomenon of technology is the coming together of art (*tekhné*) and science (*logos*). This is what is new about modernity and technology. Culture, therefore, cannot be separated from technology. For if what Peter L. Berger (like Grant) claims is true— that "the essential factor in the process of modernization, and *ipso facto* the core of modernity (which is the product of the modernization process) is technological,"[12] then technology must also be at the core of culture.

The idea that Canadian identity is to be found in its fiction is expressed in Margaret Atwood's *Survival*. Here Atwood relates, as an indirect criticism of Northrop Frye, how she was shocked to discover that her country's literature "was not just British literature imported or American literature with something missing. . . . Canadian writers have not been trying to write American or English literature and failing; they've been writing Canadian literature," and Canadian literature, she continues, is "not equivalent with 'Canadian content'."[13] The idea that only art can save us would instantly be recognized by Grant as Nietzsche's solution to modern nihilism. We should keep in mind that Frye, Davies and Atwood, disregarding the differences between them, have always kept their eyes on the bright side of modern life. Grant, on the contrary, saw it as his mission to bring the darkness into the light as darkness.

Culture, according to Frye, consists of words or the "total structure of human creation conveyed by words, with literature at its centre. . . . It is designed to draw a circumference around human society and reflect its concerns, not to look directly at the nature outside."[14] In order to look directly at the nature outside we have the mathematical language of science. What Frye in fact says is that words, that is to say language, make all kinds of literary realism impossible. Literature cannot be a window. Canadian literature cannot reflect Canadian nature, it can only protect or insulate us from it by creating a circumference around us. Here we have the theoretical underpinning of Frye's contention that Canadian writers live in a post-Canadian world. This means that "sensibility is no longer dependent on a specific environment or even on sense experience itself,"[15] as he writes in

The Bush Garden. Such pronouncements make it feasible to compare Frye
to McLuhan.

First, however, we will have to ask whether McLuhan criticizes or
celebrates modernity. It would certainly be tempting to characterize him as
an arch-modernist when we consider his fascination with and eulogies of
modern technology. In fact, he isn't a modernist and it is simply a question
of temperament whether we prefer to call him a premodernist or a
postmodernist. At least we can say that the difference between him and
Frye is that, for McLuhan, the modern is a finished project, whereas for
Frye it is an unfinished one. McLuhan was critical of the modern project
that he identified with the Gutenberg era or galaxy. Modernity began with
Gutenberg. With Gutenberg we received an eye (I) for an ear. Modernity
privileges the eye and the individual. With the new mass media, however,
we have entered a postmodern, post-contemporary, and post-Gutenberg
age, which can be seen as a return to the beginning, or at least to a
pre-Renaissance and pre-Reformation world. Frye, as we have seen, per-
ceives an absolute dichotomy between subject and object, or between
language and nature. This dichotomy cannot be overcome. The gap between the two cultures—the arts and the sciences—is unbridgeable. It is in
this sense that Frye is modern. According to McLuhan, this gulf between
mind and nature, or subject and object, was unbridgeable in modernity.
While the Romantic poets dreamed of identity or a reconciliation between
mind and nature, they could only realize the dream poetically. But what has
happened now—after modernity or after Gutenberg—is that the rift has
been healed *in fact* not in fiction. And this has happened because television
is the externalization of all our senses; in other words, of all of us. What we
see around us is one big Subject: we see ourselves, not something alien. To
McLuhan the whole world is somewhat like the centre of Montreal, where
you can spend your whole life without going outside. This underground city
can, of course, also be described according to Frye as something that
insulates, protects, and draws a circumference around us. But Frye is aware
that it is cold outside in the winter. To conclude this section, we could say
that for Frye, the subject-object dichotomy is absolute; while for McLuhan
it is sublated. The complete identity between subject and object has been
achieved by means of technology. In this way technology fulfils an old dream
without depriving us of something essential (as was the case for Grant).

Frye's idea that culture should not be bound to economic and technological
developments implies that culture always is in danger of being bound to
them. Culture is constantly threatened. We find an echo of this in W. John
Harker who notes that "our cultural identity is by no means well secured,
an awareness of Canada in the minds of students is by no means well

established."[16] In another context, Frye demonstrated his awareness of this danger, calling culture an "anxiety structure" (in *Creation and Recreation*) or an "envelope" designed to protect us from darkness and chaos.

IV. The Ancients and the Moderns

We have heard Grant claim that the only alternative for modern can be provided by ancient philosophy. In *Lament for a Nation* we saw how he was unable, not only to formulate that alternative, but also to partake in it. He just knew it existed. To entertain the possibility of the falsity of modern assumption seemed to him the work of a madman. After writing *Lament for a Nation* he began studying Nietzsche and Heidegger. It was their interpretations of modernity that helped Grant to transcend it. According to Grant, they "are the two thinkers who have most completely thought through the modern western project from within it."[17] It was this thinking through that Grant developed in *Time as History*. His reading of the two philosophers also made it possible for Grant to read Plato again: "seeing modern assumptions laid out before me at their most lucid and profound in Nietzsche and Heidegger has allowed me (indeed only slightly) to be able to partake in the alternative assumptions of Plato."[18] The reason why it is almost impossible to share such premodern assumptions has to do with the nature of modernity.

Modernity, thinks Grant, did not develop out of the premodern or the ancient period. Modern thinkers like Hobbes or Descartes became modern by denying what their predecessors had said and believed. Ancient rationality did not develop into modern rationality. The rupture between the ancients and the moderns is absolute. Nothing was, so to speak, carried over into the modern period. At this point Grant seems to be much closer to Frye than to his two German mentors. For Heidegger, there is no such fundamental break between the modern and the pre-modern. Modern Western metaphysics began with Plato and Aristotle, and technology is nothing less than metaphysics realized or in practice. Where Grant wishes to partake in Platonic metaphysics, and hence in Christian metaphysics, Heidegger wants to destruct (*Destruktion*) metaphysics, just as Derrida desires to deconstruct the same entity. While Grant believed that modernity destroyed metaphysics, Heidegger diagnosed modernity as metaphysical.

I suggested above that Grant's understanding of modernity is in a sense closer to Frye's than to Heidegger's. The mythological year of 1968 saw the publication of Frye's *A Study in English Romanticism*. A year later, Grant gave the Massey Lectures, later published as *Time as History*. I am in no position to know if Grant had read Frye's book, but I do not find it unlikely that he was familiar with it. Although Frye did not write about sociological concept of modernity, he did write about the literary concept of Romanticism, and the words mean the same thing. This, then, is one of Frye's descriptions of modernity—or Romanticism:

> Romanticism . . . is the first major phase in an imaginative revolution which has carried on until our own day, and has by no means completed itself yet (it may look from my account as though it would be complete when everything formerly ascribed to God has been transferred to man or nature, but that would in my opinion be far too simple a solution).[19]

Frye argues, first, that Romanticism, or modernity, is an unfinished project and then indirectly defines it as the transfer of all God's attributes to man. God's creativity is transferred to man, enabling us to say: *we* make history. Romanticism is also, says Frye, the re-covery of projection, that is, of man as a projective being. Once the power of projection, and another name for this power is the imagination, has been recovered, the metaphysical concept of an eternal order as well as the metaphysical concept of God is demythologized. In a 1970 interview, Frye answered John Ayre's question "What does 'God' mean to-day in our modern world?" as follows:

> the only thing that God can possibly mean is what he really does mean in Christianity, that is to say a suffering. . . . I think it is the conception of God as the power that recreates man rather than God as the Creator of the order of nature that is the really valid element in Christianity.[20]

Grant too realized, that modernity was the rediscovery of projection and it is precisely for this reason that it has become impossible to speak of an eternal order; it would at once be called an ideal constructed out of the sky. If we are is basically projective and creative beings, if this is our true essence, then all premodern assumptions become illusory. If we make history, we have always been the makers of history. As Grant knew, since the metaphysical assumptions of ancient philosophers are also projections, we cannot share in them. *Not* to see with modern eyes would mean to see in such a way that we do not think of ourselves as creative or projective. But modern man is a lamp, not a mirror. A lamp projects its light into darkness and can receive light neither from the outside nor from Athens and Jerusalem.

V. Does Canada Make A Difference

I began by saying that the most important question about Grant's work is whether his diagnosis of modernity is right or wrong. The difficulty involved in answering this question rests on how we can decide upon such an issue. How can a diagnosis claim to be true? Can it be falsified? If Nietzsche and Heidegger are wrong, is Grant wrong too? Let us first consider if Grant has added something new to their interpretations of modernity. Has he radicalized or recuperated their understandings? I think he has done both. However, he has not gone as far as they have in their attempts to destroy Western metaphysics. As we have seen, their analyses had the opposite effect, they helped Grant transcend modernity and partake in Platonic metaphysics. He also differs from them insofar as he does not himself propose alternatives. Heidegger's philosophy is meant as an alternative to what is technically called subject-philosophy or the philosophy of consciousness. In this way Grant is less "constructive" than Heidegger.

The next question to ask is whether the fact that Grant is a Canadian has made any difference. Is his reading of the two philosophers a "Canadian" reading, however problematic that adjective seems to be? If there is a Canadian literature, as Atwood has said there is, is there also a Canadian philosophy? Frye, in contrast to Atwood, has argued that a new country does not produce a new literature. If a new country doesn't produce a new literature neither does it produce a new philosophy—only new content—if we follow Frye's train of thought.

In his book *Technology and the Canadian Mind: Innis/McLuhan/Grant*, Arthur Kroker has argued that the Canadian contribution to North American thought consists of "a highly original, comprehensive, and eloquent discourse on technology."[21] What has made this contribution possible is the situational context of the Canadian mind: "the Canadian mind is that of the *in-between*: a restless oscillation between the pragmatic will to live at all costs of the Americans and a searing lament for that which has been suppressed by the modern, technical order."[22] Kroker seems to think that there *is* something new and unique in Canadian philosophy, as Atwood believed to be the case in Canadian literature.

Leslie Armour and Elizabeth Trott, in their *The Faces of Reason*, convincingly demonstrate that at least there once *was* a distinctive Canadian philosophy, a philosophy which was an amalgam of British, German, and American idealism. They describe Canadian philosophy as philosophical *federalism*. According to Leslie and Trott, while philosophy does not mirror the national mind, "philosophies are very often responses to what one thinks the world needs rather than reflections of the way in which it is."[23] This is a very important remark. If we apply it to Grant's work, we can say that he doesn't so much tell us the way it is as respond to what he thinks Canadians need to be told. We may therefore conclude that while Grant has imitated certain continental philosophers, he has also added a new content. This new content, or different emphasis, can be accounted for by his in-between position (as Kroker stated). And finally, he responds to what he thinks Canadians need to be told. They need, or the world needs, to be told the unvarnished truth about modernity as the will to mastery. We need to be told that technology is not a neutral instrument we can either use for good or for bad. We need to be told that art cannot be a haven in a heartless technological world. Grant's philosophy is not a survival kit. It is a summons to face up to the facts of modern life and uncover its truth. But the question still remains. Is Grant telling us the truth about modernity?

VI. A Diagnosis of Grant's Diagnosis of Modernity

Grant's *Time as History* is dedicated to his son, William, "who taught me to read Nietzsche." In one of the conversations in Larry Schmidt's book, *Grant in Process*, Grant tells the interviewer:

> I started reading Nietzsche because one of my children was greatly influenced by him, and I wanted to know why. Till recently it has been almost impossible for English-speaking people to take Nietzsche seriously. He seemed to be a poet who was somehow related to the ghastliness of the Nazis. In fact he is the great understander of the modern.[24]

In his *English-speaking Justice*—the text of his Josiah Wood Lectures at Mount Allison University in 1979—he comments on Nietzsche:

> Nietzsche was not taken by the English as the great critic of Rousseau's politics, but as an obscurantist pseudo-poet. They did not need to look at his lucid analysis of what we were being told about human and non-human beings in the advancing technological society. Both for good and ill, the English thinkers were sheltered from the extremities of European political thought because of their successes under bourgeois constitutional liberalism.[25]

What was happening, and what has happened—and Grant's reading of Nietzsche is a symptom of it—is that Nietzsche and Heidegger have become immensely popular in North America, as they have been in France since the War. Their analyses of modernity and their critiques of rationality and subjectivity have been accepted by the academic community. Structuralism, post-structuralism, deconstruction, and American pragmaticism are names for this general acceptance of Nietzschean and Heideggerian modes of thought. Suddenly we find Grant in the same interpretive community as Derrida, Foucault, Lacan, Hillis Miller and Richard Rorty. One should pay close attention to *where* Nietzsche and Heidegger came to be regarded as the great understanders of the modern; in the United States and France, but not Germany or Britain. Grant, it now appears, is part of a fashionable trend. Probably despite his intentions, he has moved from the periphery to the centre.

Nietzsche and Heidegger are much more popular in France and North America than in Germany, where their philosophies have been questioned. The current Heidegger "controversy" or scandal, in the wake of the publication of Victor Farias's *Heidegger et le nazisme* is just one example.[26] A recent German publication, entitled *Die Heidegger Kontroverse* (1988), is dedicated to a certain Georges-Arthur Goldschmidt who, it is said, never tired of drawing attention to the *scandal* of Heidegger's influence in France ("der nie mude wurde, den Skandal von Heideggers Einfluß in Frankreich anzuprangern"). Will Grant's importation of Heidegger to Canada once be so described? Will it affect our assessment of Grant if Heidegger's entire philosophy is inseparable from Nazism?

Certain major and influential German philosophers have convincingly shown that Nietzsche's and Heidegger's diagnoses of modernity are quite simply wrong. One of these German philosophers is Dieter Henrich. For the last fifteen years he has, in several books, tried to show how and why Heidegger's diagnosis of modernity is wrong. I cannot go into detail here about Henrich's alternative description of modernity. All I can say is that it has something to do with a re-reading of the German Idealist tradition in philosophy in general, and with Fichte in particular. The discussion is extremely complex and technical. I shall attempt to formulate it as simply as I can. If we return to Frye's description of Romanticism, or modernity, he said something like this: modernity is the transfer of all God's attributes to man. In other words, the human subject becomes almighty as was God. The death of God is the birth of the subject. Hence, modern philosophy is a philosophy of subjectivity. The subject turns everything into an object at the subject's disposal; this corresponds to Grant's claims. Will to power is another word for what the subject is. If this is what the subject is like, one understands why several twentieth-century philosophers, from Nietzsche to Heidegger and the structuralists, including George Grant, have tried to create an alternative to subject-philosophy. Subjectivity leads to mastery over human and non-human nature.

Dieter Henrich and Manfred Frank, however, claim that the subject is not like this at all. Grant himself has, in fact, hinted at something similar and hence at another way of talking about the subject and modernity. In *English-speaking Justice* (in a discussion of Hobbes and Locke), he says that, according to them, "we must preserve ourselves."[27] In relation to his idea that English thinkers were sheltered from the extremities of European political thought "because of their successes under bourgeois constitutional liberalism," he adds that "this was for *good* because the pursuit of *comfortable self-preservation*, though not the highest end, is certainly more *decent* and *moderate* than the extremities of communism and national socialism. there are worse things than a nation of shopkeepers (my emphasis)."[28] In Dieter Henrich's article, "Die Grundstruktur de modernen Philosophie" ("The Basic Structure of Modern Philosophy"), we find his alternative diagnosis of modernity—a diagnosis that also takes its point of departure from Hobbes's concept of self-preservation.[29] The modern subject is not almighty like God; it tries to preserve itself, and if it were as powerful, as one has believed, why should it try to preserve itself? "What must preserve itself, must know that it doesn't at all times and it doesn't simply have its ground in itself."[30] The self depends; it isn't in-dependent. The dynamism of modernity is not due to the will to mastery of the almighty subject, as Grant believed. It resides in the fact that the subject does not know from where it comes, and hence its dynamism is only an expression of its wish to preserve its being. It is not my intention to develop Henrich's theses. I have mentioned them for one reason only: if our diagnosis of modernity is wrong, and according to Henrich it is if we follow Heidegger, then this explains why we cannot defend ourselves and seem so unable to cure what went wrong in modernity. Perhaps the English thinkers sheltered from the extremities of Continental political thought were right in seeing that the subject is not the will to power but only something that tries to preserve itself because it doesn't know what it is and doesn't know where it comes from. Or as Henrich states, the human being does not know "wer er ist und woher er kommt."[31] The subject is not the will to mastery; it is only the will to survival. Survival, therefore, is not a specific Canadian stance, it is the modern one.

Hans Hauge

Notes

1. George Grant, *Technology and Empire: Perspectives on North America* (Toronto: House of Anansi 1969), 139.
2. George Grant, *Lament for a Nation: The Defeat of Canadian Nationalism* (Toronto: Carleton Library 1970), 55.
3. Ibid., 96.
4. Ibid.
5. Robertson Davies, "Dark Hamlet With the Features of Horatio: Canada's Myths and Realities," in *Voices of Canada/Voix du Canada*, edited by Judith Webster. (Association for Canadian Studies in the United States 1977), 43.
6. John Webster Grant, "Religion and the Quest for a National Identity," in *Religion and Culture in Canada/Religion et Culture au Canada*, edited by Peter Slater. (CCSR 1977), 18.
7. For a discussion of John Webster Grant's thesis on Canadian literature, see my article "The Novel Religion of Margaret Laurence," in Kristjana Gunnars (ed.), *Crossing the River: Essays in Honor of Margaret Laurence* (Winnipeg: Turnstone Press 1988), 121-33.
8. George Grant, *Time as History*, The CBC Massey Lectures (Toronto: Canadian Broadcasting Corporation 1969), 29.
9. For comments on the disappearance of Canada thesis, see Eli Mandel, "History and Literature: Contemporary Canadian Writing," in *Zeitschrift der Gesselschaft fur Kanada-Studien*, 1 (1983), 9-19. Mandel identifies regionalism with nationalism. Robert Malcolm Campbell argues in his editorial, "Starting Over: The Reconstruction of Canada" in *The Journal of Canadian Studies/Revue d'études canadiennes*, 22:3 (1987), 3-4, that Canada has rejected the Keynesian political strategy of welfare and only retained its economic aspects—liberalization of trade; hence Canada is being reconstructed.
10. Northrop Frye, "Canadian Culture Today," in *Voices of Canada*, 3.
11. Robertson Davies, ibid., 45.
12. Peter L. Berger, *The Heretical Imperative* (New York: Anchor Press 1979), 4.
13. Margaret Atwood, *Survival: A Thematic Guide to Canadian Literature* (Toronto: Anansi 1972), p. 237
14. Northrop Frye, *Creation and Recreation* (Toronto: University of Toronto Press 1980), 7.
15. Northrop Frye, *The Bush Garden* (Toronto: Anansi 1971), 249.
16. W. John Harker, "Canadian Literature in Canadian Schools," *Canadian Journal of Education*, 12:3 (1987), 425.
17. Larry Schmidt (ed.), *George Grant in Process: Essays and Conversations* (Toronto: Anansi 1978), 66.
18. Ibid., 67.
19. Northrop Frye, *A Study of English Romanticism* (New York: Random House 1968), 15.
20. "Into the Wilderness: An Interview on Religion," *Acta Victoriana*, 94 (February 1970), 39.
21. Arthur Kroker, *Technology and the Canadian Mind: Innis/McLuhan/Grant* (Montreal: New World Perspective 1984), 7.
22. Ibid.
23. Ibid., 14.
24. George Grant in Process, 66.
25. George Grant, *English-speaking Justice* (Toronto: Anansi 1985), 50-1.
26. For a detailed account, see Jurg Altwegg (ed.), *Die Heidegger Kontroverse* (Frankfurt am Main: Athenaum 1988).
27. George Grant, *English-speaking Justice*, 18.
28. Ibid., 51.

29. Dieter Henrich, "Die Grundstruktur der modernen Philosophie," in *Selbstverhaltnisse* (Stuttgart: Reclam 1982), 84.
30. Ibid., 97. "Was sich erhalten muß namlich wissen, daß er nicht jederzeit und vor allem nicht schlechthin seinen Grund in sich selber har."
31. Dieter Henrich, *Konzepte* (Frankfurt am Main: Suhrkamp 1987), 135.

Diane Lamoureux

Le mouvement des femmes: entre l'intégration et l'autonomie

Résumé

En abordant le féminisme contemporain à travers le prisme de l'oscillation entre le moderne et le postmoderne, cette communication vise à rendre compte de ce qui pourrait, à première vue, constituer une ambiguïté du féminisme contemporain, à savoir sa double valorisation de l'égalité et de l'autonomie. L'analyse aborde, dans un premier temps, l'importance qui a été accordée à la conquête de l'égalité juridique et le cheminement à travers les institutions qui a accompagné ce processus. Dans un second temps, l'accent est mis sur les pratiques autonomistes du mouvement des femmes. Enfin, la présence simultanée de traits relevant du moderne et du postmoderne est mise en lumière à travers une évaluation critique des rapports du féminisme au politique.

Abstract

This paper, which traces contemporary feminism through its vacillations between modernism and postmodernism, examines what could, at first glance, seem to be its essential ambiguity—the valorization of both equality and automony. The article reviews the importance of the fight for legal equality and its institutional application, and discusses the autonomous practices of the feminist movement. It concludes with an examination of modern and postmodern characteristics within the movement, via a critical evaluation of the relationship between feminism and politics.

Lorsqu'on examine l'état actuel du mouvement des femmes au Québec, au moins deux phénomènes apparaissent marquants. D'une part, le nombre de groupes de femmes est extrêmement important allant, selon certaines informations, jusqu'à atteindre le nombre impressionnant de 1 500 associations féminines. D'autre part, il y a un décalage relatif entre les capacités mobilisatrices de ces groupes et leur audience au sein de l'appareil d'État. Tout cela pour dire que nous assistons à une certaine vitalité à la base en

125

même temps qu'à une capacité de pénétration dans les structures décisionnelles de l'appareil étatique.

Ce phénomène a amené certaines observatrices à en conclure à une double dynamique du mouvement des femmes[1]. Malgré la séduction que peut exercer une pareille représentation, elle recèle quelques pièges analytiques dans la mesure où elle postule une capacité du mouvement des femmes à gérer consciemment une stratégie qui se déploie simultanément sur plusieurs plans. Cette position me semble difficile à tenir puisqu'elle implique une cohérence que le mouvement des femmes est loin de posséder et un rapport maîtrisé tant à la mobilisation qu'aux institutions, rapport qui me semble contredit par ses pratiques et certains de ses débats. J'aurais plutôt tendance à parler d'une tension entre intégration et autonomie en me servant heuristiquement de l'interprétation dont j'ai fait mention. En même temps, il me semble important de préciser que si le mouvement n'a pas trouvé de moyens techniques d'assumer consciemment cette double stratégie, puisqu'il ne possède aucune instance de mise en commun de ses expériences, la politique de respect mutuel et, dans certains cas, de collaboration entre les autonomistes et les intégrationnistes nous montre que ce genre de préoccupation ne lui est pas étranger.

Il importe d'abord de préciser les deux termes d'intégration et d'autonomie. Par intégration j'entends toutes les formes d'action à l'intérieur des institutions ou des réseaux déjà formalisés. On peut donc parler d'intégration lorsqu'on fait référence à des pratiques de participation politique directe, que ce soit sur le plan électoral ou sur celui du lobby, à la présence dans l'organigramme étatique, que ce soit par le biais d'organismes consultatifs ou de réseaux à l'intérieur de la structure administrative (comme les répondantes à la condition féminine dans les divers ministères) ou encore à la participation à l'intérieur d'organismes déjà insérés dans la structure politique formelle tels les syndicats ou les partis politiques.

Quant à ma conception de l'autonomie, elle recoupe les diverses pratiques qui vont dans le sens de l'expérimentation sociale et qui enracinent le mouvement sur le terrain de la société civile, participant de ce que Melucci qualifie de post-politique[2], le qualificatif de post-politique référant ici à une stratégie de contournement de l'État au profit de l'ordre de l'«ici et maintenant» et d'une volonté de changer la vie plutôt que les institutions.

Je poserais donc comme hypothèse que certains secteurs du mouvement des femmes ont orienté leur action dans le sens de l'autonomie alors que d'autres ont privilégié l'intégration mais sans que ce choix n'ait été consciemment assumé par le mouvement, ce qui a permis des alternances dans le temps entre ces deux stratégies. En outre, j'aimerais souligner que c'est justement cette tension entre intégration et autonomie qui permet de comprendre les oscillations du féminisme contemporain entre le moderne et le postmoderne. Dans ce cadre, je soutiendrais l'hypothèse que nous devons distinguer deux composantes majeures dans le mouvement féministe contemporain, en reprenant la classification proposée par Drude Dahlerup[3] entre d'une part un mouvement pour les droits des femmes (women's right movement) qui participerait du moderne et un mouvement de libération des femmes (women's liberation movement) qui serait précurseur d'une politique postmoderne.

Les droits comme mode d'intégration des femmes à l'ordre politique

Depuis la Révolution française, nous avons assisté à une tentative d'exprimer les revendications des femmes sur le plan du droit et à une volonté de faire reconnaître par les institutions politiques existantes l'égalité entre les sexes et de parvenir à une codification législative qui n'opère aucune distinction entre les sexes. Mentionnons par exemple des textes classiques comme *La Déclaration des Droits de la Femme et de la Citoyenne* d'Olympe de Gouges, la *Défense des droits de la femme* de Mary Wollstonecraft, la Déclaration des sentiments adoptée lors de la conférence féministe de Seneca Falls en 1848, la revendication suffragiste qui s'est développée au tournant du siècle et, plus près de nous, le document *Pour les Québécoises: Égalité et indépendance*, produit par le Conseil du statut de la femme en 1978.

Dans une large mesure, la résurgence du féminisme contemporain s'est faite à l'enseigne du droit. Ce phénomène a été clairement mis en lumière par Juliet Mitchell, qui montrait à quel point c'est le sentiment d'être les laissées pour compte de la société égalitaire qui a nourri la récente vague féministe:

> Dans cette idéologie égalitaire, des pratiques ouvertement dis-criminatoires scandalisent. L'idéologie égalitariste ne sert pas à masquer l'écart entre l'illusion et la réalité, mais est justement le mode sous lequel la discrimination autant que son refus sont vécus. Le fait de croire à la possibilité et à la justesse d'une telle égalité a permis aux femmes de se sentir trompées, et a été la condition de base de leurs protestations initiales.[4]

D'autre part, c'est à partir du moment où un certain nombre de droits sont acquis qu'il semble possible de mesurer l'écart entre l'égalité formelle et l'inégalité réelle. Le choc était d'autant plus grand dans le Québec des années 60 que l'idéologie égalitaire faisait partie intégrante tant du discours modernisateur de la Révolution tranquille que de celui de la «société juste» de Pierre Elliott Trudeau. Aussi, dans leur étude sur le Front de libération des femmes et le Centre des femmes, Véronique O'Leary et Louise Toupin situent-elles les premières féministes québécoises comme appartenant à la première génération ayant fait les frais de cet écart entre mythe et réalité lorsqu'elles soutiennent que:

> ... le contraste entre la théorie, le droit, et la réalité devenait trop grand. Théoriquement, nous étions les égales des hommes, mais pratiquement, nous demeurions toujours inférieures. Celles qui avaient eu la chance d'accéder à ces droits (droit au travail, droit à l'éducation, droit à une sexualité «sécuritaire») ont vu que tout cela n'était qu'illusion, voire mystification.[5]

Il n'en reste pas moins que ce sont dans les lois que plusieurs féministes québécoises ont cherché à inscrire leurs revendications. Cette croyance dans la force de la loi et dans l'inscription législative des revendications féministes est clairement mise en lumière par Lise Payette, qui explique ses motivations comme ministre déléguée à la condition féminine de la façon suivante:

> Il y avait longtemps, en 1976, que j'avais constaté qu'en dehors de la crise profonde des mentalités, la solution à nombre de problèmes identifiés par les femmes quant à leur statut inférieur se trouvait dans les parlements. Égalité juridique, égalité des chances au travail comme dans l'éducation, contrôle de la santé et accès aux services qui favorisent l'autonomie des femmes comme les garderies et les congés de maternité, les solutions étaient souvent à Québec.[6]

Dans une large mesure, on peut parler de modernisation de la condition féminine par l'État, sous la pression des groupes féministes, à tel point qu'au début des années 80 certaines allaient même jusqu'à affirmer qu'il existait au Québec un féminisme d'État. Et c'est partiellement vrai: une partie du mouvement des femmes oriente de plus en plus clairement son action dans le sens d'un groupe de pression classique. Par ailleurs, l'État, à travers ses organismes, a partiellement intégré institutionnellement le féminisme.

On connaît bien sûr le Conseil du statut de la femme, qui constitue la forme la plus visible mais également la moins insidieuse des rapports entre l'État et le mouvement des femmes. Car le rôle du Conseil est clair et énoncé sans ambages: traduire en termes étatiques les revendications des femmes. Cela se vérifie particulièrement bien dans le document dont j'ai déjà parlé, *Pour les Québécoises: Égalité et indépendance,* dont la méthode est la suivante: procéder à un découpage systématique de la réalité qui corresponde à la division ministérielle, établir un diagnostic des inégalités concernant les femmes et proposer des solutions qui s'apparentent largement à une liste d'épicerie revendicative. On peut parler dans ce cas de «traduction/trahison» puisque le féminisme est complètement dépouillé de sa substance critique pour se transformer en prêt-à-porter réformiste dont l'État est seul juge de l'à-propos.

Dans un tel contexte, il devient évident que l'opportunité se détermine essentiellement en fonction des priorités étatiques ou des considérations électorales plutôt que de la dynamique des luttes ou encore des besoins des femmes. On dépasse alors le simple stade de la traduction technique des revendications, qui traversent désormais un autre collimateur: la césure avec leur base d'expression. Le féminisme cesse à ce moment d'être un mouvement social ou un courant critique et certains aspects de son discours sont intégrés, après aseptisation, par la machine étatique. C'est là une forme des plus classiques de la récupération en ce sens qu'on assiste à une positivation d'un courant social critique.

Il est certain, par ailleurs, que ce processus a comporté des éléments de renforcement de la position des femmes et que les transformations législatives induites par le féminisme contemporain sont loin d'être négligeables. Qu'on prenne en considération les domaines de la reproduction où le changement majeur est certainement l'absence, à tout le moins provisoire[7], de toute loi concernant l'avortement, ou celui de la famille où en moins de vingt ans les femmes québécoises sont passées de l'autorité maritale à la direction collégiale de la famille, ou encore celui du travail où, malgré des discriminations persistantes, certains principes comme l'équité salariale ont été renforcés légalement et de nouveaux, tel l'action positive, ont été créés, ou finalement celui de l'intégrité physique puisqu'il existe des recours un peu plus efficaces contre la violence ou le viol conjugal, on s'aperçoit que l'oeuvre législative du féminisme contemporain a largement contribué à une certaine égalité entre les sexes dans notre société.

Mais que valent les droits dans une société inégalitaire? Quelle est la force réelle des recours fournis par la loi? Toute stratégie qui reposerait essentiellement sur l'action législative et judiciaire soulèverait trois types de problèmes auxquels le féminisme a d'ailleurs été confronté. D'abord l'appareil judiciaire lui-même: loin d'être neutre, il semble plus réceptif à certaines voix qu'à d'autres et organisé en fonction d'une logique qui désavantage tous les groupes socialement discriminés, y compris les femmes: le traitement des plaintes concernant la violence conjugale est assez éloquent à cet égard. Ensuite, si tous les groupes ont leurs droits, le droit peut-il encore avoir une prétention à l'universel et jouer un rôle dans la régulation sociale? Finalement, les stratégies de type juridique impliquent une intégration aux institutions car il ne s'agit pas seulement de faire voter une loi, mais de faire en sorte qu'elle soit appliquée.

Il n'est en outre pas surprenant que cette insistance sur les droits et les transformations législatives ait surtout été le fait des grandes organisations féminines comme la Fédération des femmes du Québec et l'Association féminine d'éducation et d'action sociale, sur le scène provinciale, et le Comité national d'action, sur la scène fédérale. De plus, ce type de stratégie a trouvé certains échos dans les comités de condition féminine de certains syndicats et dans certains partis politiques.

Les tentatives de construction de l'autonomie des femmes

On ne saurait cependant réduire le féminisme à ce type de pratiques. Dans le même temps où se développait l'action législatrice, on voyait apparaître d'autres types d'action qui misaient essentiellement sur la solidarité entre femmes pour construire une réalité sociale différente qui ne se contenterait pas de l'égalité mais reposerait sur l'autonomie personnelle, sociale et politique des femmes. C'est cette composante qu'on peut qualifier de mouvement de libération des femmes. Elle prend plusieurs formes, que ce soit les groupes de conscience, les mouvements d'auto-affirmation ou les groupes de services. J'insisterai cependant sur ce dernier type de pratique dans la mesure où il a été le plus visible et le plus soutenu au cours des années 80 et qu'il correspond par ailleurs à une tendance présente dans l'ensemble des mouvements sociaux qui ont évolué du révolutionnarisme au radicalisme de l'autolimitation en cherchant «à politiser les institutions de la société civile dans des directions non balisées par les institutions politiques représentatives et bureaucratiques et de ce fait à reconstituer une société civile qui n'est plus dépendante de plus de régulation, de contrôle et d'intervention»[8].

La notion d'autonomie dans le mouvement féministe se développe sur plusieurs plans. Je ne m'attarderai pas à celui de l'organisation (non-mixité des organisations et indépendance par rapport aux groupes mixtes) qui constitue un «acquis» depuis l'émergence de la dernière vague féministe. Ce qui m'intéresse particulièrement, c'est l'autonomie politique et programmatique. Ce que cela implique, c'est à la fois le côté autosuffisant du mouvement, dans le sens où la lutte des femmes n'a pas à se rapporter à aucune autre et est pleinement signifiante en elle-même, et la possibilité pour les femmes de définir comme elles l'entendent, sans en référer automatiquement à d'autres problématiques sociales, le contenu de leurs luttes.

C'est là un aspect crucial des conceptions autonomistes du politique, aspect commun à l'ensemble des «nouveaux mouvements sociaux». Le monde et l'action politiques n'y sont pas perçus comme étant organisés par une seule logique sociale (ce qui est à la base d'une stratégie intégrationniste); le pouvoir y apparaît comme un lieu vide ou plus exactement comme suffisamment décentralisé pour ne pas pouvoir être conquis par un acte unique ni obéir à une seule logique. Bref, la pensée autonomiste table sur l'hétérogénéité du social et, par conséquent, sur la multiplicité des lieux et des temps d'intervention.

À partir du moment où l'accent est mis sur l'hétérogénéité, deux mutations majeures s'opèrent au sein des pratiques féministes. D'une part l'insistance ne porte plus ni sur un projet d'avenir, ni sur un projet articulé de réformes sociales, mais sur un travestissement du présent. Il s'agit de commencer à construire, sans attendre le grand soir ou les modifications législatives, ces lendemains qui chantent, et de cesser de poser comme préalable des changements de structures ou de cadres législatifs dont on ne sait quand ils surviendront. D'autre part, cela implique de traquer le pouvoir dans toutes ses manifestations, y compris les plus infimes et les plus intimes, et d'entreprendre de changer la vie dès à présent.

L'autonomie implique également un type de rapport particulier entre théorie et pratique. Contrairement à la conception usuelle, le féminisme tire justement sa radicalité du fait qu'il ne procède pas d'une théorie forclose. Comme le soulignait Christine Delphy, découvrir l'oppression quelque part ne témoigne que de son existence, pas de son étendue ni de sa profondeur, ce qui l'amenait à préciser que «la lutte féministe consiste autant à découvrir les oppressions inconnues, à voir l'oppression là où on ne la voyait pas, qu'à lutter contre les oppressions connues»[9].

De la même façon qu'il existe une hétérogénéité du social, il y a de multiples façons d'aborder une question; surtout, la problématisation ne doit pas viser à enclore le champ de la réflexion mais laisser la voie libre à des dérapages et des digressions qui constituent souvent le lieu de la création.

Dans ce sens, la théorie est amenée à se construire au fur et à mesure que les pratiques se développent puisque, à travers les pratiques, ce sont des aspects insoupçonnés d'un problème qui émergent, ce sont des liens, qui n'apparaissaient pas toujours à l'analyse abstraite, qui s'imposent à l'esprit.

C'est dans ce contexte qu'il convient de situer le développement des services féministes. Pour celles qui s'y sont engagées, de telles pratiques correspondaient à la fois à une expérimentation de rapports sociaux différents et à une volonté d'imposer une rupture radicale du train-train quotidien. Sans attendre que la société en vienne à reconnaître que l'avortement ou la violence contre les femmes, par exemple, constituent des problèmes sociaux et non des traits de comportement individuel, il s'agissait pour ces militantes d'imposer simultanément leur vision sociale et d'offrir des alternatives aux femmes afin qu'elles puissent sortir du cercle vicieux de la victimisation.

Cette double dimension n'est pas anodine. On a beaucoup insisté, dans la récente vague féministe, à travers le slogan «le personnel est politique», sur le fait que nombre de situations auxquelles sont confrontées les femmes ne résultent pas de rapports interpersonnels mais plutôt de rapports sociaux de sexe. Construire des alternatives sociales vis-à-vis de ce qui était alors perçu comme des comportements individuels, c'était donc imposer, dans la réalité des pratiques sociales, une partie de ce qui était supposé par le slogan. En même temps, cela répondait à un impératif de changer la vie dès maintenant, sans attendre que le consensus social parvienne à des solutions largement acceptables.

Ces pratiques de services ont permis d'accroître de façon substantielle la diffusion des thématiques féministes. Longtemps cantonné à un mouvement d'idées, à une bataille idéologique, ou encore à un groupe de pression plutôt minoritaire, le féminisme allait enfin pouvoir, par des pratiques effectives, rejoindre la masse des femmes. Et c'est exactement ce qui s'est passé. Les services ont rendu possible la jonction entre un certain discours féministe et la réalité de bon nombre de femmes. Cela allait permettre de faire la preuve que la «condition féminine» n'est pas un donné immuable mais un produit social, susceptible, par le fait même, de faire l'objet d'un nouveau contrat.

Cependant, cette jonction s'est opérée dans un contexte où le mouvement était en pleine expansion, où ses terrains d'intervention se multipliaient et où son action se déployait au moins sur un double registre assez consciemment assumé en termes de division du travail. D'un côté, des pratiques permettant d'expérimenter dès à présent des réalités sociales nouvelles. De l'autre, des revendications politiques se poursuivant à la fois sur le terrain institutionnel et sur celui des luttes sociales. La mise sur pied des services correspond donc à une certaine apogée du féminisme, tant sur le plan de la théorie que sur celui de la pratique. Ce n'est qu'une des facettes du mouvement. Cependant, à partir du moment où le mouvement délaissera de plus en plus le terrain de la société civile, les services vont également poser la question de l'intégration à l'appareil d'État, tant en ce qui a trait au financement qu'en ce qui a trait aux pratiques réelles du service.

Dans une large mesure, on peut dire qu'aujourd'hui les services féministes sont devenus une annexe déconsidérée financièrement mais politiquement valorisante de l'appareil d'État. Du fait de leur caractère privé, ces services coûtent très peu cher à l'État: moins de béton, de moindres salaires, pas de charges sociales et possibilité de recours au bénévolat et au financement communautaire.

Quant à la valorisation politique, elle vient du fait qu'avec une présence minimale de l'État (principalement au moyen d'un financement aléatoire), des services sont effectivement offerts et qu'on se sert même de leur existence pour montrer que l'État fait beaucoup pour les femmes. Et puis, les divers énoncés de politique n'hésitent pas à s'appuyer sur l'expertise qui a été développée au cours des ans par les féministes, sans bien sûr reconnaître explicitement leur contribution. De plus, dans un contexte de remise en cause partielle de l'État-providence, ces services entrent tout à fait dans la logique de prendre appui sur le communautaire plutôt que d'étendre les services sociaux étatiques.

Dans ce cadre, les féministes ont essayé de répondre par une intégration parallèle à l'intégration étatique. Des regroupements provinciaux se sont créés et l'autogestion du début fait de plus en plus place à une complémentarité des interventions. Cependant les difficultés de financement permettent et même rendent nécessaire le déplacement partiel des enjeux du côté du social et cela laisse la porte entrouverte pour une nouvelle avancée de l'autonomie des femmes.

L'hésitation entre le moderne et le postmoderne

Cela m'amène à aborder la question de l'oscillation entre le moderne et le postmoderne dans le mouvement des femmes, c'est-à-dire l'hésitation entre l'intégration à la société existante et l'imagination d'une société non sexiste. Pour ce faire, je m'appuierai sur une réflexion de Françoise Collin qui introduit le même débat:

> Le féminisme est le premier mouvement à poser la question politique par excellence, celle de l'absence de droits dans un État de droit. Et c'est fondamentalement la notion de liberté qui le travaille, plus que celle de l'égalité comme égalisation. Pourtant, à ses débuts, le féminisme a succombé partiellement à l'illusion d'être un mouvement social, calqué sur les mouvements sociaux du monde moderne, en instituant les femmes comme genre, animé par une volonté supposée générale. Ainsi, le pernicieux concept de sororité est-il venu accentuer les ambiguïtés du concept de fraternité, barrant la voie au dialogue au nom d'un unanimisme postulé. Or le ressort du politique, Arendt le dit très justement, ce n'est pas l'amour, toujours aléatoire, mais le respect.[10]

Mouvement pour les droits, le féminisme l'a été en ce sens que le droit à l'avortement, le droit au travail (formulation on ne peut plus malheureuse mais typiquement moderne), l'égalité des droits civils, la protection légale contre la violence «privée» (viol, violence conjugale, harcèlement sexuel, pornographie) ont été au coeur de sa résurgence contemporaine. Mais il y aurait également lieu de lire ces revendications dans un sens d'individuation et d'autonomie sociale et personnelle. On pourrait ainsi parler de contrôle de son corps, de l'accès autonome aux ressources matérielles, de lutte contre la puissance maritale et du droit à la sûreté garanti par l'État.

À cet égard, la contribution essentielle du féminisme aura été de montrer que ces «droits de l'homme» qui sont à la base de la modernité politique reposent sur une conception éminemment exclusive de l'humanité. À l'origine, plusieurs catégories sociales en sont exclues. Étendre ces droits aux femmes, c'est donc en subvertir partiellement la logique, comme l'avait déjà pressenti Olympe de Gouges lors de la rédaction de sa *Déclaration des Droits de la Femme et de la Citoyenne*, et poser pratiquement la nécessité d'un nouveau contrat social qui reposerait sur l'inclusion.[11]

Est-ce par ailleurs un mouvement social au sens classique du terme? Dans un certain sens oui, puisque son action il l'a située essentiellement sur le terrain de la société civile, à partir d'une catégorisation sociale imposée, la «condition féminine». Non, parce qu'il n'a pu faire l'économie du politique, même si le politique constitue probablement la principale cause de sa léthargie actuelle et cela à plusieurs titres. D'abord, parce qu'il a été partiellement happé par les institutions. Ensuite, parce que ses succès ont fait voler en éclats, si tant est qu'elle ait jamais existé, l'homogénéité de la «condition féminine», obligeant à une reconsidération de la notion de sororité qui aille dans le sens de la reconnaissance de l'autonomie personnelle de chacune. Enfin, parce qu'il n'a pas trouvé de moyen de règlement de ses différends internes, oscillant entre l'unanimisme et la paralysie.

En même temps, il est un mouvement social par définition éphémère, non pas parce qu'il est intrinsèquement incapable de réussir l'intégration politique qui lui permettrait de se perpétuer dans la durée, mais parce que son objectif le plus évident est de saper la catégorisation sociale qui lui a donné naissance. Car l'objet essentiel du mouvement des femmes est la disparition de la condition féminine, telle qu'elle a été réarticulée par les révolutions fondatrices de la modernité occidentale, pour faire accéder les femmes de plain-pied à l'humanité.

C'est dans un tel contexte qu'il importe de prendre la mesure de la signification de la formule «le personnel est politique» dans une perspective postmoderne. Ce qu'il importe de retenir, c'est qu'il faut être une individue, acquérir une stature personnelle sans avoir constamment à en référer à une catégorie sociale dans le sens où la féminité est loin d'épuiser notre identité, pour pouvoir agir comme sujet politique. À travers le féminisme, les femmes comme groupe social ont accédé au droit à la parole publique. Il s'agit maintenant de contribuer à l'élaboration d'un espace public de débat pluriel de façon à pouvoir nommer, avec les autres, mais en son nom.

Il ne s'agit pas, de cette manière, de revenir à la *polis* grecque chère à Arendt, puisqu'elle suppose l'homogénéité du politique. Il s'agit plutôt de tenir compte de la fragmentation postmoderne du social et d'instaurer des espaces de débat afin que des mondes communs puissent constamment se constituer et que l'avenir reste encore possible. En rupture avec le mode binaire des confrontations agonistiques, si caractéristique de la modernité et de ses diverses philosophies de l'histoire, le féminisme veut instaurer une ère de débats reposant à la fois sur la pluralité et l'égalité, garantissant ainsi l'imprévisibilité de l'avenir[12]. À sa façon, le féminisme peut donc contribuer au réenchantement critique du monde.

Notes

1.   Je pense principalement au texte que Nicole Laurin-Frenette et Danielle Juteau-Lee ont préparé pour la Commission canadienne de l'UNESCO en 1983.

2. Voir son article «Mouvements sociaux, mouvements post-politiques» paru dans la *Revue internationale d'action communautaire*, 10/50, 1983.

3. Voir son introduction à l'ouvrage collectif publié sous sa direction, *The New Women's Movement*, New York, Sage, 1986.

4. Juliet Mitchell, *Women's Estate*, New York, Vintage Books, 1973, p. 40 (traduction française, *L'Age de femme*, Paris, Éditions des femmes, 1975, pp. 45-46).

5. Véronique O'Leary et Louise Toupin, *Québécoises deboutte!*, tome 1, Montréal, Éditions du remue-ménage, 1982, p. 47.

6. Lise Payette, *Le pouvoir? Connais pas!*, Montréal, Québec-Amérique, 1982, p. 60.

7. Depuis la tenue du colloque, le Parlement canadien a en effet été saisi d'un projet de loi restrictif concernant le droit à l'avortement. Ce projet de loi n'était pas encore adopté au moment des corrections finales de ce texte mais tout laissait prévoir qu'il le serait, ce qui représente un recul important pour les femmes canadiennes.

8. Claus Offe, «New Social Movements: Challenging the Boundaries of Institutional Politics», *Social Research* 52(4), Winter 1985, p. 820 (ma traduction). Cette position était également soutenue par Jean Cohen dans sa communication au colloque intitulé «État-providence et société civile» qui a eu lieu à Ottawa en janvier 1989.

9. Christine Delphy, «Nos amis et nous», *Questions féministes*, n° 1, 1977, p. 30.

10. Françoise Collin, «Introduction», *Cahiers du GRIF*, n° 33, 1986, p. 6.

11. Pour une analyse détaillée du caractère exclusif du contrat social moderne, voir l'ouvrage de Carole Pateman, *The Sexual Contract*, Stanford, Stanford University Press, 1988.

12. Cette question est abordée de façon plus détaillée dans mon dernier ouvrage, *Citoyennes? Femmes, droit de vote et démocratie*, Montréal, Éditions du remue-ménage, 1989.

Charles L. Jones, Lorna R. Marsden and Lorne J. Tepperman

The Individualization of Women's Lives: Changes in Women's Roles in the Family and in the Paid Labour Force

Abstract

Over the past 150 years, women have increasingly moved from the private to the public sphere. This major social change is most easily seen in the rise of married women's labour force participation rates. The paper shows how this happened in Canada and sets the process in the context of demographic trends and changes in the family. We document the growth of choice, or variety, in women's public lives, the change of choice, or fluidity and the personalization of choice, or idiosyncrasy. We coin the term "individualization" to summarize these changes in the adult female role. We make comparisons between Canada and other countries. Finally, we discuss the new "individualised" adult role of women and its implications for the family and social policy.

Résumé

Au cours des 150 dernières années, les femmes sont passées en nombre croissant de la sphère privée à la sphère publique. Ce changement social majeur est particulièrement évident dans l'accroissement de la proportion des femmes mariées dans la main-d'oeuvre. Nous verrons de quelle façon ce changement s'est produit au Canada en tâchant de le situer dans le contexte des tendances démographiques et de l'évolution de la famille. Nous analyserons tour à tour l'augmentation des choix, ou variété, dans la vie publique des femmes, le changement dans les choix, ou fluidité, et la personnalisation des choix, ou idiosyncrasie. Nous utilisons le mot «individualisation» pour résumer ces changements dans les rôles féminins. Nous faisons aussi quelques comparaisons entre le Canada et d'autres pays. Enfin, nous examinons les conséquences sur la famille et les politiques sociales de ces nouveaux rôles «individualisés».

Charles L. Jones, Lorna R. Marsden and Lorne J. Tepperman

This paper is about changes in the life cycle of the adult Canadian woman.[1] Briefly, we are concerned with:

—the growth of choice, or *variety* in women's public lives;

—the change of choice, or *fluidity;*

—the personalization of choice, or *idiosyncrasy.*

Over the past 150 years, women have increasingly moved from the private to the public sphere.[2] In the public arena, they now hold a wider variety of social and economic positions than in the past. They move more easily between these different positions than was the case before, so they exhibit more fluidity. Finally, their movements between these public positions are becoming more difficult to predict, and in this sense they are more idiosyncratic. We use the term "individualization" to summarize these changes in the adult female role.

Changes in Canadian Women's Lives

As in other countries, there has been a long term decline in fertility over the last one hundred years. This was interrupted by the baby-boom years of the 1950s, but reinstated around the same time as the introduction of oral contraception in the late 1960s. There has also been an increase in life expectancy. Taken together, these trends make it possible for women to spend many more years in the paid labour force.

Canada's total fertility rate today is well below the level of 2.1 births needed to renew or replace generations (Statistics Canada 1987). A pattern of older childbearing is also emerging. More women are having their first child after the age of 30. Although the youngest birth cohorts (Canadian women born after 1952) may not bear enough children to replace themselves, some are merely delaying, not denying, parenthood. Finally, Quebec's fertility rate, for a long time Canada's highest, is now its lowest at 1.4 births per woman (Peron *et al.* 1987). This accords with Quebec's lowest-in-Canada rate of marriage, but views differ on precisely why Quebec women have changed so radically.

Demographers disagree about the likely future level of childbearing in Canada. The most believable "constant fertility assumption" holds that, after dropping more or less steadily for a century, Canadian fertility has started to level off at a sub-replacement level. Reaching about 1.66 children per woman by 1996, it will remain constant thereafter (Statistics Canada 1985).

Major changes in parenthood have already begun and are likely to continue into the foreseeable future (Gee 1986, 277). For example, where women in earlier generations bore children over ten to fifteen years, women today bear children for only five years or less. The number of years when one or more children are present in the home has dropped from thirty to twenty years.

A woman has more options in how she can use her "extra" non-domestic time. She may take this extra time earlier or later: delay childbearing until her 30s, or get it over with in her early 20s. Delayed marriage, delayed house purchase, delayed childbearing is one set of options. Another is doing all of these in their 20s, so that the mortgage is paid off and all the children are gone by the time parents are aged 50. Whichever choice they make, people will spend more years alone with their spouse than in the company of children, the opposite of what most married women have experienced in the past century and a half and, perhaps, for most of human history.

Smith (1988) has published estimates of working-life tables for Canadian men and women. These cover the period from 1921 to 1981 and show how changes in life expectancy combine with increased participation rates. Women's life expectancy at age fifteen has increased from 53.4 in 1921 to 65.0 in 1981 and the overall participation rate has gone up from 18% to 52% over the same period.[3] Twenty-year old Canadian women can now expect to have 37 years of working life—only five years less than comparable men. Smith's analysis also shows that, by 1981, the working-life expectancy of married women was only three years less than that for single women.

Trends in Canadian Family Life

It may be impossible today to talk about the typical family or the typical marriage. Major trends include declining family size, increasing numbers of lone-parent families, increasing numbers of families created by remarriage, more multiple-earner families, and more people living alone (*Canadian Social Trends* 1986, 6, 7).

The old-style "monolithic family" model no longer applies. Rates of first marriage have fallen to an all-time low in Canada (Statistics Canada 1987,

19). This declining national marriage rate has been led by large declines in Quebec which "has not only the lowest rate of all the provinces but one of the lowest rates in the world" (Eichler 1981). To some extent, traditional engagements have been replaced by common-law unions. By 1984, about one adult respondent in six had been in a common-law partnership at one time or another (Burch 1985, Table 4A). Among young people aged 18-29, the proportion was much higher: about one man in five and one woman in four. In fact, "[On] Census Day in 1981 approximately 6% of the couples enumerated were not legally married, and half of the 704,000 or so persons involved were between 20 and 30 years of age" (Statistics Canada 1987, 25).

The trend of younger people toward opting for common law unions over marriage, partly explains the decline in marriages. There is evidence that people are merely delaying and not rejecting marriage, so that the average age at first marriage is increasing. In 1984, the average age of brides at first marriage was 24.3 years, close to the highest ever age of 24.9 recorded in 1942, during the Second World War. The average age of grooms at first marriage, 26.6 in 1984, is still far from the all-time high of 28.3, recorded in the worst part of the Great Depression, 1938. Still, the average age at first marriage is inching upward (Nagnur and Adams 1987).

Only one type of marriage is growing much more common: remarriage. The number of marriages in which at least one of the spouses had previously been married has more than doubled since 1968 when divorces became easier to get. And, combined with fewer first marriages, the increasing remarriages have come to represent over twice as high a proportion of all marriages in 1985(%) as they did in 1968(%) (Statistics Canada 1987, Table 5).

Canadian vital statistics show that rates of divorce remained fairly steady at about 200 divorces per 100,000 married women aged fifteen and over, each year from 1952 through 1968. With law reforms that made divorcing a spouse easier after 1968, the rates shot up five-fold to 1,000 divorces per year per 100,000 married women by 1978. Rates levelled off in the 1980s, and then started to fall (Statistics Canada 1987, 22). By 1984, when Statistics Canada conducted a Family History Survey (Burch 1985), one man in ten and one women in eight who had ever been married had divorced at least once.

Among ever-married men and women who were aged 40-49 in 1984 (people who had experienced adult life for 16 years after the 1968 divorce law reform), nearly one man in seven and one woman in six has been divorced (Burch 1985, Table 3A). The risk of divorce upon marrying is at least

15-16% if current rates continue to prevail; and these rates may rise. Another 4-5% of ever-married persons reported in 1984 that they had separated but not divorced (Burch 1985, Table 3C). These statistics should be interpreted with some caution because the risks of marital breakdown vary widely among different regions and educational levels. Divorce rates are much lower than average in the Atlantic Provinces and Quebec and much higher than average in British Columbia (Burch 1985, Table 19). Likewise people completing a postsecondary education are about half as likely to ever divorce as are people with no more than a secondary school education (Burch 1985, Table 20). Estimates of future divorce over the life course, which assume that present age-specific rates will continue, range between 30% and 40%, with a few even higher.

Labour Force Participation Trends in Canada

Partly in response to the increased risks of dissolution, people marrying today do not accept the same kinds of family roles as in the past. An important indicator of the change is female participation in the labour force. Over 60% of Canadian "economic families" have two or more wage earners. Even mothers of small children (under three years old) are more likely to work outside the home than in past years. The percentage of such mothers who go out to work rose from 31% in 1975 to 52% in 1984, a two-thirds increase in only nine years. Working wives currently contribute about one-quarter of the average family income. Indeed, "a family's income level is directly related to the number of earners" and, "of families with incomes in the top 20% (or highest quintile), 87% reported two or more earners, compared to 21% of families with incomes in the bottom 20% (or lowest quintile)" (*Canadian Social Trends* 1986, 9).

Being married and having children does not hold a man back from progressing to a good job (Boyd 1985, 271, 273), but it definitely handicaps a woman in this respect. Boyd's calculations (1985, 283) show that marital status has no effect on women in the full-time labour force who do not bear children. However, the birth and presence of children holds back the occupational careers of women largely because of the effects of interruptions to employment.

Townson (1987) comments that economic studies "have consistently underestimated the strength of women's increasing labour force participation." In 1975, the percentage of married women aged 20-44 participating in the paid labour force was 51%, and doubts were expressed whether the figure could go higher. Yet in 1986, the participation rate was 70%. Statistics Canada reports labour force participation rates for women who are either heads of households or the spouses of heads of households, that is to say for most adult women. Overall, this participation rate was 56.1% in 1986, similar to the rate for married women in Britain.

The basic processes that have increased the demand for women's work over the last century have been:

1) The growth of demand for nurses and elementary school teachers—jobs already thought compatible with women's caring role in the family. Later, this was extended to the growth of occupational specialties in rehabilitation medicine, occupational therapy, librarianship, etc.

2) Three general social trends:

— what Davis (1987) calls "The Big Change," from a rural society based on primary industries to an urban society based on service industries:

— Massive expansion of demand for clerical, sales, and service workers

— The general increase in the size of work organizations.

These general trends have led to the redefinition of certain jobs as being suitable for women, rather than for men only. This applies especially to clerical work—white collar and white blouse employment. More recently, it applies also to pharmacists, doctors and lawyers. In all cases, such redefinition is not simply cosmetic. It accompanies a more refined specialization and simplification of job descriptions within the occupation; women being allocated to these more limited positions (Lowe 1980; 1987).

3) Legislation and collective agreements which made gender discrimination more difficult for employers and unions (Baker and Robeson, 1981).

4) Most recently, the removal of traditional discouragements to married women being in paid work, and the formalization of arrangements allowing part-time work so that women with family responsibilities could combine them with paid work.

How it used to be

We can see how far Canadian women have come by using Katz's (1975) study of Hamilton, Ontario, between 1851 and 1861. As might be expected, women's opportunities were limited:

> In each year [1851 and 1861] most of the employed women did menial work: 72 per cent were servants in 1851 and 59 per cent ten years later; in both years about 14 per cent were dressmakers, seamstresses, or milliners, occupations suitable enough in terms of the ideology of female domesticity, but offering irregular work at low wages. Few women . . . could be positively identified as prostitutes, but undoubtedly there were very many more. . . . In 1851, perhaps 4 per cent of the women might have been considered marginally middle-class (teachers, innkeepers, grocers, clerks, tax collectors): by 1861, that figure was 11 per cent, including even one physician. At the same time, women followed a somewhat greater variety of occupations, forty-one in 1851 and fifty-four in 1861. (Katz 1975, 58)

The only independently successful women in Hamilton at this time were madams: the owners and managers of brothels. Their financial success was not accompanied by social respectability.

Women have always worked—in many cases without any money wage being paid at all. Wives and daughters worked on the farm or in a family business such as weaving, or in the myriad tasks involved in cooking, preserving food, looking after a house and bringing up children. In Catholic communities, a significant number of young women became members of religious orders, several of which had teaching or nursing vocations, and staffed schools and hospitals. The Hôtel-Dieu hospital in Quebec City was founded and run by nuns. Midwives and nurses learned and practised their trades informally in rural areas.

Home production

We must also note the ways in which women brought in family income in the "private" domestic sphere. When the family farm was the source of family income, women's contribution was very clear. But even off-farm, women at home generated income in cash and kind. This was important to their livelihood and it provided a combination of variety, fluidity and

143

idiosyncrasy within the adult role of "housewife" which has never been captured by official data sources. Tò understand this hidden aspect of the economic lives of women we must explore historical accounts, biographies and literary descriptions.

Bradbury (1984) gives an account of such work in Montreal in the period from 1860 to the late 1890s. Domestic animals were kept in the households of many Montreal families to supplement whatever income could be gained elsewhere. Boarders were kept mainly in the more prosperous households which had an extra room available and sufficiently clean and attractive surroundings.

Boarders were a major form of income earned by women at home (see also, Katz 1975). Taking in boarders is still a form of economic contribution to the household for some Canadian women. Hollingsworth and Tyyska (1989) indicate that boarders were found in about eight percent of Canadian households in 1961. Previous censuses show a much higher proportion, especially in the 1930 Depression years. By keeping boarders in their households, women acquired another adult role of landlady.

In this period, women worked extensively as seamstresses in their homes. They either visited their clients for fittings and measurements, or their clients came to them. Official data sources do not tell us a great deal about such paid work since it was seldom recorded. However, biographies and personal records tell a good deal about this adult role of "seamstress."

In her autobiography, the novelist Gabrielle Roy describes how her mother kept the family going in the 1920s by her work as a landlady, seamstress, gardener, and in other ways in St Boniface, Manitoba. When Gabrielle required an operation for which her parents had to pay—a very serious consideration for them—her mother came to visit her in the hospital, and said:

> Listen to this, now. Yesterday, as I was leaving the hospital, who d'you think I met? Madame Berubé, whose daughter's getting married next month. She needs a dress for the wedding and so does her sister-in-law. So there I am with two big orders, just because I went out by one door rather than another . . . (Roy/Claxton 1987, 23).

The Individualization of Women's Lives: Changes in Women's Roles in the Family and in the Paid Labour Force

The Rise of Paid Employment

The two World Wars of this century each brought about a shortage of labour and a mobilization of women into the paid work force. The mobilization was more extreme for the Second World War than for the First. Only single women were recruited for heavy industry in the 1914-18 war. Towards the end of the 1939-45 war, married women with children were being recruited for such war work and Federal-Provincial child-care agreements were made, resulting eventually in the setting up of day nurseries in Ontario and Quebec (Anderson 1988; Chenier and Labarge 1985). In 1917, around 35,000 women worked in central Canada's munitions factories, compared to around 261,000 in 1943.

After both wars, pressure was put on women to give up their jobs so that these could be taken up by returning servicemen. The policy was motivated by an ideology that a married woman's place was in the home and by fear of the political consequences of male unemployment. Susan Prentice (1989) has shown how federal, provincial, and municipal funding was withdrawn from day-care programmes in Toronto, until by 1952, all the gains in day-care provision that had come about during the war had disappeared. (See also, Kerr 1973).

Despite superficial similarities, the two World Wars had different contexts. During and after World War I, domestic service was still the most common occupation for a woman. The percentage of women working as domestics did not fall below 20% until the 1920s, when the clerical and sales sector continued to expand and to become more feminized. Throughout the 1930s, the Great Depression caused women to be laid off before men and to revert to nineteenth-century methods of domestic production, taking in lodgers, etc. It also caused fertility rates to drop to unprecedentedly low levels.

There has been an increase in the availability of part-time and part-year work, and this kind of work is particularly attractive to students and to married women (Langlois 1989). Between 1971 and 1981, the number of women who had worked for at least part of the preceding year grew from 3.5 million to 5.2 million. As we have seen, women have always done a great deal of what amounts to part-time work in household production and in the informal sector of the economy. Since work in the household and informal sectors has decreased relative to the massive increase in the formal part of the economy, women do many of the same part-time economic activities, but do them outside the home and for an official paycheck.

Charles L. Jones, Lorna R. Marsden and Lorne J. Tepperman

There is no doubt that employers used to discriminate against women. Part of this discrimination was directed particularly against hiring married women and was bound up with ideas about the proper place of husbands and wives in marriage. Employers also believed that women were talented at painstaking, detailed work. Prejudiced thinking can be found in the rationalizations that were made either for not hiring women at all or for confining them to very low level jobs, many of which had been created specifically as "job ghettos" for women (Lowe 1980). Since the 1960s, such prejudices are no longer accepted as rationalizations for action.

Organized labour exerted influence to prevent women being employed in the occupations over which it had control (Baker and Robeson 1981). The rationalizations were similar to those used by employers. Certainly, the "marriage ban" continued to be enforced in British industries, at the insistence of organized labour (Hakim 1987). Change in such policies has resulted in women being more likely to obtain jobs in areas that had previously been male preserves. The general disappearance of the marriage ban means that women can continue to work for pay after their marriage.

Much of Canadian legislation has been provincial, but in general, similar provisions spread through the provinces. Equal pay for equal work came into effect in the 1950s. Throughout the 1970s, significant "employment standards" legislation began to affect women's rights to work in certain occupational and industrial settings. For example, women no longer had to be transported home after late shifts and could therefore work at night.

There has been a long term trend towards less occupational segregation and it is now fairly easy to find female doctors and lawyers in Canada. Nevertheless, the 1981 census found that Canadian women were still concentrated in secretarial and clerical work, sales, services, health, and elementary school teaching. Fox and Fox (1987) conclude that, while segregation by gender remains high in absolute terms, the chief reason for its decline between 1971 and 1981 was that significant numbers of women entered occupations that had been almost exclusively male.

What kind of jobs are made available to the new generation of married women who in previous years would have never have re-entered paid work? There is considerable evidence that they are largely confined to *unsheltered* jobs in the clerical, sales, and service sectors.

Unsheltered jobs never require more than minimum training, are relatively low paid, offer few benefits or security of tenure, and demand few skills. They are an extension of eighteenth- and nineteenth-century systems of

hiring casual labourers by the day, and of unskilled factory work that could
be done by children. What is new in the prosperous West is that factory
systems of production and distribution have de-skilled many jobs that
previously demanded expertise. The skills of a trained cook are not required in fast food delivery systems.

Today, women are changing their labour force statuses more frequently and
rapidly than in the past. Movements between pairs of labour market
statuses (per unit time) are more frequent and varied than ever before.

Le Bourdais and Desrosiers (1988) have used the Family History Survey to
focus on the dynamics of marriage, divorce, and employment. Their report
emphasizes the discontinuity of women's employment in Canada, the low
level of the jobs, the prevalence of part-time employment, and the
pauperization of women in female-headed households. Their conclusion is
essentially that, notwithstanding any advances made since 1950, it is still
women who pay the price of the family (see also, Dooley 1988).

Many writers about the future have believed that the relentless march of
technology and capitalism would result in a society where the vast majority
of the population would be unemployed or merely employed in routine jobs.
Current debates about the declining middle class revive the spectre of a
society polarized between those protected in sheltered careers and an
expanding, increasingly feminized sub-middle class working in one unsheltered job after another (Leckie 1988).

Towards Individualization of Women's Lives

Our summary statement that women's adult lives have become
"individualized" is consistent with the proposition that women increasingly
work in unsheltered labour markets or in *periphery* industries—especially
services. They work in a wider *variety* of jobs than ever before, and because
of the way these jobs have been organised—as part-time and/or as limited
contract jobs—they are more *fluid* in moving more rapidly from one job to
another. As moves are also more *idiosyncratic* or apparently random, we
find it more difficult to predict their behaviour.

With individualization as we have defined it comes the appearance, if not
always the reality, of choice. Lives are less predictable and less similar to
each other. There is a growing gap between the lives of women and those

of their female friends, a growing discontinuity between generations of women and a growing dissimilarity between the lives of women and men.

When gaps like these open up, certain consequences are inevitable. One is confusion: Women will ask "Where is this process heading? Is it good or bad? If bad, can we stop it, and how? Why am I getting the life I am, and not the one I had planned?" Another consequence is *anomie*, or normlessness: Women will ask "What are the rules of living in this new order? Are there to be new ideas of good and bad, right and wrong? How should I plan my own life, and help my daughter to plan hers?" A third is disorganization: Women will ask "How can people organize a happy, comfortable family life under these circumstances? How can we balance the demands of work, parenthood and marriage? Is there any possibility of planning for the future?"

Today, ever-married women have more years in which to work for pay. They are better educated than previous generations, and some of them have jobs which give non-monetary satisfaction. Alongside an increased demand for clerical, sales, and service workers, there is now very little scope for household production. In many cases, the household income is no longer sufficient to support the lifestyle women have been taught to regard as adequate. In some cases, being an earner may confer some clout in household decision making. In other cases, earning plays another role. Women who are divorced or separated are largely responsible for the care of children; such women have no alternative but to work.

Once age, marital status and childbearing are no longer the prime influences, public policy variables assume a great deal of influence over women's lives. By combining with women's personal characteristics in a multitude of almost unique ways, they contribute significantly to the making of idiosyncratic lives.

Interpretations

Why does women's paid work show increasing variety, fluidity and idiosyncrasy? And what changes have been taking place in the lives of men and of young people just entering the labour market?

In one major theoretical approach, these changes are viewed as stemming from the logic of modern capitalism. On this account, women are seen in terms of the social class relations that emerge from capitalist relations of production. See for example, Hamilton and Barrett (1986). The principal effect examined is the exploitation of all working-class people, men and women alike. In a fusion of Marxist and feminist perspectives, the exploitation of women in domestic labour as well as in the paid labour force is seen as qualitatively different from that of men, because of women's role in childbearing and childrearing. This exploitation results in alienation, which applies equally to men and women, though they experience it in different forms.

Other theoretical traditions in sociology have been less developed from a feminist perspective (Sydie 1987). The Weberian tradition views male dominance in all cultural and economic matters as a major cause of inequality. Patriarchy is an expression of power relations based in marriage and the household (Sydie 1987). In the feminist approach to this tradition, changing or destroying capitalism is no solution to the problem of women's historical and contemporary inequality. The problems of inequality must be worked out between women and men themselves, in their collective as well as interpersonal relations. Weberians argue that it is not only the objective conditions under which women live that are alienating, but also the subjective ones.

The meaning of the term "patriarchy" is still being debated (Fox 1988). There is both historical and contemporary interest in this debate about the subjective, structural, and organizational dimensions of male-female differences and the social production of power (Mann 1986; Rueschmeyer 1986; Sydie 1987).

In the sense of community too, the situation of women is viewed as unequal. In the communities in which Durkheim found the expression of social orderliness in our societies, women played a limited role in the division of labour. Such Durkheimian ideas dominated sociologists' thinking about gender in American sociology's period of structural functionalism. In response to the question, "How is social order possible?", the answer was often—only when women maintain the family, undertake socialization tasks and have complementary, not competitive, statuses with men (Sydie 1987).

The problem of social order is now seen as less interesting. Once again, as when Marx, Weber and Durkheim wrote about society, we face major changes in the ways the community, the state, and the lives of individuals are organized. We must ask the same sorts of questions as were asked by the early theorists. In particular, we must ask about the causes of change in women's lives and the social reaction to them; of the organizational shifts that not only structure women's lives but also adapt to the changes in those lives; and the extent to which these changes will bring about other social changes -- for example in patterns of child care, marriage, and job-holding.

Charles L. Jones, Lorna R. Marsden and Lorne J. Tepperman

Are the changes we see in employment and family life the result of alienation in the Marxian sense of the word? That is, are they the result of capitalist relations? Or are they the result of anomie, the loss of meaning in the lives of women and men? Are women as a class having to reinterpret their roles in adult life without the help of social institutions, such as the church, the arts or politics, that might help men, the poor, new immigrants, or other groups which also experience change?

In Canada, as well as other countries, we see changes in the family and other social institutions which have left adult women without an important role, or at least *as* important a role in daily life as they had before. These changes include easier divorce, decline in fertility, and the maintenance of old people by the state rather than by the family. Changes in family life have combined with a major shift to a service-oriented economy and increasing demand for women's labour in the paid labour force (Oppenheimer 1970). As these processes have proceeded, it has become more and more apparent that women must be prepared to support themselves.

This requirement that women provide support for themselves in the paid labour force has occurred since the 1960s in the Western industrial societies. Now girls must learn at an early age that they cannot assume the support of husbands as they go through their child-bearing years. Both the state and their arrangements with their employers will be more important to them. In this context, the exercise of economic rights by women to hold property, bank accounts, inheritances, etc. becomes vitally important.

For men, the changed pattern of adult women's lives represents a major challenge to their established ways of doing things. Increasingly, men are rearing children on their own or on an intermittent basis. Employers can no longer assume that men will always have domestic arrangements such that the employer has a full call on their time.

One might explain these shifts simply as the product of structural change in the economy. It is also possible to see them as the pulling of women more completely into capitalism so that employers no longer have to be concerned with any concept of the "family wage" but only with individual employees. In this model of explanation, women are being forced into paid employment because the family requires a second wage. In entering into this arrangement with capital, the last vestiges of freedom which women had in bearing and rearing their children are put into the cash nexus.

From a Weberian point of view, what is happening is a process of rationalization with, as a consequence, the further alienation of women's lives. On

150

this account, the state bureaucracy continues with the rationalization of law and of the economy based on a liberal democratic notion of individual life chances and freedoms. The increasing complexity of the division of labour, the rising entitlements, and the increasing pressure on all individuals to occupy all social statuses available works to the disadvantage of the relatively less powerful (Rueschmeyer 1986).

Is Individualization Really Fragmentation?

Ours is, admittedly, a liberal position arising out of functionalist theory that holds, ultimately, that increasing social complexity means more choice (i.e., more liberty, if not more equality) for more people. But perhaps women "choose" housework and part-time work because they cannot get decent full-time work at fair pay and lack affordable day-care and spousal cooperation. In keeping with this alternative, non-functionalist viewpoint, what we are witnessing today is not a growth of individualization, but a progressive fragmentation of women's lives.

Men's lives, by this reasoning, continue to keep their unitary character. By contrast, women's lives—always vulnerable to patriarchal control and economic hardship—reflect problems of advanced capitalism and the breakdown of the traditional family. Thus the growth of variety may reflect the growth of a female marginal workforce largely unprotected by unions, deprived of security and benefits, ill-paid, and driven into part-time work by the need for wages at almost any cost. Part-time work is the employer's way of getting workers without paying good pay and benefits.

A growth of fluidity may merely reflect the marginality of part-time or short-term jobs—their insecurity and unattractiveness compared to housework—and the unavailability of good full-time work. Fluidity, by this reasoning, results not from the exercise of worker choice but from the instability of the economic system and discrimination against women. The observed growth of idiosyncrasy is the result of long-term, nearly random fluidity in which women bob about on a sea of uncontrolled influences. There is some support for this interpretation; for example the rising proportion of involuntary part-time workers (Akyeampong 1989). However, we lack the data that would tell us how voluntary female choices really are and how choice patterns are likely to change in response to easier access to adequate day-care, greater spousal cooperation at home, and more effective legislation governing the pay, hiring, and promotion of women.

On the other hand, some believe that the growth of individualization reflects a growth of choice and opportunity for women. In practice we see a great deal of support for both interpretations. We can test the two approaches, since if social vulnerability is really the main factor driving individualization, then the most vulnerable women of all—those with the least choice—should be most various, fluid, and idiosyncratic. This would include women with little education or other human capital, older women, women without husbands, and women whose husbands earn little or no income. By this reasoning, poor and working-class women should be increasingly fluid, and women in the middle and upper classes should remain unchanged.

If what is growing is choice, not fragmentation, then women with the opposite characteristics—those possessing the most "human capital"—should be leading the most individualized lives.

Concluding Remarks

One question to be clarified is the relationship between "individualization" and "improvement." Some might confuse "individualization" with what developmental psychologists have called "individuation": the growth and strengthening of a person's sense of self. We do not claim that individualization, as we define it here, necessarily contributes to individuation, nor even that individualization is a good thing in any respect. We only want to describe and understand what has happened to women's lives, by comparing today's lives with earlier women's lives. Then we can see better what women have gained and lost.

A second question is the relationship between "individualization" and "equality." We have already signalled that we see little evidence that male and female lives are converging; so they are not likely to become equal by becoming the same. Will individualization make women's and men's lives different (and separate) but equal? That is a harder question to answer.

We do not assume that individualization either ensures or rules out gender equality. In fact, gender inequality seems to be a social or cultural universal: it appears in all societies of any complexity and size beyond the simplest hunter-gatherers. Moreover, we see no sign of a linear trend towards gender equalization in our society. If anything, the signs indicate that the Canadian state is retreating on this issue. So long as this gender inequality exists to a marked degree, women will enjoy a wider choice of lives simply because what they give up is worth little—certainly less than what a man would have to give up to get a change of similar magnitude. Women float in and out of gaps in the domestic and paid economies.

Given the opportunity to choose among equally limited or undesirable alternatives, women will move about more frequently to meet more idiosyncratic needs, respond to new opportunities, and solve new problems resulting from large-scale social change.

We have focussed on changes in the realm of work: specifically, on changes in the pattern of women's work. However the process we are discussing in relation to work—individualization—is occurring in other domains as well. Patterns of marriage, parenthood, and recreation, to name only a few, are also individualizing. The individualization of work is part of a general individualization of women's lives. It can be taken to illustrate the overall process.

More than that, the individualization of work influences, and is influenced by, individualization in the other domains. We often refer to the connection between changing patterns of marriage and childbearing, and their influence on female work. Ultimately, the history of individualization is the story of an unfolding relationship between family life and the economy.

Space does not permit us to compare the Canadian experience with that of women in other countries. Suffice it to say that there is abundant evidence that women's adult roles are in very rapid change in the USA and in Western European countries (Bergmann 1986; Bianchi and Spain 1986; Delacourt and Zighera 1988; Glenn 1987; Jenson 1988; Joshi 1989; Mintz and Kellogg 1988; *Canadian Social Trends* 1989).

Almost all industrial countries have seen their rates of female participation in the labour force increase markedly since 1950 (*Journal of Labour Economics*, January, 1985). The growth, mostly due to the changing behaviour of married women with children, is one of the most dramatic social changes of the century. The 1983 OECD Employment Outlook (page 48) reports a close relationship between overall female participation rates and the evolution of part-time employment across countries. There have been other social and economic trends, such as increasing divorce rates, declining fertility, the growth of service industries, and (in many countries) chronically high levels of unemployment and government programs to stimulate employment. While there are important differences in traditions and social institutions, we believe that our findings for Canada apply in general to the USA and to most Western European countries.

Charles L. Jones, Lorna R. Marsden and Lorne J. Tepperman

Notes

1. The ideas discussed in this paper are developed at greater length in a book with the provisional title, *Lives of Their Own*, to be published by Oxford University Press, Canada. We thank Simon Langlois, Vappu Tyyska and Barry Wellman for valuable comments. The research was funded by Health and Welfare Canada, by Labour Canada and by the Social Sciences and Humanities Research Council. Author order is alphabetical.
2. As their public lives have grown more complex, many aspects of women's family lives have become simplified and more standardized.
3. Labour force participation rates for Canadian women over 15 years old were: 17.6 in 1921, 19.6 in 1931, 20.7 in 1941, 24.1 in 1951. They then began to take off, to 29.7 in 1961, 39.9 in 1971 and 51.8 in 1981 (Smith, 1988).

References

Adams, Owen and Dhruva Nagnur (1989) "Marrying and divorcing: a status report for Canada." *Canadian Social Trends* (Summer), 24-7.

Akyeampong, Ernest B. (1987) "Involuntary part-time employment in Canada, 1975-1986," *Canadian Social Trends*, 26-9.

Anderson, Doris (1988) "Status of Women." *The Canadian Encyclopaedia*. 2nd Edition. Edmonton: Hurtig, 2072-4.

Baker, Maureen and Mary-Anne Robeson (1981) "Trade union reactions to women workers and their concerns." *Canadian Journal of Sociology* 1, 19-32.

Bergmann, Barbara R. (1986) *The Economic Emergence of Women*. New York: Basic Books.

Boyd, Monica (1985) "Education and occupation attainments of native-born Canadian men and women." In Monica Boyd *et al., Ascription and Achievement: Studies in Mobility and Status Attainment in Canada*. Ottawa: Carleton University Press, 229-95.

Burch, Thomas K. (1985) *Family History Survey: Preliminary Findings*. Ottawa: Statistics Canada. Catalogue 99-955.

———— (1987) "Age-sex roles and demographic change: an overview." *Canadian Studies in Population*, 129-46.

Bradbury, Bettina (1984) "Pigs, Cows and Boarders: Non-wage forms of survival among Montreal families, 1861-91." *Labour/Le Travail*, 9-46.

Canadian Social Trends (1986) Ottawa: Statistics Canada, Catalogue Number 11-008E, Summer.

Canadian Women's Educational Press (1974) *Women at Work: Ontario 1850-1930*. Toronto: Canadian Women's Educational Press.

Coale, Ansley J. (1969) "The decline of fertility in Europe from the French Revolution to World War II." In *Fertility and Family Planning*. Edited by S.J. Behrman, L. Costa and R. Freeman. Ann Arbor: University of Michigan Press, 3-24.

Chenier, Nancy Miller and Dorothy Labarge (1985) *Towards Universality: an historical overview of the evolution of education, health care, day care and maternity leave*. Ottawa: Report for the Task Force on Child Care. Series 2, Catalogue No. SW43-1,2E.

Davis, James A. (1987) *Social Differences in Contemporary America*. New York: Harcourt, Brace, Jovanovich.

Davis, Kingsley *et al.* (eds., 1987) *Below-Replacement Fertility in Industrial Societies: Causes, Consequences, Policies*. New York: Cambridge University Press.

Delacourt, Marie-Laurence and Jacques A. Zighera (1988) "Situation au regard de l'emploi des femmes chefs de ménage ou conjointes de chef de ménage pour dix pays de la Communauté Européene en 1985." *CASSF*. Université de Paris X-Nanterre à Nanterre.

Dooley, Martin D. (1988) "An analysis of changes in family income and family structure in Canada between 1973 and 1986, with an emphasis on poverty among children." Hamilton: McMaster University. QSEP Research Report No. 238.

———— (1989) "Changes in the market work of married women and lone mothers with children in Canada: 1973-1986." Hamilton: McMaster University. QSEP Research Report.

Economic Council of Canada (1984) *The Changing Economic Status of Women*. (J.A. Boulet and L. Lavallée.) Ottawa: Ministry of Supply and Services.

Eichler, Margrit (1981) "The inadequacy of the monolithic model of the family." *Canadian Journal of Sociology* 6:3, 367-88.

Fox, Bonnie J. (1988) "Conceptualizing Patriarchy." *Canadian Review of Sociology and Anthropology* 25:2 (May), 163-82.

Fox, Bonnie, J. and J. Fox (1987) "Occupational gender segregation of the Canadian labour force, 1931-1981." Toronto: York University, Institute for Social Research.

Gee, Ellen M. (1986) "The life course of Canadian women: An historical and demographic analysis." *Social Indicators Research* 18, 263-83.

Glenn, Norvall D. (1987) "Continuity versus change: sanguineness versus concern: views of the American Family in the late 1980s." *Journal of Family Issues* 8:4 (December), 348-54.

Gower, David (1988) "Annual update on labour force trends." *Canadian Social Trends* (Summer), 17-20.

Hakim, Catherine (1979) "Occupational segregation: a comparative study of the degree and pattern of the differentiation between men's and women's work in Britain, the United States and other countries." London: Dept of Employment Research Paper, No. 9.

———— (1987) "Trends in the flexible workforce." *Employment Gazette* (November), 549-60.

Hamilton, Roberta and Michele Barrett (eds., 1987) *The Politics of Diversity, Feminism, Marxism and Nationalism*. Montréal: Book Centre.

Hollingsworth, Laura and Vappu Tyyska (1989) "The hidden producers: women's household labour during the great depression." *Critical Sociology* (Spring), 2-39.

Jenson, Jane, Elizabeth Hagen and Ceillaigh Reddy (eds., 1988) *Feminization of the Labour Force: Paradoxes and Promises*. Toronto: Oxford University Press.

Joshi, Heather (1989) "The changing form of women's economic dependency." In *The Changing Population of Britain*. Edited by Heather Joshi. Oxford: Basil Blackwell, 157-76.

Katz, Michael B. (1975) *The People of Hamilton, Canada West*. Cambridge, MA: Harvard University Press.

Kerr, Virginia (1973) "One step forward—two steps back: child care's long American history." In *Child-Care—Who Cares?: Foreign and Domestic Infant and Early Childhood Development Policies*. Edited by Pamela Roby. New York: Basic Books, 157-71.

Labour Canada (1983) *Part-time Work in Canada*. Report of the Commission of Inquiry into Part-time Work. Ottawa: Supply and Services. (Joan Wallace, Commissioner).

Langlois, Simon (1989) "Le travail à temps partiel: vers une polarisation de plus en plus nette." Québec: Institut québécois de la recherche sur la culture. Mai.

Le Bourdais, Céline and Hélène Desrosiers (1988) "Trajectoires démographiques et professionelles: une analyse longitudinale des processus et des déterminants." Montréal: INRS-Urbanisation.

Leckie, Norman (1988) "The declining middle and technological change: trends in the distribution of employment income in Canada 1971-1984." *Economic Council of Canada Discussion Paper*, No. 342.

Lowe, Graham S. (1980) "Women, work and the office: the feminization of clerical occupations in Canada." *Canadian Journal of Sociology* 5:4.

——— (1987) *Women in the Administrative Revolution: The Feminization of Clerical Work*. Toronto: University of Toronto Press.

Mann, Michael (1986) *The Sources of Social Power. Volume I: A History of Power from the Beginning to A.D. 1760*. New York: Cambridge University Press.

Mintz, Steven and Susann Kellogg (1988) *Domestic Revolutions: A Social History of American Family Life*. New York: Free Press.

Nagnur, Dhruva and Owen Adams (1987) "Tying the Knot: an overview of marriage rates in Canada." *Canadian Social Trends* (Autumn), 2-4.

Oppenheimer, Valerie K. (1970) *Employment Outlook 1983*. Paris: OECD.

——— (1979) *The Female Labour Force in the United States*. Westport, Conn.: Greenwood Press. Reprint.

Parliament, Jo-Anne B. (1989) "Women employed outside the home." *Canadian Social Trends* (Summer), 2-6.

Peron, Yves, Evelyne Lapierre-Adamcyk and Denis Morissette (1987) "Le changement familiale: aspects démographiques." *Recherches sociographiques* 28:2-3, 317-39.

Pierson, Ruth R. and Marjorie Cohen (1986) *"They're Still Women After All": The Second World War and Canadian Womanhood*. Toronto: McLelland and Stewart.

Prentice, Alison, Paula Bourne, Gail C. Brandt, Beth Light, Wendy Mitchinson and Naomi Black (1988) *Canadian Women: A History*. Toronto: Harcourt, Brace Jovanovich.

Prentice, Susan (1989) "Daycare organizing in Toronto: 1946-1951." Paper presented at the Canadian Sociology and Anthropology Association Meetings in Quebec City, May.

Robinson, Patricia (1986) "Women's occupational attainment: the effects of work interruptions, self-selection and unobservable characteristics." *Social Science Research* 15, 323-46.

Rueschemeyer, Dietrich (1986) *Power and the Division of Labour.* Cambridge: Polity Press.

Scott, Joan W. and Louise A. Tilly (1975) "Women's Work and the Family in Nineteenth-Century Europe." *Comparison Study in Society and History* 17:1 (January), 36-64.

Smith, Pam (1988) "Working life and unemployment tables for males and females: Canada, 1981." Edmonton: University of Alberta, Population Research Laboratory. Discussion Paper No. 55.

Statistics Canada (1983) *Report on the Demographic Situation in Canada.* (J. Dumas.) Ottawa: Ministry of Supply and Services.

———— (1984) *Fertility in Canada: From Baby Boom to Baby Bust.* (A. Romaniuc.) Ottawa: Ministry of Supply and Services.

———— (1985) *Family History Survey: Preliminary Findings.* Catalogue No. 99-955. Ottawa: Ministry of Supply and Services.

———— (1985) *Population Projections for Canada, Provinces and Territories, 1984-2006.* Ottawa: Ministry of Supply and Services.

———— (1987) *Interim Household and Family Projections for Canada, Provinces and Territories to 2006.* Ottawa: Ministry of Supply and Services.

Sydie, Rosalind A. (1987) *Natural Women, Cultured Men: A Feminist Perspective on Sociological Theory.* Toronto: Methuen.

Townson, Monica (1987) "Women's labour force participation, fertility rates and the implications for economic development and government policy." Institute for Research on Public Policy, Discussion Paper No. 87.A.11.

Karen Gould

A Revolution in Literary Theory: Recent Texts by Nicole Brossard and France Théoret

Abstract

This essay focuses on two recent theoretical texts whose appearance signals a new phase in the discussion of women's writing in Québec: Nicole Brossard's La Lettre aérienne *(1985; trans. as* The Aerial Letter*), and France Théoret's* Entre raison et déraison *(1987). When considered together, their rather different approaches to the problems and discoveries of women's writing today, as well as their perspectives on an emerging feminist literary aesthetics, suggest a new self-confidence among feminist theorists in Quebec who are no longer dependent on American or French theory to legitimize their own work. The essays presented in these two collections underscore the connections for women between theory and writing, feminism and language, subjectivity and ideology.*

Résumé

Cet article porte sur deux textes théoriques récents qui semblent marquer une nouvelle étape dans le débat sur l'écriture des femmes au Québec: La Lettre aérienne *de Nicole Brossard (1985) et* Entre raison et déraison *de France Théoret (1987). Lorsqu'on les étudie ensemble, ces deux approches théoriques des problèmes et des conquêtes de l'écriture des femmes aujourd'hui, aussi bien que leurs points de vue sur l'émergence d'une esthétique littéraire féministe, témoignent d'une nouvelle assurance chez les théoriciennes du féminisme au Québec, qui n'ont plus à se référer aux modèles théoriques américains ou français pour justifier leur propre travail. Les essais réunis dans ces deux ouvrages soulignent les rapports entre théorie et écriture, féminisme et langage, subjectivité et idéologie.*

> . . . la théorie féministe évoluera si l'on est capable de parler de la féminité en tenant compte des différences entre les femmes.
>
> Louise Dupré, *Au noir de l'écriture*

159

It is impossible to speak of women's experimental writing in Quebec today and over the past two decades without recourse to the word "theory." Indeed, many of the questions and the discourse of contemporary feminist thought have provided the conceptual bases and the poetic impetus for what we now refer to as *écriture au féminin*. This term has come to designate a variety of experimental writing practices in Quebec since the mid-1970s that have sought to place female experience and a feminist consciousness at the core, if not at the origin, of language itself. Whether we consider the works of Nicole Brossard, Louky Bersianik, France Théoret, Madeleine Gagnon, Louise Dupré, or others—and despite the acknowledged differences in their respective literary projects and political outlooks, we are talking about a group of Québécoises writers who have approached the act of writing from the point of view of gender and of engendered identities in order to articulate something new about women—about their place in language, in history, and in the culture at large. Such forms of writing are always situated on the side of subversion or outright opposition to patriarchal thinking and to the theory it has generated, promulgated, and preserved over the centuries. Viewed from this angle, the project of "writing in the feminine" can be understood as a collective literary attempt to reclaim the realm of the symbolic as women's rightful place of creative activity and political struggle. For as Louky Bersianik has argued, "Le symbolique est la place que s'est donnée l'homme mâle là où il n'était ni sollicité, ni réclamé, pour cela, il a pris la place de l'autre, c'est-à-dire de la femme. Aussi peut-il dire qu'elle n'existe pas."[1] (The symbolic is the place the male has accorded himself, a place where he was neither solicited nor required, and in doing so, he has occupied the place of the other, which is to say, the place of woman. He can then say that she doesn't exist.)

While the direction of Quebec literature in the 1970s was profoundly altered by the disruptive power of feminist analysis and by an increasing number of women-centred texts of fiction, poetry, "fiction-theory" and other mixed forms, the 1980s have been no less deeply marked by the publication of numerous essays and essay collections on feminist literary theory itself.[2] Theoretically inspired poetic and fictional writings have, in turn, generated more theory on the project as a whole. What is striking, if not surprising, in the increasing attention given to the realm of theory per se is the extent to which the writers themselves have also emerged as some of the most articulate and important voices in the development of a new critical discourse on feminist theory and women's writing.

I have chosen to comment in this essay on two works of theory from Quebec: Nicole Brossard's *La Lettre aérienne*,[3] which appeared in 1985, and France Théoret's *Entre raison et déraison*[4] published in 1987. While this selection has been made for purposes of comparison and contrast, and because of the recognizably theoretical nature of Brossard and Théoret's work as a whole, there is a personal motivation as well since my own critical approach to contemporary women's writing has developed as a result of a constant negotiation between the respective artistic visions and theoretical positions of these two writers in particular.

Both *La Lettre aérienne* and *Entre raison et déraison* are excellent examples of politically motivated gender-marked theory. Both are also retrospective works in that each one allows us to re-consider a series of published and unpublished essays written during the last decade. Thus, although we may have read some of the essays before, the very structure of the essay collection as a compilation of prior texts moves us out of the present perfect and into an evolutionary past—although Théoret's text is less chronological in presentation than is Brossard's, and no doubt intentionally so. In each collection, we are in fact asked to retrace the theoretical paths of a feminist writer and theoretician who has demonstrated "the capacity to 'think from the outside'," as Bersianik puts it, and to move beyond the "purely literary" in any restricted sense of the term toward a broader view of the political functions of theory and, more generally speaking, of cultural production as well.

While Brossard and Théoret have published numerous other theoretical essays, the appearance of these two works nevertheless marks a turning point in the conscious formulation and development of feminist literary theory in Quebec. Indeed, with the publication of these two texts, along with the recent collaborative work, *La Théorie, un dimanche* (1988), as well as Madeleine Gagnon's *Toute écriture est amour* (1989), and Gail Scott's *Spaces Like Stairs* (1989), it would seem that the time has now come to acknowledge the extent to which "theorizing in the feminine" in Quebec has come of age—a point also made by Lori Saint-Martin in the October 1989 issue of *Spirale*. With less recourse to French or American theoretical influences than was formerly the case during the 1970s, feminist literary theory in Quebec appears to be charting its own distinct intellectual and political history. It is, moreover, a history in which Brossard and Théoret have already been among the most visible and influential participants.

Writing and theory have been virtually intertwined throughout most of Nicole Brossard's literary career. Her interest in theory dates back, as we know, to her early poetic explorations and initial work at *La Barre du jour* in the late 1960s. Even then, she viewed theory not only as a means of explaining the need for contemporary innovations in formal experimentation, but also as a means of promoting a radically new view of the text's "materiality" and of generating the process of writing itself. From the outset, then, Brossard's emphasis on theorizing about her own writing practice would prepare the way for her subsequent integration of various theoretical discourses within feminism into her women-centred texts. Hence her involvement with and contributions to the literary project of *la modernité* provided Brossard with much of the theoretical grounding needed to contest the authority of traditional literary forms and with a theoretically oriented writing practice that would eventually expand the field of theory itself in her subsequent feminist texts.

Returning now to the 1980s and to *La Lettre aérienne*, it is worth noting that this is not the first time Brossard has published a collection of texts that are indicative of the major phases in her own theoretical development as a writer. In fact, the essays re-presented in *Double impression*,[5] which appeared in 1984, also cover the early years of her poetic reflections on *la modernité*, as well as the subsequent move to feminist theory. But *Double impression* is just that—a double impression of poetry and theory, with the taste for the modern *texte* serving as preamble to a nascent feminine desire for modes of inscription that consciously take female subjectivity into account. On the other hand, theory is preeminent in *La Lettre aérienne*. And yet, like *La Lettre aérienne*, *Double impression* is a text that records both the theoretical basis for Brossard's approach to writing and the emergent voice of a writer-theoretician for whom the word *femme* can no longer be trivialized or neutralized. "Parler femme, c'est d'abord composer son sujet. Tisser une fiction du sujet. Tramer le drame. Faire sa première scène de montage" (67). (To woman-speak means composing her subject first. Weaving a fiction of the subject. Plotting the drama. Creating her first edited scene.)

In the essays that comprise *La Lettre aérienne*, however, the "sujet à composer" or subject-to-be-composed is thoroughly conceived relatively early on and the theoretical drama eventually moves well beyond "une première scène de montage" or initial scene such as the one Brossard repeatedly played out in "la scène blanche" of *Picture Theory*,[6] which appeared in 1982. While Brossard underscores her preoccupation with the construction of a "female subjectivity traversed by a feminist consciousness," many of the essays assembled in *La Lettre aérienne* also push us further still, beyond the construction of the female subject per se and toward the trajectory or elevating movement of the female subject in a space theoretically conceived and poetically fashioned as her own creative territory. The word "space" is appropriate here because, as I argue elsewhere, "The space of women's creativity and spatial configurations have assumed important poetic and theoretical functions in Brossard's writing from *le centre blanc* of her early poetry to the whirling spirals in *Amantes*[7] and *Le Sens apparent*[8] and finally to the wonder of the hologram in *Picture Theory*"[9] and the expanse of the horizon in *Le Désert mauve*. As the aerial movement evoked in the text's central essay and in its title—*La Lettre aérienne*—suggests, the space in which the woman writer explores and delivers her own letter-text is symbolically significant—in theory and in reality. For Brossard, the image of the air-born letter also conveys the need to make fundamental connections by establishing an overview of her experience and her world from space, from an uprooted and free-floating position; it promotes the notion of a global vision of body-text and skin, of history and gyn/ecological memory, of theory and the fictions it engenders. Finally, the aerial letter rises above conventional, one-way sense in order to make sense of *les sens* and place *le sens* in perpetual movement. Like the hologram in *Picture Theory*, the aerial letter is technology in the hands of the female artist:

> La lettre aérienne, c'est le fantasme qui me donne à lire et à écrire en trois dimensions, c'est mon laser. Espace-temps-mobilité dans l'Histoire avec cette vision qui permet de voir l'Histoire à même sa peau, de manière à pouvoir distinguer les moments où nous en sortons, ceux où il nous est nécessaire de la réintégrer, si possible pour en changer le cours. Sortir de sa peau veut dire alors *partir* pour s'acheminer lentement et difficilement vers d'autres fictions, vers ce qui se calibre théoriquement. (65-66)

> (The aerial letter is the fantasy which permits me to read and write in three dimensions; it is my laser. Space-time-mobility in History with this vision equipped for seeing History right down to the skin, in a manner that lets us distinguish those moments where we step out of it, moments where it is essential that, where possible, we reintegrate it, to change the course of it. To take leave of one's skin also means *to depart*, to make one's way slowly and with difficulty toward other fictions, toward that which in theory calibrates [Wildeman, 86].)

Yet despite this appeal to thoroughly contemporary and futuristic imagery, theory in *La Lettre aérienne* does not rely on a grid or on other elements attributable to advanced engineering. It is neither scientific nor reductionist in its presentation. On the contrary, and as the collected essays over the past decade demonstrate, the ascending, expanding space of Brossard's theoretical writing has nurtured her poetically and has also served as a springboard for political intervention in the realm of the real as a *woman who loves women* and as a writer in search of new ways to inscribe this amorous fact. A theoretician both of women's experimental writing and of lesbian inscription, Brossard insists on combining intellect, emotion, and sexual desire at all levels of her own theoretical discourse. In so doing, she refuses the canonical distinctions that have historically separated and hierarchized these same aspects of the writing subject and the writing process. The result in Brossard's text has therefore been a conscious tempering of history, reason, and so-called "knowledge" with the sensorial, the sexual, and the imaginary. As Brossard herself remarks, "Si la question du texte tourne autour du savoir, la question de l'écriture, quant à elle, tourne autour de l'énergie comme une continuité spatio-temporelle dans laquelle il faut nous immiscer avec toute l'attention combinée des sens et du cerveau, rythmiques" (63). ("If the question of text revolves around knowledge, the question of writing revolves around energy, like a spatio-temporal zone we must work our way into, be attendant to with brain and senses combined, rhythmic" [Wildeman, 84].)

For the reader already versed in contemporary critical discourse and in the critical jargon that usually accompanies it, Brossard's essays highlight the inherent deficiencies of more conventional theoretical writings that repeatedly privilege a removed rationality over the body's lived experience. While intellectual theorizing is unquestionably rigorous in *La Lettre aérienne*, the rigor itself is, nevertheless, of a different nature. Her theorizing here does not forget her own female body or the structures of the feminine imaginary; rather, it moves outward from them, always citing them as the origin of creative movement and invention, returning to them for inspiration, analyzing and theorizing their power, their resources. Thus, she celebrates a change in the angle of vision of "theorizing in the feminine," from modernity's abstract thinking about *the* body to her own female body "thinking at the speed of light"—to use her image. In an effort to assume her lesbian identity through writing, skin, vitality, and reasoning are thus unavoidably intertwined—as are fiction and theory. Brossard has, in fact, placed selected brief passages from her poetic and fictional works at the end of each essay to underscore the close links between the evolution of her theoretical writings and her other texts.

Along with the necessity for personal inscription, Brossard privileges the status of the lesbian writer in a number of essays in *La Lettre aérienne* because of the lesbian's courageous divergence and conscious revolt from the heterosexual norm and because, as Brossard herself affirms, "the lesbian makes patriarchal dogma invalid" (Wildeman, 122). But like Louky Bersianik, Brossard also constructs a liberating image of lesbian creativity by emphasizing the lesbian's role as a political "instigator" and artistic "explorer"—capable of working from the political and artistic margins with a heightened sense of purpose and emotional intensity. "The lesbian," affirms Brossard, "is a mental energy which gives breath and meaning to the most positive of images a woman can have of herself" (121). The politics of sexual preference and a women-identified culture are thus underscored and accorded explicit value in Brossard's literary theorizing, while at the same time the magnetic and homogenizing force of heterosexual, male-identified culture is continually assailed.

In her insightful introduction to the English translation, *The Aerial Letter*, Louise Forsyth points out that "The theoretical texts of Brossard are not detached intellectual exercises seeking to reveal unchanging truths. They claim no authoritative status. They assume the relativity of having been written in the fullness of personal experience. They call out to the fullness of other lucid subjects. They insist on the central importance of sensation, pleasure, anger and desire felt intensely and immediately."[10] The essays found in *La Lettre aérienne* help us re-envision what theory could become for women who seek an integrative approach to feminist politics, aesthetics, and literary production. Rather than lament this intentional textual criss-crossing of the theoretical, the personal-corporeal, and the political, as Quebec critic Louise Milot and others have sometimes done in the name of an unmixed, unsullied *texte*,[11] we should view this expansive and constantly shifting metaphorical space as a welcome admission that theory—whether feminist or not and whether consciously or not—is always tied to the larger picture; moreover, we should not be surprised when the very language of theory sets out to emphasize this point.

In the final pages of *La Lettre aérienne*, the focus on the contours and territory of women's writing shifts to a series of reflections on the space of *reading in the feminine*—a revelatory space of intimate encounter and openness for the woman who reads another woman's text. Brossard's female reader is a cultural interpreter, a translator of the original text who, like the young narrator Maude Laures in her most recent novel, *Le Désert mauve*,[12] affirms the importance of women's interpretive role in art and in all aspects of life. She is, in fact, a crucial mediator between the word as sign and the world, between forms of feminine inscription that address women's experiences and a culture that would deny them in the most violent fashion:

> Les mots que nous remarquons s'appliquent à nous et nous remplissent d'inquiétude et de plaisir. Ces mots sont révélations, énigmes et adresses. Nous les transformons selon une méthode d'approche qui échappe à notre conscience et pourtant notre

conscience s'en trouve éclairée. Lectrices, nous devenons l'allusion et la tendance d'un texte. (153)

(The words we notice speak to us and they fill us with unrest and pleasure. These words are revelations, enigmas, address. We transform them by an unconscious method, yet our consciousness finds itself enlightened by the process. Women reading, we become the allusion and the tone of a text.) [156]

This poetic staging of the woman reader in her recent texts corresponds to Brossard's increased interest in the act of reading as an important site of self-affirmation and creative expression for women. No doubt she has also learned that feminist writers need to promote the construction of a female reading subject who is an active and inventive ally. For the lesson of *Le Désert mauve* suggests that without the reader, Maude Laures, the text of Laure Angstelle might easily remain undiscovered—and unconfronted. Brossard's recent emphasis on the female reader and on the aesthetics of feminist reception explains, perhaps, the increased "readability" of *Le Désert mauve* itself. Moreover, the concluding essay in *La Lettre aérienne* underscores the significance of the woman reader as the emerging source of Brossard's poetic vision and ongoing theoretical project. "Toute lecture," she tells us, "est une intention d'images, une intention de spectacle qui nous donne espoir" (154). ("All reading, every reading, is a desire for image, an intention to re/present, which gives us hope" [157].)

While the essays France Théoret presents in *Entre raison et déraison* echo Brossard's interest in theorizing the contours of feminine inscription, they also counterbalance and complement Brossard's project with somewhat different concerns. However, Théoret's analysis of the initial appearance and *raison d'être* of *l'écriture au féminin* in Quebec clearly parallels Brossard's own perceptions of this important literary event. Both explain the emergence of various attempts to write in the feminine as a response to the erasure of social, historical, individual, and gender-specific forms of inscription in the experimental writings of *la modernité*. And both emphasize the role of language as a strategic place of identity-formation and exploration for women. As Théoret notes,

La prise de conscience des femmes en tant que femmes a fait chercher une inscription dans le langage. Les écrivaines ont exploré le langage stratégiquement, c'est-à-dire comme peut le faire tout désir différent. . . . Le langage au féminin a ouvert la brèche entre l'énonciation et l'énoncé, brèche fermée dans le formalisme. Le langage au féminin a posé ses problématiques du côté de l'énonciation. (146)

(Women's developing awareness of themselves as women has triggered the search for an inscription in language. Women writers have explored language strategically, that is to say, as a different desire might do. ... Language in the feminine has revealed the gap between the process of enunciation and the word, a gap closed-off in formalism. Language in the feminine has posed its questions in terms of the enunciation.)

In her theoretical reflections on writing, Théoret repeatedly speaks of her "combat with language," viewing this painful struggle at the level of enunciation as the central dynamic in her work. The anxiety that results from efforts to locate words and reshape linguistic patterns to communicate this malaise remains virtually constant in Théoret's theoretical thinking over the past decade, as does her sense of discomfort and restlessness when searching for a language of approximation and protest. Recognizing the gulf that exists between her own internal pulsions and the available structures of coherent thought, Théoret views the affirmation of female subjectivity in language as "une appropriation au sens d'une conquête" (7), ("an appropriation with the feel of a conquest"). "Appropriation" as "conquest" because subjectivity itself belongs to the domain of the father, who guards it like an annexed land, and because, as in any struggle to regain a conquered, colonized domain, this seizure of subjectivity from the hands of men rarely occurs amicably. Re-possession of subjectivity thus constitutes the re-claiming of women's stolen territory.

Although Théoret's theoretical discourse is sometimes rarefied, it can also be extremely down to earth. Unlike Brossard, Théoret frequently places herself and her autobiographical past at the centre of her own theoretical investigations. She speaks, for example, of her family, youth, and personal struggles with writing and teaching, and reviews her own naiveté and periodic disillusionment as a writer with some anguish. Ironically, even though she continually reminds us of how difficult it has been to assume her own subjectivity in language and say "je," the first person pronoun is highly visible in her own theoretical writing. But the "je" in these essays is often an unstable construction continually battling for a place from which to speak. Even in her most recent essays, the fear of self-contradiction and negative judgment remains strong, "il n'y a pas meilleure que moi pour connaître d'avance ce qu'on peut m'objecter lorsque je suis en train de réfléchir" (26). (No one knows better than I do what people could object to while I'm thinking things through.)

167

If Brossard's recent theorizing calls attention to the intense concentration that inhabits her political commitment to, and amorous desire for, a visibly women-centred writing practice, the act of concentration is itself problematized in Théoret's theoretical discussions as a difficulty that is grounded in personal, cultural, class, and gender considerations. The same can also be said of the act of reading in Théoret's text: "Dans mon enfance, lorsqu'on me surprenait lisant en cachette, on disait que je tirais du grand. Lire était une activité empruntée, distante du milieu auquel j'appartenais. Au Québec, être une lectrice, c'était se prendre pour quelqu'un d'autre" (12). (As a child, when they found me secretly reading, they said I was trying to be a big shot. In Quebec, to be a female reader was to pretend to be someone else.) How, then, does the young female reader come to the text on her own terms, and the woman writer come to her writing, when they have already learned to occupy that space in the guise of another?—as a rich girl rather than a poor one, as a man rather than a woman? This is a problem feminist critics in the United States such as Judith Fetterley, Elaine Showalter, Annette Kolodny, and Nancy Miller have already addressed from various stances and at great length. Théoret continues to fight against this erasure of the female subject in the act of reading and writing even in her most recent essays.

In *Entre raison et déraison* (*Between Reason and Unreason*), the theoretical space Théoret carves out is that of the interval—the dis-connected point, the space of the in-between. By insisting on this state of in-between-ness, she necessarily calls attention to *where* the female self is located in the communal setting and in culture, since it is culture that determines what reason is as well as what positions are *reason*able and who is most capable of reasoning well. This interspace appears to function as an escape hatch for Théoret, furnishing an exit out of the weight of conventional reason and correctness, while also making it possible to avoid the dreaded plunge into madness. For in madness, the woman writer's revolt cannot be consciously directed. Théoret does not want to relinquish control altogether nor is she interested in romanticizing the revolt of madness—the way Breton and other male "visionaries" have done, and so often, as we know, at the expense of a woman. In *Entre raison et déraison*, women's writing is described as a site of self-exploration and self-knowledge that necessarily approaches the realm of reason, even as it resists conforming to its codes and to its implicit hierarchizing of certain experiences over others.

> Entre raison et déraison, il n'y a qu'un pas. Le sens commun fluctuant selon les variables de l'époque marque le coup rapidement.... Écrire, pour une femme, c'est toucher la raison. Il arrive que l'interstice entre rationalité et irrationalité fasse l'objet de

longues méditations, voire d'errances, qu'il vaut alors mieux mettre radicalement à distance dans le language, pour échapper à la fiévreuse répétition, à la maladie ordinaire qui livre au Tout. Dans chaque processus psychique, il y a matière à connaissance. (35-6)

(Between reason and unreason there is only a step. Common sense fluctuating according to the variables of the period marks time swiftly. To write, for a woman, is to approach reason. It can also happen that the interstice between rationality and irrationality gives rise to long meditations, even wanderings, which must then be radically re-positioned in langage, in order to escape feverish repetition and the daily sickness to which one submits. In every psychic process there is material for self-knowledge.)

As far as Théoret is concerned, the space in between reason and "unreason," between the rational and the irrational, and between correctness and un-reasonableness, has long been women's cultural territory. The implications of this rootless and estranged middle ground are certainly not without interest for many of the literary practices commonly associated with "writing in the feminine" in Quebec. For the act of writing often appears to heighten the woman writer's awareness of her own condition of psychic limbo, as Théoret in fact acknowledges: "Écrire un roman quand on est femme, c'est aller vers la pensée, pour mieux l'oublier au fur et à mesure de l'écriture, c'est-à-dire pour être dans l'enjeu verbal" (24). (Writing a novel when you are a woman is like approaching thought itself—if only to forget it again during the process of writing, which is to be in the play of language.)

The nostalgia for unity so in keeping with much postmodern writing also traverses Théoret's text, although it too has been given a decidedly feminine cast. It is perhaps best exemplified in the series of essays that deal with what Théoret calls "la turbulence intérieure," an interior disturbance resulting from ongoing conflict among the internalized voices of cultural authority and the emerging sounds of individual resistance:

La turbulence intérieure, pour être précise, je ne sais pas s'il s'agit d'une manière d'être au monde typiquement femme, je sais que j'ai connu cette turbulence et que je l'ai aperçue chez d'autres femmes. Je sais aussi que toutes les femmes ne connaissent pas cette turbulence. Ce que j'appelle la turbulence intérieure, c'est un envahissement psychique par des contraintes extérieures réelles et/ou imaginaires intériorisées par le moi qui devient incapable d'agir. . . . Beaucoup plus que d'un monologue intérieur, il faudrait parler d'un dialogue au moment où se produit le malaise. La voix est puissante, répétitive, sans qu'on puisse repérer le phénomène de la répétition, elle est envahissante. (49-50)

(Interior turbulence, to be precise, I don't know whether it's a mode of being in the world that is typical to women or not, I know that I have experienced this disturbance and that I have observed it in other women. But I also know that all women do not experience this inner turbulence. What I call interior turbulence is a psychic invasion by exterior constraints—real and/or imaginary—which are interiorized by a self that becomes incapable of acting. Much more than an interior monologue, it should be viewed as a dialogue at the point at which uneasiness occurs. The voice is forceful, repetitive, without our being able to locate the phenomenon of repetition, it is invading.)

Théoret goes on to say that the interior disturbance some women experience may also be viewed as a form of resistance that occurs when the female self attempts to think independently.

In her focus on the existence of interior voices struggling to become vocalized, Théoret approaches both the archaeological writing of another Québécoise writer-theoretician, Madeleine Gagnon, and Julia Kristeva's interest in a pre-linguistic, feminized space. Théoret uses theory to mediate between the as-yet-unspoken or unspeakable and the fully vocalized. At the same time, however, her analysis relies on the credibility of the experiential, since, as she freely admits, *la turbulence intérieure* cannot be satisfactorily represented in writing because it is essentially a pre-verbal phenomenon. In Théoret's theory and in her fictional and poetic works as well, the univocal subject is unlocatable precisely because it is not experientially lived and therefore no longer imaginable in language. Thus, while she does express some sense of loss over the disappearance of a unified writing subject, Théoret has come to accept this fragmented, plurivocal state of female selfhood and of her own subjectivity in writing as unavoidable—at least for the time being.

Théoret's assessment of the difficulties of inscribing the lived experience of the female subject in language as evoked in the space of the in-between is a far cry, to be sure, from the air-born female subjectivity *imaged* and imagined in Brossard's *Lettre aérienne*. But if Théoret is unable to embrace without hesitation Brossard's utopian view of female subjectivity and feminist literary inscription, and if she continues to argue that the new female writing subject cannot as yet be re-constituted as "whole," she nevertheless concurs with Brossard that constructive strategies for female self-inscription are needed if women are ever to succeed in displacing the male symbolic system. In so doing, she too is calling on women to extend the meaning of knowledge beyond the constraints of paternal *reason* and beyond the conventions of tradition-bound thinking. Although considerably more cautious in her metaphorical constructions and in her relation to the discourse of theory in general, Théoret is, in the end, also involved in a rehabilitative cultural rereading of the female writing subject and, ultimately, of writing itself: "We must take the risk of constructing a new speaking subject," affirms Théoret, "which can retain through memory the knowledge that fragmentation is everywhere, that there is no centre, and nevertheless survive" (96).

Notes

1. Quoted by Nicole Brossard in "Mais voici venir la fiction ou l'épreuve au féminin," *La Nouvelle Barre du jour* 90-91 (May 1980), 65.
2. In addition to the two texts discussed in this essay, see for example: Nicole Brossard *et al.*, *La Théorie, un dimanche* (Montréal: Remue-ménage 1988); Madeleine Gagnon, *Toute écriture est amour: Autographie 2* (Montréal: VLB Éditeur 1989); Shirley Neuman and Smaro Kamboureli, eds., *A Mazing Space: Writing Canadian Women Writing* (Edmonton: Longspoon/NeWest Press 1986); Gail Scott's *Spaces Like Stairs* (Toronto: The Women's Press 1989); and the special issue on "Le Forum des Femmes" in *La Nouvelle Barre du jour* 172 (March 1986).
3. Nicole Brossard, *La Lettre aérienne* (Montréal: Remue-ménage 1985). References to this work will parenthetically in the text. There is an English translation: *The Aerial Letter*, translated by Marlene Wildeman (Toronto: The Women's Press 1988).
4. France Théoret, *Entre raison et déraison* (Montréal: Les Herbes Rouges 1987). References to this work will appear parenthetically in the text.
5. Nicole Brossard, *Double impression* (Montréal: L'Hexagone 1984).
6. Nicole Brossard, *Picture Theory* (Montréal: Nouvelle Optique 1985).
7. Nicole Brossard, *Amantes* (Montréal: Les Quinze 1980).
8. Nicole Brossard, *Le Sens apparent* (Paris: Flammarion 1980).
9. See Karen Gould, *Writing in the Feminine: Feminism and Experimental Writing in Quebec*. (Carbondale, Illinois: Southern Illinois University Press 1990), 94.
10. Louise H. Forsyth, "Errant and Air-born in the City," in Brossard's *The Aerial Letter*, 15.
11. See Louise Milot's critique of Brossard's politicizing of *la modernité* in "Nicole Brossard: Une influence coûteuse," in *Modernité/Postmodernité du roman contemporain. Cahiers du département d'études littéraires*, no. 11. Edited by Madeleine Frédéric and Jacques Allard (Montréal: Université du Québec à Montréal 1987), 77-86.
12. Nicole Brossard, *Le Désert mauve* (Montréal: L'Hexagone 1987).

R. Alex Kizuk

Wrestling with the Angel: Political Continuities in Canadian Poetry in the Times of Carman, Smith, Layton, and Davey

Abstract

The paper suggests that at least since the 1890s (when Bliss Carman began importing to America attitudes of the Yellow Book school of the English Aesthetes), poetry in Canada has been an expression of competing would-be orthodoxies masquerading as avant-gardes. I discuss this long-standing struggle as a problematic of political interest in Canadian poetry. I argue that such Canadian poets as Carman, A.J.M. Smith, John Sutherland, Louis Dudek, Irving Layton, James Reaney, and, most recently, George Bowering and Frank Davey, wrestling with their often inherently equivocated activism, have created a condition of perpetual unrest and upheaval in Canadian literature.

Résumé

L'auteur suggère qu'à partir des années 1890 (alors que Bliss Carman commençait d'importer en Amérique les manières de penser de l'école des esthètes anglais), la poésie au Canada a été l'expression d'orthodoxies rivales se faisant passer pour des avant-gardes. Il considère ces querelles de vieille date comme une problématique d'ordre politique. Il soutient que des poètes canadiens tels Carman, A.J.M. Smith, John Sutherland, Louis Dudek, Irving Layton, James Reaney et, plus récemment, George Bowering et Frank Davey, luttant avec leurs tendances à un activisme ambigu, ont créé dans la littérature canadienne un état d'agitation perpétuelle et de malaise incessant.

In Canadian literature today, as Frank Davey has recently said, we "construct value in differing and historically understandable ways." "What is worthwhile" is a question of "textual production of particular ideological positions—positions which envisage or assume specific epistemologies, forms of social organization, regional relationships, institutional structures, and political practices" (1988, 7). This strategic positioning of political interest leaves its mark on art and culture to the extent that various interests compete for dominance even within a single poem. Thus, in this sense of literary value as determined by interest, poems worth writing and reading are multivalent. Interests such as youth and newness for their own sakes, self-unction, passion, and the Prince of Wales, or the interests of such institutions as the academy, criticism, publishing, and the media, individually or in combination, particularize Canadian poems. This particularity also reifies ideological positions inherent in style and technique. In reading any literary text, conservative or avant-garde, one should, on this line of argument, be aware of the various interests that percolate through manifest allegiances to society and temporal continuity or the high world of art and myth. In this paper, however, I want to suggest that this problematic may not so much reflect contemporary literary political awareness as it does a long-standing historical struggle between Canadian literary avant-gardes and their often shadowy adversaries. At least since the 1890s (when Bliss Carman began importing to America attitudes of the *Yellow Book* school of the English Aesthetes), poetry in Canada has been an expression of competing would-be orthodoxies masquerading as avant-gardes.

The avant-garde as a literary term usually connotes a small group of like-minded writers who regard themselves as a visionary elite locked in heroic struggle with the past and an indifferent present. Often, though not always, such groups are made up of young men and women ("Young Turks") who share a perception of each other's writing as no less than a spiritual liberation. It is economical to present this aspect of the avant-garde in Canadian poetry by contrasting two poets writing nearly a century apart on fellow freedom-fighters in verse. In 1891, thirty-year-old Archibald Lampman described the effect that Sir Charles G.D. Roberts' *Orion and Other Poems* (1880) had had upon him as an undergraduate at college:

> Like most of the young fellows about me I had been under the depressing conviction that we were situated hopelessly on the outskirts of civilization . . . and that it was useless to expect that anything great could be done by any of our companions, still more useless to expect that we could do it ourselves. I sat up all night reading and re-reading *Orion* in a state of wildest excitement. . . . It seemed to me a wonderful thing that such work could be done by a Canadian, by a young man, one of ourselves.

Lampman goes on to say that "It was like a voice from some new paradise of art calling to us to be up and doing . . . everything was transfigured for me," so that radiance, beauty, and magic were reclaimed from the local and the here and now (Daymond & Monkman 1984, I:137). Nearly a century later, George Bowering, at twenty-nine, speaks similarly about Frank Davey's "influence on our art" (Davey 1974, 89). Without Lampman's affective language but with a certain philosophical affectation, Bowering strikes the same chords of camaraderie and visionary liberation. For Bowering, reading Davey is an experience of "entering"—"one enters & on entering discovers a person wholly confessed" (86). Having entered, the reader "discovers" a wholeness or plenitude of self, by which Bowering means "not a thing but process," requiring "not the pulse of the soul, but the flight of spirit" (87).

One does not, however, properly speak of continuities when dealing with a series of literary avant-gardes. Avant-gardes typically make a clean break with the past, including past avant-gardes. "Indeed," as Charles Russell puts it in his recent history of the literary avant-garde from Rimbaud to postmodernism, "since total liberation and transformation can only be achieved in the future, the present moment can only be suffered as a personal sacrifice" (1985, 37-8). This sacramental and precipitous aspect has profound consequences for Canadian poetry. This is so because the brief history of our literature has been shaped by no less than six successive generations of literary shock troops living the literary life on the edge of the abyss since the time of Bliss Carman.

As odd as it may seem today, accustomed as we are to regarding him as a late-Victorian cross between Poe and Browning, Bliss Carman's poetry does satisfy Richard Kostelanetz' three discriminatory criteria of avant-garde art (1982, 3). As an undergraduate in 1887, Carman allied himself with anti-materialist interests, combatting "the growing trend of standardization in art," which he feared would subordinate art to business interests in literary circles (Miller 1985, 45-6). His *Songs of the Sea Children* (1904) and *Sappho: One Hundred Lyrics* (1904), moreover, transcend turn-of-the-century poetic conventions of decorum and taste regarding poetical representations of sexuality.[1] No one else had been so bold outside of Oscar Wilde and a few others of the notorious *Yellow Book* school of writers in London. Hence it should not be surprising that John Lane of The Bodley Head, publisher for many of the works of this school of English Aesthetes and Decadents, actively pursued the thirty-one-year-old Carman in 1892 as a potential Bodley Head author (Miller 1985, 78). Though Carman declined, as he felt unready for such a venture, he and Lane's literary reader Richard Le Gallienne made the New York society pages five years later by attending the opera together in shockingly Bohemian livery (160). Carman's social life, which later included such people as Isadora Duncan (225), his self-consciously avant-garde literary editorship of the little magazines *Current Literature* and *The Chapbook*, his Delsarteanism and his feminism, and his anti-middle class, all-for-the-here-and-now, open-road lyricism, combined to make Carman a significant avant-garde figure in England and America from the 1890s to World War I.

Kostelanetz's second criteria is that the public remains indifferent toward avant-gardes for a considerable time before their influence begins to be felt. Canadian readers certainly did not catch up with Carman until the early 1920s, when his best and boldest work was long done. Indeed, it took a media-blitz sparked by near-fatal tuberculosis in 1919 to awaken the reading public to Carman's significance in North American art and culture (Miller 1985, 235-44). The third criteria is that avant-gardes inspire creative work of successive generations, and this is true of such Canadian poets as Ernest Fewster, Arthur Stringer, F.O. Call, Arthur Bourinot, and several others. Al Purdy paid tribute to Carman in his early books *The Enchanted Echo* (1944) and *Pressed on Sand* (1955), and has recently discussed Carman's lyricism as a "remote counterpoint" to his own poetic voice.[2] Carman's verse elevated a *fin-de-siècle* anti-materialism, shaped and coloured by a youthful, sensuous Vagabondianism, to the status of a definition of what makes a poem worth making, reading, and writing about. This concept of poetry as and only as avant-garde expression reappears particularly strongly in the works of poets like Arthur Stringer. Forty years old when Carman was in his mid-fifties, Stringer wrote a manifesto for Canadian avant-garde poetry in 1914, the "Foreword" to his *Open Water*, one of the first books of modern free verse in Canadian literature.

Stringer is all but forgotten as an early twentieth-century poet and novelist, yet his "Foreword" is often cited in discussions of the beginnings of modernism in Canadian poetry. He became a literary star at the age of twenty-nine on publication of his first novel *The Silver Poppy* (1903). He married the original Gibson girl, Jobyna Howland, and after much more writing, a divorce, time spent on a ranch in Alberta and in Hollywood on his series "The Perils of Pauline," he married again and settled down as a writer and fruit farmer in upstate New York. His poetic career spans a dozen books from the turn of the century to the 1940s. A true son of Carman, the English Aesthetes and the French Decadents, his "Foreword" blasts conservatism in poetry. *Open Water* itself abandons metrics for a verse of sensuous, vernacular speech, and the "Foreword" scorns any technical formalism that forces on the poet "an instinctive abhorrence for anything beyond the control of what he calls common sense" (Stringer 1974). Poetry must return to the "more open movement of the chant, which is man's most natural and rudimentary form of song."

F.O. Call struck another avant-garde blow for poetic experimentation and primitivism six years later in his "Foreword" to *Acanthus and Wild Grape* (1920). Like Stringer, Call champions *vers libre* by way of a rhetorical storm of militaristic metaphors (Call 1974). Call, however, demanded wholesale change in how poets perceive the world, whereas Stringer was more concerned with self-discovery and the expression of strong, private emotion. For Call, forty-two in 1920, modernism was a means of reconciling emotion to thought. Stringer's foreword somewhat resembles Pound's more famous *Blast*, and shares with the writings of later poets like Raymond Souster, Dennis Lee, and Frank Davey a deep concern for open forms and the vernacular voice in poetry. Call's foreword recalls that metaphysical fusion of thought and feeling that so intrigued Eliot and the New Critics, and Canadian poets like A.J.M. Smith, F.R. Scott, and A.M. Klein, the leaders of the next avant-garde movement in Canadian poetry.

Call later turned away from his rebellious manifesto to become a highly conservative writer of visionary, self-consciously regional sonnet sequences and a professor of history at Bishop's University in the Eastern Townships. Stringer, too, rejected his avant-garde stance and returned to metrical prosody. Even in *Open Water*, Stringer admitted that he had been too long in the dungeons of song, that "after my moment of light," he must "go back to the Dark,/ Since the Open still makes me afraid" ("The Revolt," 94-96). Poetry is but "a note in the chorus . . . a wave on the deep," an "eternal failure" ("The Echo," 101-02). Twenty years later, Stringer declared that "Time teaches us that this shifted fetter known as Freedom is not always the final solution of the artist's problem" (Lauriston 1948, 262).

Carman, Stringer, and Call were unable to bear the thrust of Canadian literary activism past their middle years. The same is true of A.J.M. Smith and John Sutherland, representative figures of the next two avant-gardes in Canadian poetry. Each of these innovative and influential poets eventually took up positions behind the front lines.

True, the self-consciously militaristic bombast of the two 1920s avant-garde forewords is born again in the literary political rivalries of Canadian "little magazines" during and between the two World Wars. And Smith and Sutherland were the most visible of those editors, the most successful in acquiring an audience. By observing the practices of modernist avant-gardes abroad, they had learned that control over their own periodicals was politically necessary "to publish proclamations and programs or a series of manifestos, announcing the foundation of a new movement." They also adopted the antagonism toward the public and tradition, "the most noticeable and showy avant-garde posture" of the modernist *milieu artiste* (Poggioli 1968, 21, 31). Yet for all their modernist activism, for all the agitation and controversy over the issues of cosmopolitanism and local pride in Canadian poetry, they each came to represent what Smith in 1961 called "an easily isolable phenomenon: the quick and almost forced development of a compact and self-contained literary tradition," an "orthodoxy" that editors and critics like themselves must support (8-9).

After his conversion to Roman Catholicism, Sutherland wrote an entirely sympathetic book of criticism on E.J. Pratt, probably the most conservative of Canadian poets, praising those stable Prattian "virtues—courage, loyalty, steadfastness, and self-sacrifice" (1956, 10). W.E. Collin wrote in 1982 that Smith's mid-century compromises in critical stance reflect his "progress out of a fractured world into a world of unified sensibility such as T.S. Eliot would endorse." Waxing eloquent, Collin pictures Smith in his last moments as "a Knight with his sword drawn, seasoned in war between flesh and spirit, fortified in the faith that he is the absolute, ideal figure of Christian man" (97).[3]

Canadian literature is now perhaps indelibly marked by its growth and development as a series of avant-gardes willing to risk all for the sake of power and influence in literary circles while still young enough to enjoy it. The controversies of our literary movements have always been secondary to the desire to effect if not control the reading tastes of a generation. Victorian or Georgian other worlds, modernist technical experimentation, mid-century mythopoesis, the contemporary interest in linguistic structure —none of these issues have proved terribly durable. All are but sacrificial lambs hoisted high above the gulfs of whatever conservatism and complacency can have been established in the ten or fifteen years since the last Canadian literary revolution. In such a situation, it is not surprising that Irving Layton in 1977 chose to pin his hopes on laughter, thirty years after Sutherland's *Other Canadians* (1947) presented him, Souster, and Dudek as an alternative to the Smith, Scott, and Klein of *New Provinces* (1936). Layton wrote that though poets confront "the moment of significant change when old values and institutions are crumbling into hypocrisy and cowardice . . . nothing finally endures except truth, and laughter is mankind's best purgative. It remains my best hope" (1977, xiv-xv).

Bliss Carman's vision, A.J.M. Smith's technique, James Reaney's mythopoesis, none of these achievements *repeat* in Canadian literature. We do not speak of a Carman or a Smith tradition in the same way that Americans, for instance, speak of a Whitman and a Pound tradition. I submit that one reason for this may be that Canadian avant-gardes have been too successful in fixing the reader's attention on idealizations of what

Canadian poetry can or will be in the future. Davey's first editorial of the present-day avant-garde periodical *Open Letter*, for example, launched its exploration of language in these prophetic tones: "Fifteen hundred years finds the total magic of the English language still untapped. . . . the written sign is always open, always unexplored. THE OPEN LETTER begins its explorations" (Daymond & Monkman 1984, II:494). A sense of tradition is simply impossible in this condition of precipitousness and sacrementality that generations of highly effective literary politicking have made chronic in our literature. Furthermore, the essential violence of this aspect of the avant-garde can be gleaned from a letter of Smith's to Raymond Knister in 1927. Here, Smith, twenty-five years old, outlines the plan of his campaign:

> Critical standards must be thoroughly overhauled and some counter irritant provided to offset the traditional gentility of journals like *The Canadian Bookman* and *The Canadian Magazine* which are vitiating public taste and distorting literary values. I think Canada needs a group of writers who will shock her literature out of its present complacency. . . . We've got to do a lot of destroying before we begin to lay the foundation. (Burke 1982, 122)

Poetic achievements may not repeat in Canadian literature, but that "destroying" of the present (and concomitantly any sense of tradition), in which Sir Smith would engage, certainly does.

In an unpublished autobiographical fragment, Sutherland, twenty-three when Smith was in his forties, explains why he quoted Nietzsche on the title page of the first *First Statement* in 1942:

> "Ye say it is the good cause which halloweth war; I say unto you, it is the good war which halloweth every cause." By this [Sutherland] meant to imply that the literary disease of Canada was the brotherly love which authors forever spouted over the tea-cups and beer-mugs; the only thing that would put Canadian literature on its feet was a first-class literary war. (Quoted by Fisher 1974, 32-3.)

During the 1940s, controversial avant-garde in-fighting became an end in itself, however. Sutherland attacked the cosmopolitanism of Smith's group, Smith counterattacked, and the well-known "native and cosmopolitan" debate began. As editor of the would-be house organ of an avant-garde self-consciously in opposition to "the McGill movement," Sutherland wanted to expose the neocolonialism of the cosmopolitan school for merely substituting T.S. Eliot for Tennyson or Keats. Ironically, Sutherland's policy is of course open to the same charge, allied as it is to currents in American poetry that produced William Carlos Williams' answer to Eliot's sophisticated wasteland.

Nevertheless, a decade later Smith and Sutherland were easing themselves into conservative editorial positions on *The Oxford Book of Canadian Verse* and *Northern Review* respectively. In 1952, Louis Dudek wrote the first editorial of his own little magazine *Contact*, later as influential as Smith's anthologies and Sutherland's two magazines:

> Poetry in Canada needs a new start. To the young, the field is wide open. Our younger poets are getting grey about the temples. The work of the forties is by now old and yellow: it was a good beginning, but not yet the real thing (Daymond & Monkman 1984, II:394-5).

Thus, the voice of the angry young poet shaking foundations (that never stood firmly for more than a decade at best) passes on from one avant-garde to the next.

By way of concluding, I want to suggest here that this call for "the real thing," that is, poetry as and only as avant-garde expression, has been answered at least twice since *Contact*. Frye's mid-century theory of literary archetypes (recently republished in Richard Kostelanetz' *The Avant-Garde in Literature*), and the poetry and criticism that it immediately influenced, are, I suggest, yet another privileging of the avant-garde initially set in motion as a historical force in Bliss Carman's time. In 1960, James Reaney, thirty-four years old when Dudek was forty-two, launched *Alphabet*, a little magazine meant to challenge the clout of periodicals like *Contact*, whose policy was to accept experimental writing that reflected the American Pound-Williams tradition. Reaney saw his magazine as the mainstay of a regional liberation front, and sought poems for publication that were in his opinion "real poems." Like Carman and Smith before him, Reaney wanted to convince the reading public that "metaphor is reality" and that the time had come to *begin* an exploration of the "powerful inner life" of the "secret alphabet or iconography or language of symbols and myths" (Daymond & Monkman 1984, II:438-9).

True to form in the history of Canadian poetry, the Frye-Reaney avant-garde immediately developed its "counter-irritant" in the poetry and literary politicking of those young Vancouver Vagabonds of the 1960s, Frank Davey, George Bowering, Fred Wah, Lionel Kearns, and others of this school. The house organ of these self-consciously anti-myth, anti-metaphor poets, *Tish,* edited initially by Davey, set out to destroy the trend Frye set in motion by subverting the mandarin dignity of the Frygean literary universe. Their strategy was to deploy the ideas and language of the American Black Mountain poets so that, as Warren Tallman put it in 1961, Allen Ginsberg could say "'Taste my mouth in your ear,' . . . as he tongues a groovey bridge between" (Daymond & Monkman 1984, II:448).

As the *Tish* movement is well-known and meticulously documented, I will only say here that its entirely evangelical concern for the human voice in poetry is in fact a repetition of the stance taken by Stringer in the first decade of the century. Similarly, Davey's distinction between humanist and universist positions in Canadian poetry repeats the tendentiously avant-garde stance (the form if not the content) of Smith's native and cos-mopolitan distinction. In 1975, Davey had decided that the *Tish* poets belonged:

> to the "universist" line of Lampman, Carman, W.W.E. Ross, Klein, Souster, Layton and Purdy, rather than to the humanist and rationalist one of Goldsmith, Sangster, Pratt, Smith, F.R. Scott, Finch, LePan, Reaney, Mandel and Gustafson. . . .

> The universist line is by far the dominant one at the moment in Canadian poetry. Whether this dominance has been partly due to the influence of *Tish* is difficult to determine. (Gervais 1976, 156)

Davey's essay "Louis Dudek and Raymond Souster" makes it clear, how-ever, that in his view the older (non-*Tish*)"universists" failed to relinquish a "belief in the existence of something transcendentally 'true' or natural that acts as a ground or benchmark for all experience." Consequently, for Davey, "their opposition to our society's dominant consumerist ideology is seriously compromised" (Davey 1988, 60-1). Yet in this Davey is apparently unaware of his own compromises, his own mythical thinking. As with the earlier avant-gardes, Davey sacrifices the present moment to the dream of a future "defeat" of bourgeois commoditization and fetishization of poetry and the poetic text.

Canadian avant-gardes tend to transform themselves into orthodoxies as the leaders mature and acquire power in literary and academic circles. Davey, forty-nine, is now Head of the Department of English at York University and one of the finest critical minds in the country. Yet Davey had been dogmatic even in his twenties and thirties, indeed quite as dogmatic as Smith or Frye in their days. Keith Richardson argued in 1976 that Davey's editorship of *Tish* was entirely unyielding toward other, non-Black Mountain points of view (37). In 1978, Jean Mallinson attacked his *From There to Here* (1974) in these words: "This is normative and prescriptive writing, exclusive in its intention and designed to establish a canon of approved writers on the basis not of style but of the 'values' or attitudes which Davey condones" (97). Davey's response to this is instructive: What's wrong with "normative? Is it blameworthy to be 'prescriptive' and 'exclusive'?" (1978, 286).[4] I submit that what's wrong is wanting to be avant-garde while at the same time wanting to be approved and approving. Successive waves of such inherently equivocated activism have created a condition of perpetual unrest and upheaval in the literary culture of this country. This situation implies a society in which individual poetic accomplishments cannot become a bridge to some supreme consolidation of past successes—a society balked this side of the River Jabbok, as it were. The best one might hope for, to take a dim view, would be just one jazzy dead end after another. The Canadian avant-gardes have operated on the false assumption that there are conservative values in place that can or should be dislodged. This is not the case. The avant-gardes have from the start wrestled with their own failed bids for orthodoxy in Canadian writing. But perhaps a more precise analogy for the problematic of political interest in Canadian poetry would be the practise of shadow boxing. In the absence of any real opposition, Canadian avant-garde poetry wins bout after bout with the shadows on the wall.

Notes

1. Many commentators note Carman's sensuality, but most often move on to discussions of local colour. Bentley's is the only considerable study of Carman's "fleshly" poetry ("Threefold" but see also "Pan"). The most immediate influence of Carman's liberated attitude toward sex in literature is of course Stringer's verse play *Sappho in Leucadia* (1907).
2. I have explored this topic in a paper presented in the 1989 Ottawa Bliss Carman Symposium. My remarks here bear closely upon the other papers in the symposium, including Purdy's.
3. Smith and Sutherland eventually formed a kind of intellectual coalition, as Smith records in "Confessions of a Compulsive Anthologist," (1977) having recognized finally that they were really after the same thing all along: the side of power, that is, influence over the reader's perception of what makes a poem worthwhile.
4. Davey has become dogmatically non-dogmatic in recent theoretical writings. An important lecture delivered at the University of Alberta in 1987, "Reading Canadian Reading," insists that "Critical theory should be recognized as inevitably a field of conflict—a field in which two of the greatest dangers are illusions of harmony and the attainment of hegemony by any one of the contestants" (Davey 1988, 17). Surely, this attitude is the only way Jacob can appease Esau: a wholesale and timely investigation of the interests that poems serve in our society.

Works Cited

Bentley, D.M.R. (1979) "Pan and the Confederation Poets." *Canadian Literature*, 81, 59-71.

———— (1985) "Threefold in Wonder: Bliss Carman's *Sappho: One Hundred Lyrics*." *Canadian Poetry*, 17, 29-58.

Burke, Anne (ed. 1982) "Some Annotated Letters of A.J.M. Smith and Raymond Knister." *Canadian Poetry*, 11, 98-135.

Call, Frank Oliver. (1974) "Foreword to *Acanthus and Wild Grape*." In Dudek & Gnarowski (1974), 21-3.

Collin. W.E. (1982) "A Few Pages in the History of Canadian Literature." *Canadian Poetry*, 11, 93-7.

Davey, Frank (1974) *From There to Here: A Guide to English-Canadian Literature Since 1960*. Erin, Ont.: Press Porcepic.

———— (1978) "A Response to Jean Mallinson's 'Poetry and Ideology'." *Studies in Canadian Literature*, 3, 286-7.

———— (1988) *Reading Canadian Reading*. Winnipeg: Turnstone.

Daymond, Douglas M. and Leslie G. Monkman (eds. 1984) *Towards a Canadian Literature: Essays, Editorials and Manifestos*. Vols. 1, 1752-1940 and 2, 1940-1983. Ottawa: Techumseh Press.

Dudek, Louis and Michael Gnarowski (eds. 1974) *The Making of Modern Poetry in Canada: Essential Articles on Contemporary Canadian Poetry in English*. Toronto: Ryerson.

Fisher, Neil H. (1974) *First Statement 1942-1945: An Assessment and An Index*. Ottawa: Golden Dog Press.

Gervais, C.H. (1976) *The Writing Life: Historical & Critical Views of the Tish-Movement*. Coatsworth, Ont.: Black Moss Press.

Gundy, H. Pearson, (ed. 1981) *Letters of Bliss Carman*. Kingston and Montreal: McGill-Queen's University Press.

Knister, Raymond (1976) "Canadian Letter." In *The First Day of Spring: Stories and Other Prose*. Edited by Peter Stevens. Toronto: Toronto University Press.

Kostelanetz, Richard (1982) "Introduction: What is Avant-Garde?" In *The Avant-Garde Tradition in Literature*. Edited by Richard Kostelanetz. Buffalo: Prometheus Books, 3-6.

Lauriston, Victor (1948) "Arthur Stringer." In *Leading Canadian Poets*. Edited by W.P. Percival. Toronto: Ryerson, 255-64.

Layton, Irving (1977) "Foreword." In *The Covenant*. Toronto: McClelland and Stewart, xii-xv.

Mallinson, Jean (1978) "Ideology and Poetry: An Examination of Some Recent Trends in Canadian Criticism." *Studies in Canadian Literature*, 3, 93-109.

Miller, Muriel (1985) *Bliss Carman: Quest and Revolt*. St. John's, Nfld: Jesperson Press.

Poggioli, Renato (1968) *The Theory of the Avant-garde*. Translated by Gerald Fitzgerald. London: Belknap.

Richardson, Keith (1976) *Poetry and the Colonized Mind: Tish*. Ottawa: Mosaic Press.

Russell, Charles (1985) *Poets, Prophets, and Revolutionaries: The Literary Avant-garde from Rimbaud through Postmodernism*. New York: Oxford University Press.

Smith, A.J.M (1961) "Eclectic Detachment: Aspects of Identity in Canadian Poetry." *Canadian Literature*, 9, 6-14.

———— (1977) "The Confessions of a Compulsive Anthologist." In *On Poetry and Poets: Selected Essays*. Toronto: McClelland and Stewart, 106-22.

Stringer, Arthur (1974) "Foreword to *Open Water*." In Dudek & Gnarowski 1974, 5-9.

Sutherland, John (1956) *The Poetry of E.J. Pratt: A New Interpretation*. Toronto: Ryerson.

Notes on the authors

Boris Alekhin was born in the Soviet Union in 1946. He graduated with a BA in economics from Moscow State University in 1971. After three years of postgraduate research at the Institute of the USA and Canada, he finished his first Ph.D in international economics in 1976 and his second Ph.D in 1990. Dr Alekhin is now a senior research fellow at this institute. Dr Alekhin's long standing interest in the Canadian economy and Canada's foreign economic relations has led to articles in professional journals, monographs and contributions to other books. His major publications are *Canada in World Trade* (Moscow: Nauka 1986) and *Canada: Monopolies and Science Policy of the State* (Moscow: Nauka 1982). Dr Alekhin's current research deals with various aspects of Canada's interaction with the world economy.

Karen Gould is Director of Women's Studies and Associate Professor of French at Bowling Green State University in Ohio. She is the author of *Writing in the Feminine: Feminism and Experimental Writing in Quebec* (Southern Illinois University Press 1990), *Claude Simon's Mythic Muse* (Summa 1979), and co-editor of *Orion Blinded: Essays on Claude Simon* (Bucknell University Press 1981). She has published widely on Quebec women writers in journals such as *Voix et images*, *L'Esprit Créateur*, *Signs*, *The French Review*, *Modern Language Studies*, and *The American Review of Canadian Studies*, as well as in edited collections. She is also the editor of *Québec Studies*, an interdisciplinary journal devoted to the study of Quebec society and French Canadian culture.

Hans Hauge was born in 1947. Since 1976 he has been Associate professor of English at the University of Aarhus, Denmark and part-time Research Fellow at the Centre for Cultural Research. He has published books and articles on English, American, and Canadian literature, as well as on philosophy and theology.

Diddy Hitchins is Professor of Political Science and Director of Canadian Studies at the University of Alaska, Anchorage. British born and educated, she has a BA from the University of Southampton, and a MA and Ph.D from the University of Essex. She taught at the University of Ghana, Legon during the early 1970s while studying development and aid programs in

West Africa. After a period focusing on European Community aid, she is now increasingly interested in development in the Asia-Pacific region.

Charles L. Jones is Professor of Sociology at the University of Toronto. He has an honorary appointment at McMaster University. He was educated at Cambridge University, the London School of Economics and Edinburgh University. Previous books include *The Images of Occupational Prestige, Class and Hierarchy* and *Images of Social Stratification*.

R. Alex Kizuk presently holds a Leave-Replacement Assistant Professorship at the University of Western Ontario. The scholarship, criticism, and teaching of Canadian literature constitute his main field of interest. He has published over a dozen articles and two books of poetry, *millions of acres* (Folks Upstairs Press, 1984) and *Microphones* (Brick Books, 1987). His articles on such writers as Margaret Atwood, Robertson Davies, Robert Kroetsch, Dorothy Livesay, A.J.M. Smith, W.W.E. Ross, E.J. Pratt, Marjorie Pickthall, and others have appeared in the refereed Canadian scholarly journals.

Diane Lamoureux, Professor of Political Science at Laval University since 1986, has studied history, political science and sociology. Her work focuses on women's methods of developing individual and collective autonomy. She has had two works published to date: *Fragments et collages, essai sur le féminisme québécois des années 70* and *Citoyennes Femmes, droit de vote et démocratie* (both by Editions du remue-ménage). As well as being on the editorial committee of the journal, *Recherches féministes*, and regularly contributing to the international journal, *Les Cahiers du GRIF*, Ms Lamoureux has also published several articles examining the political stakes of feminism.

Bertil Liander is Professor of International Marketing and also Associate Director of the Institute for North American Trade and Economics at the University of Massachusetts at Amherst. Swedish born, he has a MBA from the Stockholm School of Economics and a Ph.D from the University of Massachusetts. He has lived and worked in Sweden, France, Italy, and the USA.

Lorna R. Marsden is a member of the Senate of Canada and is also Professor of Sociology at the University of Toronto and a fellow of Massey College. She was educated at the University of Toronto and Princeton University. Previous books include *The Fragile Federation: Social Change in Canada*.

186

Jean McNulty is Senior Policy Advisor in the Broadcasting Office, Communications Division, of the Ontario Ministry of Culture and Communications. From 1984 to 1987, she taught mass communications at York University and, before 1984, she was research associate and project coordinator of the Telecommunications Research Group at Simon Fraser University. Her research interests are in communications policy, technology and social change, and communication theory. As well as writing numerous reports and articles on communications policy topics, Jean McNulty has co-authored two books: *The Tangled Net: Basic Issues in Canadian Communications* (1977) and *Mass Communication in Canada* (1987).

Lorne J. Tepperman is Professor of Sociology at the University of Toronto and a fellow of New College. He was educated at the University of Toronto and Harvard University. Previous books include *Social Mobility in Canada* and *Choices and Chance: Sociology for Everyday Life*.

Martin W. Thunert is a member of the Association for Canadian Studies in the German-speaking Countries and a doctoral candidate in Political Science at the University of Augsburg, Germany. He has been a visiting graduate student at the Political Science Departments of Queen's and McGill Universities. He currently works as an academic assistant at the Center for North American Studies and Research, Goethe University, Frankfurt. He is co-author (with R.O.Schultze) of *German Students in Canada: An Empirical Evaluation* (Bochum, FRG 1989) and has written on Canadian politics in German publications. Fields of concentration: Comparative and German Politics, Political Theory.

Roy Turner, Professor of Sociology at the University of British Columbia, has published many articles on sociolinguistics. His current work, employing a hermeneutic perspective, is concerned with the contemporary cultural ambivalence towards history as this is expressed in current discourse on, for example, cultural identity, the place of museums and art galleries in public life, heritage movements, urban revitalization, etc.

José Woehrling, Professor of Law at the University of Montréal since 1971, has published works on constitutional, international, and comparative law.

Notes sur les auteurs

Boris Alekhin est né en Union soviétique en 1946. Il a obtenu un baccalauréat ès arts (économie) de l'Université d'État de Moscou en 1971. Après trois ans de recherche à l'Institut des États-Unis et du Canada, il obtint un premier doctorat, en économie internationale, en 1976, et un second doctorat en 1990. Boris Alekhin est chercheur principal associé du même Institut. Il porte un intérêt de longue date à l'économie et aux relations économiques internationales du Canada. Ses principales publications sont *Le Canada et le commerce international* (en russe), Moscou, Nauka, 1986, et *Canada: monopoles et politique d'État en matière scientifique* (en russe), Moscou, Nauka, 1982. Ses recherches en cours portent sur divers aspects de l'interaction entre le Canada et l'économie mondiale.

Karen Gould est directrice des Études féministes et professeure de français à l'Université d'État Bowling Green en Ohio. Elle est l'auteure de *Writing in the Feminine: Feminism and Experimental Writing in Québec* (Southern Illinois University Press, 1990), *Claude Simon's Mythic Muse* (Summa, 1979), et a aussi publié en collaboration *Orion Binded: Essays on Claude Simon* (Bucknell University Press, 1981). Elle a publié de nombreux articles sur les écrivaines du Québec, notamment dans *Voix et images*, *L'Esprit Créateur*, *Signs*, *The French Review*, *Modern Language Studies*, *The American Review of Canadian Studies*, aussi bien que dans des ouvrages collectifs. Elle est également directrice de *Québec Studies*, revue interdisciplinaire consacrée à l'étude de la société québécoise et de la culture canadienne-française.

Hans Hauge (né en 1947) est depuis 1976 professeur adjoint d'anglais à l'Université d'Aarhus au Danemark. Il est aussi chercheur associé au Centre d'études culturelles. Il a publié des ouvrages et des articles sur les littératures anglaise, américaine et canadienne, et sur la philosophie et la théologie.

Diddy R.M. Hitchins est professeure de science politique et directrice des Études canadiennes à l'Université de l'Alaska à Anchorage. Née en Grande-Bretagne, elle est diplômée de l'Université de l'Essex. Elle a enseigné à l'Université du Ghana au début des années 70 alors qu'elle étudiait les programmes de développement et d'aide en Afrique occidentale. Ses recherches ont également porté sur l'aide de la Communauté européenne et elle s'intéresse actuellement au développement dans la région de l'Asie du Pacifique.

Charles L. Jones est professeur de sociologie à l'Université de Toronto et professeur honoraire à l'Université McMaster. Il a fait ses études à l'Université Cambridge, à la London School of Economics et à l'Université d'Édimbourg. Au nombre de ses publications, mentionnons: *The Images of Occupational Prestige, Class and Hierarchy* et *Images of Social Stratification*.

R. Alex Kizuk est actuellement professeur substitut à l'Université de Western Ontario. Son champ d'intérêt principal est l'étude, la critique et l'enseignement de la littérature canadienne. Il a publié une douzaine d'articles dans des revues savantes, notamment sur Margaret Atwood, Robertson Davies, Robert Kroetsch, Dorothy Livesay, A.J.M. Smith, W.W.E. Ross, E.J. Pratt et Marjorie Pickthall, et deux livres de poésie, *millions of acres* (Folks Upstairs Press, 1984) et *Microphones* (Brick Books, 1987).

Diane Lamoureux a fait des études en histoire, science politique et sociologie. Depuis 1986, elle est professeure au Département de science politique de l'Université Laval. Ses travaux portent principalement sur les modalités de constitution de l'autonomie personnelle et collective des femmes. Elle a déjà publié *Fragments et collages, essai sur le féminisme québécois des années 70* et *Citoyennes? Femmes, droit de vote et démocratie*, aux Éditions du remue-ménage. Elle est membre du comité de rédaction de la revue *Recherches féministes* et collabore à la revue internationale *Les cahiers du GRIF*. Elle a également publié plusieurs articles sur les enjeux politiques du féminisme.

Bertil Liander est professeur de marketing international et directeur adjoint de l'Institute for North American Trade and Economics à l'Université du Massachusetts à Amherst. Il est né en Suède et a obtenu son MBA de la Stockholm School of Economics et son Ph.D. de l'Université du Massachusetts. Il a vécu et travaillé en Suède, en Angleterre, en France, en Italie et aux États-Unis.

Lorna R. Marsden est membre du Sénat canadien et également professeure de sociologie à l'Université de Toronto et au Massey College. Elle a fait ses études à l'Université de Toronto et à l'Université Princeton. Elle a entre autres publié *The Fragile Federation: Social Change in Canada*.

Jean McNulty est conseillère principale à la Division de la radio-télédiffusion au ministère de la Culture et des Communications de l'Ontario. De 1984 à 1987, elle enseignait les communications de masse à l'Université York et, avant 1984, elle était chercheure associée et coordonnatrice de projet au Telecommunications Research Group de l'Université Simon Fraser. Ses champs de recherche sont les politiques gouvernementales en matière de communications, la technologie et les changements sociaux, et la théorie en communications. En plus de produire de nombreux rapports et articles sur les politiques gouvernementales en matière de communications, Jean McNulty est coauteure de deux ouvrages: *The Tangled Net: Basic Issues in Canadian Communications* (1977) et *Mass Communications in Canada* (1987).

Lorne J. Tepperman est professeur de sociologie à l'Université de Toronto et au New College. Il a fait ses études aux universités de Toronto et Harvard. Il est l'auteur de *Social Mobility in Canada* et *Choices and Chances: Sociology for Everyday Life*.

Martin W. Thunert est membre de l'Association d'études canadiennes dans les pays de langue allemande et candidat au doctorat en science politique à l'Université d'Augsbourg. Il a fait des stages d'études aux universités Queen's et McGill. Il travaille actuellement comme assistant au Center for North American Studies and Research, à l'Université Goethe de Francfort. Il est coauteur (avec R.O. Schultze) de *German Students in Canada: An Empirical Evaluation* (Bochum, RFA, 1989) et a écrit des articles sur la politique canadienne dans des publications allemandes. Ses champs d'intérêt sont la politique allemande, la politique comparée et la théorie politique.

Roy Turner, professeur de sociologie à l'Université de Colombie-Britannique, a publié plusieurs articles dans le domaine de la sociolinguistique. Ses travaux en cours, où il utilise une approche herméneutique, portent sur l'ambivalence culturelle contemporaine envers l'histoire telle qu'exprimée dans le discours contemporain sur, par exemple, l'identité culturelle, la place des musées et des galeries d'art dans la vie publique, les mouvements «héritage», la revitalisation urbaine, etc.

José Woehrling est professeur de droit à l'Université de Montréal depuis 1971. Il publie dans les domaines du droit constitutionnel, du droit international et du droit comparé.